Taking Rational Trouble Over the Mysteries

Taking Rational Trouble Over the Mysteries

Reactions to Atheism

Edited by Nicola Hoggard Creegan
and Andrew Shepherd

PICKWICK *Publications* • Eugene, Oregon

TAKING RATIONAL TROUBLE OVER THE MYSTERIES
Reactions to Atheism

Pickwick Publications
An Imprint of Wipf and Stock Publishers
199 W. 8th Ave., Suite 3
Eugene, OR 97401

www.wipfandstock.com

ISBN 13: 978-1-4982-6269-9

Cataloguing-in-Publication data:

Taking rational trouble over the mysteries : reactions to atheism / edited by Nicola Hoggard Creegan and Andrew Shepherd

xviii + 248 pp. ; 23 cm. Includes bibliographical references.

ISBN 13: 978-1-4982-6269-9

1. Apologetics. 2. Atheism. 3. Religion and science. I. Hoggard Creegan, Nicola. II. Shepherd, Andrew. III. Title.

BL2775.3 H544 2013

Manufactured in the U.S.A.

Contents

Illustrations and Tables

Neil Broom

Wilf Malcolm

Jeff Tallon

Yael Klangwisan

Contributors

Dr. Irene Alexander is a lecturer in counselling and psychology in Brisbane, Australia, as well as Asia. She is also a spiritual director and author of several books, and is passionate about living the kingdom in the real world. She has two adult sons.

Prof. John Bishop is Professor of Philosophy at the University of Auckland, New Zealand. He is the author of *Natural Agency* (Cambridge University Press, 1989) and *Believing by Faith* (Oxford University Press, 2007), and of articles in philosophical journals in the areas of the philosophy of action and the philosophy of religion.

Prof. Neil Broom holds a Professorship in the Department of Chemical and Materials Engineering, University of Auckland. His research interests are in the areas of joint tissue and spinal biomechanics. He has also written extensively on the Science-God theme with his most recent book *Life's X Factor: The Missing Link in Materialism's Science of Living Things* published by Steele Roberts, Wellington, in 2010.

Dr. Judith Brown is an occasional lecturer in theology at Laidlaw College and has lectured in church history at St. John the Evangelist College. She has published on both Ernst Bloch and theology and the arts, including the work of Colin McCahon. Her current projects include a book on theological method.

Dr. Nicola Hoggard Creegan lectures in systematic theology at Laidlaw College. She is author of *Animal Suffering and the Problem of Evil* (Oxford University Press, 2013) and has written extensively in the area of science and theology. She is Chair of TANSA (Theology and the Natural Sciences in Aotearoa).

Dr. Yael Klangwisan has recently passed her PhD that explores new intersections between Continental Philosophy and the Hebrew Bible. She lectures in Education, Culture, and Hebrew Language at Laidlaw College. She has written and presently widely on the Song of Songs and Genesis.

Assoc. Prof. Peter Lineham's interests cover a range of subject areas that can loosely be categorised under history and religion. He teaches history at Massey's Albany campus, and is the Regional Director of the College of Humanities and Social Sciences on Massey's Albany campus. He has written articles on many aspects of English and New Zealand religious history and his books include *There we found Brethren*, *No Ordinary Union*, and *Bible and Society.*

Dr. Wilf Malcolm was formerly Professor of Pure Mathematics at Victoria University of Wellington and subsequently the Vice Chancellor of the University of Waikato. He is author with Nicholas Tarling of *Crisis of Identity? The Mission and Management of Universities in New Zealand,* (Wellington: Dunmore Pub, 2007). He served for five years as General Secretary of the Inter Varsity Fellowship, now the Tertiary Students Christian Fellowship.

Dr. Tim Meadowcroft is Senior Lecturer in Biblical Studies and Head of School: Theology, Mission and Ministry at Laidlaw College in Auckland, New Zealand. He has published widely on Old Testament prophets and hermeneutics, and his most recent book is *The Message of the Word of God* in the InterVarsity Press Biblical Themes series (Downers Grove, IL: InterVarsity, 2011).

Rev. Dr. Graham O'Brien is the Ministry Education Coordinator for the Anglican Diocese of Nelson, New Zealand, and a Lecturer at Bishopdale Theological College. He has a PhD in Cellular and Molecular Biology as well as an M.Th in theology. He publishes widely in the area of science and theology and is also a member of the Inter-Church Bioethics Council in New Zealand.

Dr. John Owens holds a doctorate in philosophy from the University of Munich and teaches philosophy at Good Shepherd College, a Catholic theological college in Auckland, New Zealand. He is interested in late twentieth-century philosophy in relation to the classical tradition of Plato, Aristotle, and Aquinas. He has published on such figures as D. Z. Phillips, Martha Nussbaum, and Richard Rorty.

Dr. Andrew Shepherd works as a free-lance researcher and teacher in theology and ethics. He is the author of *The Gift of the Other* (Pickwick Publications, forthcoming.) He is the Education Co-ordinator for A Rocha Aotearoa New Zealand—a Christian conservation movement.

Dr. Jeff Tallon is Distinguished Scientist at Industrial Research Ltd., a New Zealand government-owned research institute and, until recently, was concurrently Professor of Physics at Victoria University of Wellington. He is internationally known for his research, discoveries and commercialization of high-temperature superconductors—currently being developed for applications across all sectors: health, transport, energy, mining and minerals processing, telecommunications, information technology, and the research sector. Dr Tallon has received many awards for his work, including the Rutherford Medal and the Inaugural Prime Minister's Medal for science.

Acknowledgments

Nicola Hoggard Creegan

I WOULD LIKE TO thank everyone associated with the support of TANSA (Theology and the Natural Sciences in Aotearoa) over the years. This includes Laidlaw College (TANSA is a Centre within the Graduate School), Metanexus (for Local Society Initiative funds 2006–2009), and all the scientists, theologians, and students who come to monthly meetings of TANSA, together with all of those who have given of their time and talents to speak at these meetings. Particular thanks to Prof. Wilf Malcolm for advice and counsel and help with administering TANSA and chairing a number of events.

Thanks also to the Rev. John Fairbrother, Director of Vaughan Park Retreat Centre in Long Bay, Auckland. He has hosted our meetings from time to time and his enthusiasm for taking on this discourse within the church and for the church has been very encouraging.

I am grateful also to my co-editor Andrew Shepherd, an entrepreneurial theologian, environmentalist, and community worker who lives in the stunning Makarora Valley. His insights and help with editing were invaluable.

And I would like to thank Pickwick Publications, and in particular Christian Amondson, for his long patience as this project meandered its way to completion.

Thank you to all the authors in this volume. Your willingness to commit to a project which involved a very diverse group of writers is much appreciated. We hope we have managed to present a cross section of New Zealand voices on this important issue.

This book was written and edited in spaces in between other projects. I would like to thank my family for putting up with a mother and wife who is always writing. And thanks also to my writing companions, Ruth and Milu who accompanied me on writing breaks at the beach over a period of years. You both made writing such a cheerful occasion.

Andrew Shepherd

Collaborative projects, while having their challenges, are always in the end the most enjoyable. This book bears this axiom out. The project has ebbed and flowed depending on other life demands but throughout the process it has been a joy to work with Nicola. I am very grateful for her personal encouragement over the years and for her love of our family.

Thanks are also due to Ricky Waters whose invitation to deliver a lecture on hospitality and peace-building at the Massey University Peace Week in September 2010, formed the basis of my contribution to this collection.

Finally, I acknowledge the ongoing love and support of my wife Ingrid and my three daughters, Julia, Kristin and Natalie. Not only have I learnt much from Ingrid's own attention to detail and fine editing skills during the years, but it is helpful to live with someone also used to juggling multiple balls at the same time. I am thankful for both her and the children's patience in giving me time to follow my various passions.

Introduction

Nicola Hoggard Creegan

THIS COLLECTION OF PAPERS came out of a succession of conferences and seminars held under the auspices of TANSA (Theology and the Natural Sciences in Aotearoa) and in particular one seminar on God and the New Atheists, held at Vaughan Park Anglican Retreat Centre on May 29th, 2010.

Those who take part in these sorts of colloquia often experience frustration. Sometimes we seem not to be getting anywhere. There is often little progress. And certainly the last few decades have shown us that for all the schemas and taxonomies, the discourse in the margins among disciplines as diverse as biology and theology is frightfully hard. Theology often finds itself at a disadvantage, often reacting to and reflecting upon the latest scientific findings. Science differs from theology in its endlessly onward direction. Theology is as often stopping to take stock of voices from the past as it is forging new research. What is achieved, however, is a mapping of the territory. This becomes a resource for further investigation and future generations of searchers along the way. The sense of getting nowhere can also belie the question: how would we know when we have achieved some progress? There is no flat plane on which we meet between disciplines and life-worlds. Some discomfort is always going to accompany this task. There is thrill at times, however, when connections from different vistas are discovered.

And indeed the best theology from the past is often remarkably prescient. Schleiermacher's insistence upon the sense of absolute dependence is an understanding of piety that includes an acute awareness of our place in the natural world, and of our consciousness as reaching beyond and outside that world. Other voices from the past, such as Gregory of Nyssa, Augustine, Hildegaard, Aquinas, John Wesley, and Jonathan Edwards, to name but a few, were keen observers of nature and of God's hand in nature. But Christianity must also take stock of the mixed fruits of religious belief, perhaps not a surprising state of affairs in a "wheat and tares" world. Even there, though, we must take note of the breadth and diversity of belief, and of how close to belief are some forms of unbelief. There are stark differences among believers, but not always lying along preconceived boundaries.

Yet this volume is not one that includes only theologians and scientists. There are theologians, but also biblical scholars, philosophers, a psychologist and therapist, an historian, biologists, writers trained in several areas, and a physicist as well. The habits and thought forms and discipline of these multiple fields are sometimes discordant. The discord is true to life however. Each story and each approach is part of the larger picture.

Part of the discordance is associated with taking a fine grained approach as opposed to the looking at the bigger picture. Scientists are more inclined to take the specialized approach, though in some cases this intense scrutiny then becomes a way of seeing a larger vision (Broom, chap 6; Malcolm, chap 7). Philosophers also have more constrained language than do theologians. Philosophy is able to make many important distinctions and arguments that become a part of the theological landscape. Sometimes these arguments too refer back to ancient sources like Aristotle (Owens, chap 5). Theologians use philosophical arguments and draw on revelation and the voices of tradition, but always in a way that is straining to respect and approach a transcendent source. God cannot be named and defined and placed in order in quite the way ordinary subjects and objects sometimes can.

Only some of these chapters refer directly to New Atheist arguments (Hoggard Creegan, chap 1; Shepherd, chap 2; Bishop, chap 4; Broom, chap 6; Tallon, chap 8, and Meadowcroft, chap 11). The acknowledgement and countering of current prevalent arguments is an important part of the philosophical and theological task. But indirect methods count as well. They point to different spaces and vistas that the more circumscribed view omits. So, for instance, Yael Klangwisan gives a fuller, more nuanced, more transforming view of Genesis (chap 12). Genesis is arguably the most mis-read text in the Western canon. It is so often misused and misread that to have a joyous fuller reading is a gift, and an indirect way of countering unbelief.

Similarly, Irene Alexander calls for more generous understandings of knowing (chap 10), a common theme in late twentieth-century intellectual life. Graham O'Brien looks to the possibilities of spirituality in the intersection of disciplines (chap 9). Lastly, it always helps to have an historical perspective. In a volume of New Zealand voices it is particularly appropriate to have a quick purview of the varieties of atheism in one's own country. It turns out atheism has been with us a long time in different guises. There is nothing particularly new about it, as Peter Lineham explains (chap 3). In a similar way, Judith Brown's powerful essay reminds us of the mix of belief and unbelief in early twentieth-century philosopher Ernst Bloch (chap 13).

I would argue, however, that there are points of surprising resonance in all the noise that counts as science and theology. Theology has often treasured its corporate metaphors of the body of Christ and church, insistent in every age, that these metaphors ground true human life and becoming. It is therefore interesting that newer understandings of evolutionary theory are now turning to more corporate metaphors like niche, for instance. Group, and not just individual selection is discussed. Evolutionary science is discovering that altruism runs deep in human biology; evolution is not quite the nature red in tooth and claw that was once supposed. Science and theology have discovered common ground in our ecological concern and in the dangers that climate change bring to the very possibility of human existence and indeed the existence of all life in the anthropocene.

These assumptions and common metaphors might be the ground for new beginnings and directions in this dialogue in coming decades. But we must never give up the important distinctions either. Theology is funded by its deep convictions in an "otherwise," that is for want of a better word named the transcendent or the unseen. For many in this discourse it is imperative that signs of this transcendence be visible in the seen world—"images and shadows of divine things," as Jonathan Edwards described. Theology will always resist the scientist's urge to conflate God and the Universe, or God and "natural selection" or God and nature. Thus some of the important questions that theology might bring to science include the following: is it imperative that *telos* be removed from biology? What is the life principle, and has it been eclipsed by forms of naturalism? Is our understanding of consciousness deeply misleading and deceiving in some way? These also will be questions we continue to face in the future.

Perhaps what is important is that we have made progress. We have moved from defensive postures over Genesis to fuller and more spiritually rich readings. We have progressed from rebutting arguments about religious violence to new understandings of atonement, commitment to pacifism and a rich appreciation of the call to hospitality in the Christian tradition. We have begun to dig deeper in matters of theodicy, retreating at last from the burdens that the old story of Adam and Eve placed on us, to an understanding of nature as much more "wheat and tares," as tinged with tragedy and wonder in a mysterious and blessed mix. Possibly we have also moved from the position of stark polar alternatives, belief vs. unbelief, to a more nuanced understanding of the great varieties of human approach to and understanding of the divine.

Introduction:
Facing Atheism and New Atheism

1

Christian Responses to Atheism in Our Time

NICOLA HOGGARD CREEGAN

TWO HUNDRED YEARS AGO the great German theologian Friedrich Schleiermacher said: "Shall the tangle of history so unravel that Christianity becomes identified with barbarism, and science with unbelief?"[1] He was prescient indeed. For today one could well argue such was the case. The world of belief and unbelief is very confusing. For every great hero of faith like Mother Theresa there appear to be ten fellow believers who espouse hatred of all manner of other human beings in the name of Christ. Sometimes believing can mean taking company one would rather not take, being associated with causes which seem to be inimical to the gospel. At the same time there are fellow travellers outside the fold. For instance, Dr. Russell Norman, leader of the Green Party in New Zealand, gave a speech in the New Zealand Parliament on December 21st, 2011 about the coming festival of Christmas, and how we should all be taking note of the values that Christ espoused. It was arguably one of the most rousing Christmas sermons given in New Zealand, and yet Norman was at pains to declare himself an atheist.[2] Norman wants a world for his children that reflects the early first-century Christian community. He took aim at the government's shallow utilitarian materialism and its seeming lack of concern for both the poor and the well-being of the planet. A world where atheists sing the praises of Christ and believers hate gays is a confusing world indeed.

In spite of the Russell Normans of this world, and in spite of the odd well-known saint, institutional Christianity is floundering. How do we

1. Schleiermacher, *On the Glaubenslehre*, 61.

2. Norman, "*Address to the New Zealand Parliament.*"

respond as believers? Is the New Atheism[3] not to be taken too seriously as Peter Lineham suggests in this volume? Is it a passing phase? Or is a *defacto* atheism as embraced increasingly by the young and educated here for the long haul? Militant New Atheism may be short lived, but I suspect milder not altogether unrelated atheism, or vague states of not caring about God are more than a passing phase. Atheism is not always linked to Darwinism, but it is closely yoked, as I will discuss further below, because evolutionary explanations for everything from life to consciousness are now so closely and scientifically argued. Where evolution once used to explain life, it now takes upon itself the explanation of religion and the very intuitions which seems to ground religious belief.

In a recent paper in the *Expository Times* Michael DeLashmutt has argued that the problem of the modern world is the presence of a naïve atheism as the default position of most people in the Western world.[4] This has replaced, he argues, the problem of previous eras which was that of an equally unreflective and naïve faith. The faith even of students who come for theological training is sometimes very brittle and vulnerable. One ex-student told me recently that she lives on an ethic of always doing what is life-affirming. She feels that her worldview is now immeasurably bigger and less provincial than the old worldview in which we educated her. No rules, no creeds, no difficult history, no fraught task of interpretation. Just life-affirmation. She, and many like her, are choosing in a sense to acquiesce with the atheist worldview, but they want to hang on to an ethic they respect; they feel they have distilled the essence and the spirituality out of the myth.

I will begin this paper, then, examining for myself in more detail why I believe in God in these circumstances of ubiquitous unbelief and, at times, barbarous belief; why I have continued to believe for so long, not without doubt, but without any conviction that God could possibly not exist. In doing this I will be examining religious intuitions that undergird faith. In subsequent sections I will argue the social, cultural, and scientific milieu of our current Western world is an unstable environment for these intuitions. It is this instability the New Atheists both encourage and exploit. I will conclude by charting possible responses—some of which are reflected elsewhere in this volume.

3. The "four horsemen" of the New Atheist movement are Sam Harris, Richard Dawkins, Christopher Hitchens, and Daniel Dennett. They have sworn war on ignorance, superstition, the belief in invisible gods, and the influence of religion in all areas of life and culture.

4. DeLashmutt, "Delusions and Dark Materials," 586–93.

The Basic Intuitions

The reasons for belief, for anyone's belief unless they are engaged in some sort of Pascalian wager, are in the first instance deeply personal and intuitive.[5] Faith requires the connected personal knowledge of which Irene Alexander speaks in a subsequent chapter, because this knowing is based upon and acknowledges the intuitions. Wolfhart Pannenberg, for instance, one of the great German theologians of the twentieth century, began his Christian life with a numinous experience which came out of the blue in a natural setting.[6] Only later did he link this experience to Christ and realized that his light filled conversion was on the Day of Transfiguration.

For many of us, however, it is not numinous experiences but more ordinary intuitions that serve faith. There is first, the intuition that human personality is derived, that it did not appear with us or with the mammalian tree a few million years ago. We have an intuition that our intelligence is similarly derived. Another intuition: When we grasp reality in any form there is also that sense of infinity within the finite, even if we do not call it that. This very concept has been an important part of twentieth-century mathematics—as Wilf Malcolm has detailed from the mathematician's viewpoint later in this volume—giving some added intellectual backing to the naïve awareness. And it was Schleiermacher, the theologian who also dabbled in mathematics, who insisted that true religion is a "sensibility and taste for the infinite."[7] This sense of the embedded infinite within the finite is perhaps related to what Jean-Luc Marion might call "excess," or Charles Taylor "fullness." It is the hunch that the ordinary and material is studded with something else, indiscernible, beyond the margins.[8] While science may at one stage have contradicted this intuition, seeing ahead the end of physics or chemistry, the exact opposite is the case today; the hard sciences are uncovering further and deeper complexity. There appears to be unlimited structure to discern, even scientifically, beneath the surface.

This excess is more than just the infinite. We also grasp the whole; we discern a coherence that is interconnected and infinitely dense. Meaning is made in these shifts of heuristic consciousness, uncanny meaning. Some ways of telling the story of origins only increase that coherence and depth. Think of the birth of the cosmos: a few laws, infinite smallness becoming

5. Evolutionary cognitive psychologists would say that these intuitions are simply the result of cognitive capacities like theory of mind which have been evolved to solve a different evolutionary problem.

6. Pannenberg, "God's Presence in History," 260–63.

7. Schleiermacher, *On Religion*, 23.

8. Marion, *In Excess*; Taylor, *A Secular Age*, 5.

unimaginable hugeness, small irregularities giving rise to suns, planets, elements, light, life. It is all quite staggering and hard to understand at a distinct level. We make it mundane, telling the story often enough that strings, quantum mechanics, DNA, all rattle off our tongues. This ordinariness numbs us to the intuition that all parts of the whole are connected to all other parts, across both time and space. Hence we have both ecology on the one hand, and speculative ideas like that Lovelock's Gaia on the other.[9]

Another intuition, again also related to excess, is that of purpose. Nature, life, doesn't just do a good enough job for what is needed now; it appears to contain resources for the future, and all life requires both meaning and interpretation. John Owens and Neil Broom in this volume, from a philosophical and scientific point of view respectively, point to the sense of purpose that life reveals at every level. We are purposeful beings and we see hints of this purpose around us, even in fact across time. Biology tells us of mutations which are later co-opted for a new function. How extraordinary. A moon and a goldilocks zone make life on earth possible: they are the womb for life and sentience.

It would, however, be hard to have purpose without meaning and meaning without interpretation. These are related concepts, and in a recent book Andrew Robinson has developed C. S. Peirce's theory of semiotics to argue that life is irreducibly signing and interpreting at its most basic levels. For Peirce there was the object, the sign, and its interpretant, present wherever even unconscious life is present. Robinson understands the enormity of this and the way in which interpretation permeates the universe, making living nature understandable as a trinitarian vestige of God and God evident in life. If we think about it, interpretation is the key to all communication and the fact of being able to interpret anything is mysterious and miraculous, as much in the amoeba as in ourselves. When we grasp the purposefulness of the living world it is possible that it is this very excess of signs we understand at some level.[10]

These intuitions together, of personhood, intelligence, infinity, coherence, and purpose lie beneath all that we call God. They are not God, but in their excess they point to God, to the Real. At various points this God appears to have communicated through human prophets, and the intuitions at that point meet and mirror and embrace the revelation, albeit not without discord and conflict. Only then can we move to the almost audacious belief in after-life with all the associated concepts of salvation this entails, and of which revelation gives us hints. On the back of all this intuition then, we

9. Lovelock, *Gaia.*

10. Robinson, *God and the World of Signs.*

dare to consider that death too has no sting, that the sense of infinity and deep purpose within us might also mirror reality.

The idea of life after death deeply impacts with and relates to the moral life of the human being here. As Kant has argued, an afterlife and God might be required to make moral sense of the injustice we experience and witness.[11] All of this means that belief is not in a single concept, like life after death, or being saved or forgiven, or the existence of an individual omni-God, or even the incarnation. Belief begins at deeply intuitive levels of first response to all that is out there, especially life; belief is nurtured by gratitude and amazement, forgiveness, release, transformation, and longing. That some of these emotions and intuitions exist also in the unbeliever, as John Bishop has argued with his section on Dawkins' Eucharistic turn, and Judith Brown's description of Bloch's longing, both in this volume, only increases the complexity of this subject, and of belief.

We cannot rely on intuitions alone, however, especially in an era of cognitive evolutionary science which looks at just these types of intuitions and examines the evolutionary story of fitness which produced them. All humans are primed, it is argued, to believe in unseen agents, and to invoke these agents to explain patterns and events. This ability is called HADD (hyperactive agency detection device).[12] Why? Well this might well be an evolutionary advantage, for prey and enemies hide behind cover. Moreover, these unseen agents might observe and sanction your behavior, with obviously cooperative advantage. Whether any of these just-so stories is true or not, cognitive evolutionary science does subtly undermine warranted Christian faith in many ways. Such science tends to flatten the explanatory terrain, subsuming theological interpretations within it or subverting them. Theology is always tempted to divest itself of the miraculous and wonderful and the counter-intuitive. This I will explore later. There remains, however, the possibility that ancient minds were very different from ours, and in some sense cognitively inaccessible. It is also possible and indeed likely from a faith perspective, that the animal which fills the God-niche would be endowed with capacities for intuiting and knowing in this space.

Jesus Christ

All of this is also a long way from the details of Old Testament justice, and those of the Christian understanding of atonement or incarnation, let alone the cultural out workings of these revelations in diverse times and places

11. Kant, *Critique of Practical Reason*, 240.

12. Guthrie suggests this idea in *Faces in the Clouds*; See also Barrett, *Born Believers*.

around the world, all of which are sometimes fodder for New Atheist tirades. I would add, however, one more reason for my own belief. The way that Christ taught us to live and the life-out-of-death example he gave does work. When people live like this they bring life and flourishing and hope to others, often against all odds or in the most degraded contexts. When we are faced with utilitarian ethics and social decisions that may increasingly be dehumanizing, the image of the Christ is important as an antidote. If we had no Christ we would not really know that weakness could outperform strength. We would not know that in the end all people are equal and equally valuable. We would not know the other grammars of the gospel, that in giving we receive, and that grace covers a multitude of sins, that we are the body of Christ. With the Gospels we are invited into a journey of discovering wholeness. With Christ and the Gospels our basic intuitions are met. And here I do not at all mean that Christ came only as an example; rather that in dying and rising he revealed hidden mysteries of God. Christ thereby showed that the teaching works. He showed that forgiveness, weakness, suffering, hope and life are all inextricably mixed. The temptations are always there, to power, influence, and magic. Christ reveals to us another way. That Christ's coming and his life with us was so inextricably entwined with the one he called *Abba* gives us another way of relating to God. In the end we reach some impasse in our journey to understand and talk about deity. Then we can turn to the one who claimed to image God in human flesh and human words.

Faith Seeking Understanding

Why can't we leave it at that then? We can, but as John Bishop has said, if we seek to interact with science, or even the scientific world and public, we need also to seek understanding. Moreover, it is science in recent times that has deeply undermined or seemed to undermine some of these basic intuitions—while nevertheless also often increasing our sense of wonder. The New Atheism is particularly virulent about the kind of God we seem to worship—one reflected in the worst of Old Testament tyranny and in the most parasitic of biological specimens like the Guinea worm. New Atheism has also relished the predicament believers find themselves in with the problem of evil and the Christian association with violence. These topics believers must address. It is a part of gaining some measure of coherence and understanding to do so. In this volume Tim Meadowcroft addresses the complex problem of Hebrew Bible violence, Andrew Shepherd examines Christopher Hitchens' retorts about the dangers of religious violence, and Yael Klangwisan shows us how Genesis, that book which is the object of so much strife and politics, can and should be read as a richly poetic, life-giving, and transforming text, but one that both encourages and allows cultural input.

These challenges in theological and spiritual life do not at all negate the dense levels of intuition by which, and in light of which, we claim to know God, but they can destabilize us. This undermining of intuition happens, I would argue, at both an unconscious insidious level and at the level of concepts and reason. I examine these in different sections below.

The Subtle Destabilization of Intuition

I have argued that people take up religious lives and practices and beliefs because of deep intuitions which find resonance in religion and belief in God. These intuitions, however, need good foundations in which to thrive and continue to be plausible. The Western world today may lack these structures and might even significantly undermine them.

The first and most obvious of the undermining effects is the need to reduce and understand everything in terms of evolutionary advantage as explained above. This applies these days to the complexities of altruism and religious belief as much as it does to biological traits.[13] Both altruism and belief are understood to be costly in terms of evolutionary effort. Thus attempts are made to understand retrospectively the survival advantage of these deep-seated tendencies. On some accounts religion is a spandrel, an unintended consequence of lower level cognitive capacities. Other cognitive scientists believe that religion fulfilled a purpose of overcoming selfishness.[14] It did this by constructing a punishing all-seeing God. This thinking does not directly undermine the content of belief, but it does reduce its value, and it suggests that the intuitions which suggest God are of use rather than being true; "natural selection" is simply using these intuitions for its own purposes. Some human intuitions are in fact deep cognitive biases which have little validity; an example might be the idea that nothing bad is going to happen to *us*. This intuition is useful to a degree, because an inordinate amount of time spent worrying about what might happen is not conducive with maintaining and living life now. An intuition, to have any claim to validity at all must have some resonance in multiple disciplines, some back-up from somewhere.

13. See Barrett, *Born Believers*.

14. See Johnson et al., "The Puzzle of Human Cooperation," 911–12.

Young children, and even babies, come into this world apparently with a capacity to believe in God and with what is called "promiscuous teleology," the tendency to think of everything in terms of what function it fulfils.[15] Thus cognitive science affirms some of our deepest intuitions, and affirms that these biases are in fact hard-wired. This might of course be because they help us interact with the world—interpret the word in Robinson's terms—accurately. Or the content might in fact be wrong, the survival crutch of an earlier and more naïve age.

I would argue though, that the fact that instincts come "naturally" does not necessarily undermine faith. Natural instincts might simply mean that there is a happy reconciliation between the way things are and the cognitive habits of the knowing primate. As someone who started life in mathematics I have enormous respect for the capacities of the human mind to usefully and perhaps even truthfully know the world, albeit not always without error. This is certainly the opinion of one such cognitive researcher in the field, Justin Barrett, though he is a strong but minority voice in a new and emerging field that is part of a long tradition of using natural selection in a way that is incidentally subtly undermining of the content of beliefs.[16]

Even without reductionist Darwinism, however, technology is the most obvious culprit in terms of the focus of our consciousness. We are yet in the early days of charting the effects of this ubiquitous aspect of our lives, and undoubtedly it has immeasurably enriched and rapidly changed our cultures. Yet technology does also cut us off from the natural world which feeds our basic human sense of wonder, and the understanding that we are a part of infinitely purposeful whole. It may in fact be the religious senses that are most affected by this change of consciousness. This is the state of affairs of which Jacques Ellul warned us in his life-long critique of technology in our lives. He argues, for instance, that with technology the positive aspects are easy to articulate and see—and indeed they are—the negative aspects are always "vague phenomena, which are significant only by their bulk and their general nature . . . but [which] eventually give a certain negative style to human life."[17]

Two more recent books continue in a similar vein, articulating this unconscious insidious change of consciousness we are experiencing due to a variety of factors from technology to the undermining of the warrants of faith in a evolutionary theory. The first is Marilynne Robinson's *The Absence of Mind,* a transcript of her Terry Lectures at Yale. She describes the way in which the faith is pulled and formed by what she calls the parascientific

15. Kelemen, "Why are Rocks Pointy?" 1440–52.

16. Barrett, *Born Believers.*

17. Ellul, *The Technological Bluff*, 47.

world, specifically by its reductionism and its positivism. Writing about the parascientific, she states: "There is a characteristic certainty that is present structurally in the kind of thought and writing to which I wish to draw attention, a boldness which diminishes its subject."[18]

In a world in which objective knowledge has long been critiqued there has never been a time when it is used more, or trusted more implicitly. And reductionist explanations only increase as evolutionary psychology and sociology seek to explain and thereby sometimes deliberately to disarm the content of belief itself, as explained above. When we are always seeking to find the *function* of something there is an almost irresistible temptation to think the *content* unimportant or even more to think it false. In this way talk of belief in a divine being becomes instead an analysis of the function such a belief might play in evolutionary fitness at an individual or group level. And here I must turn to mathematics again. There is an emerging literature now which attempts to understand the evolution of advanced mathematical ability. The possible explanations are very similar to those given for religion. Yet although mathematics is produced most often from a motive of sheer pleasure, in the end it also almost always has uncanny uses in the natural world. Perhaps, one might suggest, religion shares with mathematics as much as it shares with mating and courting behaviors more open to evolutionary explanation.[19]

Robinson says further: "Parascientific literature makes its case by proceeding, using the science of its moment, to a set of general conclusions about what our nature is and must be." Such literature, she argues shows inordinate confidence that conclusions drawn are inevitable given the science in question.[20] She goes on to say, when speaking of the materialism of the present age, that the church and theology have "accommodated the parascientific world view." In doing so theology has,

> tended to forget the beauty and strangeness of the individual soul. . . . But the beauty and strangeness persist just the same. And theology persists, even when it has absorbed as truth theories and interpretations that could reasonably be expected to kill it off. This suggests that its *real* life is elsewhere.[21]

This is very well put. Of course, something like this is happening when deep intuitions are being undermined, and we hardly see it occurring. Yet there

18. Robinson, *Absence of Mind*. 12.
19. See Devlin, *The Math Gene*.
20. Robinson, Absence *of Mind*, 32–33.
21. Ibid., 13

are also signs of hope: Robinson points to the persistence of the subjective even in a world that is always attempting to remove it.

In spite of Irene Alexander's confidence that a new way of knowing is emerging (see chapter 10), I am not so sanguine. Certainly science and law and most University disciplines are attempting to remove the personal. "The difficulty with which objectivity can be achieved, to the extent that it is ever achieved," Robinson argues, "only demonstrates the pervasive importance of subjectivity."[22] Perhaps it is this pervasive power that gives those who argue for connected/personal knowing confidence that their methods may be gaining authority. Ironically, of course, even physics no longer ascribes to the flat positivist landscape of "parascience." But the mechanistic images persist nevertheless. We wonder where on earth there is room for immortality and spirit in this flat mechanical world.

How do we counter the power of parascience? Perhaps the current interest in prayer, meditation, and mindfulness is one of the Spirit's gifts to a parascientific world. Only by insisting that experience, subjective inwardness, and personal knowing are important and valid can we counter parascientific practice. Technology, and the findings of evolutionary cognitive studies, can immeasurably enrich our lives. It is enlightening to learn that babies and young children so easily "know" God. Yet for a person weighed down by accumulating doubt the overall landscape of these findings can be undermining.

In the church we can hold up the subjective, personal knowing, the importance of intuition, the inward beauty of the inner life, and hints of immortality and otherness we carry within us as a means of resisting the default atheism of the world at large. In this fight to survive it is not the church's creeds and moral codes that are of overwhelming importance, though the insistence on an "otherwise," and a rich theological language remain important; rather it is music, compassion, a non-utilitarian ethic, hope and works of hope, inner transformation, and the symbolic world that speaks of transcendence and grace.

The other major book which speaks to this issue is *The Master and His Emissary,* written by a psychiatrist and philosopher, Iain McGilchrist.[23] Drawn from a life-time of observing human frailty and mental disorder, as well as a deep philosophical knowledge, McGilchrist delves into the fraught question of the brain's hemispheres. All human cognitive functions, McGilchrist argues, arise not only out of different areas of the brain, but out of complex networks. Nevertheless we and animals and birds all have divided brains for a reason. The right hemisphere, in most human, pays attention

22. Ibid., 14.

23. McGilchrist, *The Master and his Emissary.*

to the overall landscape, the big picture, to novelty, but also to life and the individual.[24] The left side attends to the details, to language and abstraction, and importantly to the machine. In our civilization the left brain and its skills have taken over from the right. The left brain gets obsessed over details and is very hard to derail; the left brain finds it hard to hand back the reins to the wide vista. People who have a stroke in the right brain often refuse to believe that anything is wrong. In previous eras the church was always there, to draw us back and into the wide visage again, to insist that the overall picture mattered, that life matters, and feeling, and to orient us. Thus the right brain—together with the left, but not excluding the right—is required for a sense of awe and piety.

McGilchrist notes the dangers that emerge when thinking and reflecting is done only by the left brain, especially in the realm of religion and art. Then, he says, abstraction rather than awe dominates:

> If the process ends with the left hemisphere, one has only concepts—abstractions and conceptions, not art at all. Similarly the immediate pre-conceptual sense of awe can evolve into religion only with the help of the left hemisphere: though, if the process stops there, all one has is theology, or sociology, or empty ritual: something else[;] . . . the process needs to return to the right hemisphere, so that it can live.[25]

When the right side of the brain is engaged, feeling and a sense of connection to God follow. McGilchrist's elaborate arguments give believers pause for thought. This is the type of explanation from science that is consistent with the biblical view of the world, one in which humans are easily deceived, and in which the motivations behind the deception are mimetic desire and control (as in Cain and the flood and Babel stories).

One is always impressed in the Hebrew Bible by the energy that is invested in resistance of idolatry. Idolatry then or now is not easy to define but the ancient Israelite writers describe the ubiquitous slow slide into idolatry that seems to happen everywhere. The habits of consciousness that Ellul, Robinson, and McGilchrist describe may be the road to contemporary idolatry. Belief may only be possible if the church is constantly striving to curate spaces that are creative, life-enhancing, leading us to nature, and to beauty, as well as to habits of thought which are aware of the temptations to insidious unbelief around us. In this volume Graham O'Brien encourages us

24. In some individuals, apparently, the hemispheres are reversed. In others parts of the right brain function are present in the left. See McGilchrist, *The Master and His Emissary*, 12.

25. McGilchrist, *The Master and His Emissary*, 199.

to see the interface between science and faith more generously as a domain in which spirit is common to both modalities. Perhaps both science and faith can in the end be practiced best when practiced together.

Arguments for Atheism

But the undermining of deep intuition happens also at the level of reason. Very powerful arguments from New Atheists and their friends seep into the consciousness, closing down the intellectual vista, holding us captive, in the same way that Job's friends threatened his resolve to believe in a good God. As one example, the sense of derivation is undermined by the scientifically posed possibility of self-perpetuation in biological and cosmological evolution. The universe brought into being all that there is and the universe keeps things going. God and the universe become at times indistinguishable, but one is known to be resolutely natural and the other not. One is sometimes the object of awe but not the beginning of religion. The intuition of coming after and being dependent are easily subverted by the detailed and objective stories told by the evolutionary biologist and evolutionary psychologist, stories which in their telling often become what Robinson calls parascience. It is not that these stories are wrong; rather, it is that these accounts are so dominating that they undermine other explanations—even as they have the power themselves to undermine science itself. If all intellectual pursuits are directed towards understanding how things happen "naturally" in a cause and effect sort of way then God's hand, which is in any case mysterious and perhaps ultimately ineffable is eclipsed. If God is the creator and preserver of the universe there is more happening than just what is visible. One aspect of the theological story which is eclipsed is the strong theological emphasis upon prolepsis which I will examine further below.

First, however, I will respond to what is probably the most common, and for theologians, the most sensitive area of assault, that of theodicy. New Atheists' assault on this issue comes at a time when old theodicies have been undermined by our knowledge of pre-human death, disease, aggression, and extinction. The human species did not invent any of these, even if it did enormously exacerbate them, and *homo sapiens* almost certainly did not arrive at the species boundary "innocent." In spite of the high apparent levels of violence in many parts of the world, and in our own cities, we live in times sensitized to violence. The last decades of the twentieth century revealed common associations between abuse and church authority, and the Scriptures have been read through feminist and pacifist hermeneutics.

These readings reveal in the Scriptures, and in our theologies, an ambivalence about patriarchy and violence which are sometimes disturbing.

In the past all evil, natural or moral, could be laid at the feet of Adam. Now science gives us a very disturbing view of the creation for which God has been responsible for 3–4 billion years since life emerged on this planet. At least we might ask, if God is not responsible, then who? There has apparently been a long, long history of sentient suffering, predation and extinction, and of selfish genes competing to survive. God is, to all intents and purposes a "hands off God," or so it might appear, not intervening to rescue the weak or the vulnerable. We wonder why did God create in quite this ruthless way, for God must be at least the final cause of all that is, unless there are other players.

The manifold responses to the problem of evolutionary suffering all have their place but fail in a way to measure up to the depth of the suffering and seeming gratuitous evil involved. Why could a good God not in the end create a world of kindly meerkats and affectionate straw eating lions, of wild but not too vicious hawks, leading to benign and beautiful humans? Why could we not have a world inhabited with creatures more like the bonobo than the chimpanzee? Why do we live in a solar system that is not only exquisitely tuned and primed for life, but subject to random asteroid hits that eliminate life and meaning? Narratives of hope can appear to flights of fancy when brought into focus with this God, as Dawkins and other New Atheists well know.

Neo-Darwinism also presents us with a radically purposeless "history" of 3–4 billion years. This vast timespan threatens to deconstruct the sense of purpose with which humans have invested the past paltry 4,000–5,000 years since civilization began. History itself is under attack. We may think our few thousand years of recorded history are of immense importance. But what does it matter really when compared to the vast billions of years of eventful yet seemingly purposeless pre-human lineage? Scripture is replete with images of a God who cares, who may not always intervene, but always has a part to play in the history—a part that includes dramatic rescue (admittedly after 400 years of slavery), of incarnation, of miracles and healing. And yet, nature reveals to us a God who seems not to care. We may think that nature's very purposelessness, its pure contingency, or its apparent randomness, is at odds with the story of God and the doctrine of providence. This deep purposelessness feeds the incipient and ubiquitous atheism we see around us.

I cannot in this paper do any more than chart some of the response to the problem of evil and purposelessness in Christian theology. One response which most typifies mid to late twentieth century theology is the response of hope, because God in God's human nature joined us in solidarity with our suffering.[26] We might not know the origins or necessity of suffering, but at least God has not left us alone. Allied understandings argue that God in Christ resisted the powers of evil which are inexplicably besetting the world. Others argue for some version of the "free creatures" response. That is, God cannot intervene because to do so would be to contradict our freedom, and perhaps the freedom of all conscious creatures. Along the same lines, it is argued that suffering brings character and also soul-making.[27]

Still further theories look to the nature of God. Process theology, for instance, solved the problem of evil by positing a God who lures but never coerces.[28] Christopher Southgate proposes a theory of intratrinitarian kenosis, whereby the Son is "selved" in relationship to the Father, eternally.[29] "Selving" is the task of all conscious creatures and requires suffering separation in the interests of flourishing. I have argued in a recent book, that one must take seriously the biblical emphasis upon evil, and that some measure of understanding is garnered by seeing the whole creation as wheat and tares, perfect and at the same time corrupted, the tares—and wheat—becoming more pronounced under the control of the primate who has dominion of the whole world.[30]

But I also argue in that book that the emerging alternative understandings of evolutionary biology make a "wheat and tares" approach to the whole of creation more plausible. Nature appears both perfect and corrupted; there are in the evolutionary process cooperative and interdependent "mechanisms" at work as well as the well-known phenomenon of nature red in tooth and claw. What Sarah Coakley refers to as the paradigm shift in biology is a part of the whole story.[31] And this more benign reading of the evolutionary story is a counter also to the narrative of purposelessness and randomness of evolution's Central Dogma.[32]

All of these intellectual approaches have some value, but they must be combined with a change in our way of seeing, especially the seeing of nature. Like the biblical Job we will never understand nature, and the way we see it and relate to it and participate within it may either alienate us or draw us towards the God of love.

26. Moltmann, *Theology of Hope*.

27. Murray, *Nature Red in Tooth and Claw*.

28. Suchocki, *God, Christ, Church*.

29. Southgate, *The Groaning of Creation*.

30. Hoggard Creegan, *Animal Suffering and the Problem of Evil*.

31. See Coakley, Gifford Lectures, 2012.

32. The Central Dogma of biology refers to the one-directional flow of information from DNA to proteins and not vice versa. See Crick, "Central dogma of molecular biology," 561–63.

Responses: Faith Rising Like a Phoenix

Faith often now seems to be dead in the West, weakened and swallowed up by the rising tide of humanistic secularism. But if Christian faith tells us anything it is that life comes out of death, and faith out of a desert. On the one hand, the solution is in the hands of God, literally; on the other hand, it lies with us. We must construct worlds that resist some of the insidious changes in our thinking which have kept us captive. We will find many who question the extent of evil in this God surrounded world. At other times we will insist that theology is asking fresh and different questions that challenge the consensus in the cultures and life-worlds we inhabit.

There are dual worlds, the world of evolutionary biology and the world of faith. These are the two competing views of the world today, and they have constructed two competing stories of origins. As we inhabit the world of faith we will be amazed at what evolution is and has done, not just what has survived. Why do we have a "mechanism" that changes and reproduces and gifts its individuals with a relentless passionate desire to live? What is this process that is endlessly complex and seems to think ahead, as much as backwards? Why is life like this at all?

A quick and easy synthesis between these worlds should be avoided, however. This is the strength of Van Huyssteen's work in which he advocates transversal discourse.[33] Transversality resists and precludes any premature synthesis of two disciplines, always working at different levels, but maintaining a dialogue along with the resulting tension. In the past half century theology has, as Marilynne Robinson said, accommodated itself to the parascientific views which are incompatible with its own practice. Too often theology is amazed and enthusiastic about concordant points of agreement between the two disciplines and the distinctives of the faith perspective are overlooked. This is the case whenever you hear someone say: I have no problem with synthesizing evolution and faith. Does that mean that the person is a Deist, or that they have no problem with God behind a slow and intimate but somewhat brutal process? Does this person have no problem with the mix of beauty, providence, and randomness the process seems to reflect?

Thus we must bring theological thinking to the biological table. For instance, prolepsis is central to theology, but overlooked when it comes to a meeting of the scientific and theological perspectives. If God in the future is bringing all of creation towards Godself then evolution too must bear the imprint of this future orientation or even causation. The figure of Christ is

33. Van Huyssteen, *Alone in the World?*

everywhere in Christian theology; Christ cannot disappear as the source of our inwardness when we are talking to science. Also the realism about evil that is found in the Scriptures must be faced, and not obscured. Even the words of warning that we as believers should expect hardship are very pertinent to the theological perspective in the world.

We must also find and draw out the signs of transcendence in art and the natural world, something done by several of the authors in this volume. I end then by examining as a case study, the humane, but distinctly Christian voice in one recent movie, *Of Gods and Men*. In this movie we discover a window into the world of faith, by which ordinary non-religious movie goers might "see" into the heart of the Christian. This movies present a view of faith in which the inner world, the subjective, the self, the right brain input are evident. The Christian monks in this movie struggle with God's apparent absence in the light of evil. *Of Gods and Men* shows what cannot easily be said, that God can be seen, but only through eyes of suffering and hope. In a sense this showing of faith is really the only "answer" to atheism.

Faith at the Movies

Of Gods and Men is a story of martyrdom in a Trappist monastery in Algeria. The monastery mission was to incarnate Christ in a poor Muslim community. In the 1990s these ordinary but "called" men found themselves dangerously poised between a corrupt government and a brutal uprising. Rarely do movie goers listen in to the inner world of the Christian as they ponder the point of giving your life, of allowing your life to be snuffed out by pointless violence, the ethical struggle of choosing to stay in solidarity with those who cannot leave, while at the same time intensely willing to live. And this, of course, is important. Martyrdom which is not accompanied by a deep love of living is dangerous, as Dawkins suggests.

Of all things, perhaps, martyrdom is most inconsistent with a parascientific worldview, being terribly hard to justify in terms of logic and analysis (except in terms of costly signalling).[34] Martyrdom like this might well be the end of a Christian life even if we all hope and pray that it is not. In this case martyrdom is the end of lives that are already given over to the "martyrdom" of the monastery. The film makes a compelling case that having started down a certain road, faithfulness demands that the monks continue;

34. More than that, the evolutionary psychologist will also talk in terms of "costly signalling." The martyr's life is inconsistent with evolution's usual fitness criteria, as is monasticism, but the very act of being different is a costly signal to others of the importance of a community's shared beliefs.

faithfulness demands that they not give in to the threat of violence, that they continue to live by a higher rule of peace. Yet they are human and they want to live. They have a way out; they could all go back to France. We see their inner struggles; we see the beauty of their lives and the deep symbolism of their last supper. The inner gaze is crucial because the film is mirroring everyday sacrificial Christian life; it reveals the type of inwardness, the types of reasons and reasoning that can properly be called Christian, but that are normally hidden to public viewing. There are reasons why this movie and also the documentary of silent monastic life, *Into Great Silence* have been so powerful in a secular world, why people with no faith lined up to see them both. It is in this contemplation of the inner space that the mind "understands" and resonates with other living forms, enters into their ecstasy. In speaking of *The Great Silence* which shared some of the same tenor as *Of Gods and Men* one reviewer said this of the director, Philip Groning:

> He is after the spiritual content of intense religious commitment. . . . Not the thing itself. Mr. Groning is not so vain as to suppose that a movie can provide a religious experience, but a preliminary understanding of its shape and weight.[35]

This could well be said *Of Gods and Men* as well. The movie almost incarnates the spirituality. These movies show more than can be said in words of the way in which prayer and commitment and sacrifice and faith and hope and love can change the consciousness, so that it can face even the greatest evils imaginable, and evils from which one might reasonably expect that the omni-God might deliver us. They can change the consciousness so that even if we do not grasp the mystery of God's activity and inactivity, the presence in absence of divine love is tangible enough that faith is possible.

The last words of the Prior Christian in anticipation of his death are some of the most convincing words in Muslim/Christian dialogue:

> I know the caricatures which a certain Islamic ideology encourages and which make it easy for some to dismiss the religion as hateful. . . . But such people should know that at last I will be able to see the children of Islam as He sees them—He whose secret joy is to bring forth our common humanity amid our differences.[36]

In these words is a recognition of the common inward life, the common infinite depths that religion proffers, especially in the Abrahamic religions now apparently at war with one another. He alludes to the common Christian and Muslim way of paying attention to the larger whole, to the

35. Scott, "Lives Lived at Monk's Pace Allow Life to Flourish."

36. Arnold, "Christian de Chergé."

mystery of divinity among us, and to a common expectation of meaning. The movie itself is an extraordinary example of taking the events of life and framing them within a scriptural context, as narrative theology has insisted we should do.

Conclusion

The faith of Jesus and in Jesus is a subjective faith. Jesus taught us that although faith in God has all sorts of outward fruits it is the heart that matters. Jesus' disciples, not to mention other heroes of faith like Mary, were asked to make decisions based on inward personal intuitions and trust. When faith in God is challenged there can be no complete answer at the level of propositions and argument alone. Faith can be shown to be coherent but in the end it must also be shown. Even the greatest challenge to Christian faith—theodicy and the challenges in theodicy that are associated with Darwinism—must be answered indirectly by affirming the subjectivity of the person and the intuitions that undergird faith. I began this essay, then, with the argument that faith grows out of a whole network of intuitions which may in turn be examined and considered in more rational light. I suggested that cognitive evolutionary psychology is also interested in these intuitions, for different reasons, ones that are not always consistent with faith as belief in God, and may, in their alternative viewing of a similar phenomenon in fact undermine faith.

Theology is a second order reflection on the life of faith that is already present. In our world this faith is severely challenged by an alternative great narrative, one which is extending its explanatory power in increasing circles. This narrative is also central to science, one of the most powerful means we have of understanding our world, and "knowing" nature. We cannot dismiss it. We should not want to dismiss it. We must then bring theological thinking into conversation with this other great narrative, while at the same time respecting and nurturing the intuitions that give life to faith.

Bibliography

Arnold, Johann Christoph. "Christian de Chergé: a Story of Forgiveness." Excerpt online at the *Plough* (Feb 28, 2011). Online: http://www.plough.com/en/articles/2011/february/christian-de-cherg%c3%a9-a-story-of-forgiveness.

Barrett, Justin L. *Born Believers: The Science of Children's Religious Belief.* New York: Free, 2012.

Coakley, Sarah. *Gifford Lectures, 2012.* Aberdeen Lecture no. 2. No pages. Online: http://www.abdn.ac.uk/gifford/people/.

Crick, Francis. "Central Dogma of Molecular Biology." *Nature* 227 (2007) 561–63.

DeLashmutt, Michael W. "Delusions and Dark Materials: New Atheism as Naïve Atheism and Its Challenge for Theological Education." *The Expository Times* 120.12 (2009) 586–93.

Devlin, Keith. *The Math Gene: How Mathematical Thinking Evolved and Why Numbers are Like Gossip.* New York: Basic, 2001.

Ellul, Jacques. *The Technological Bluff.* Translated by Geoffrey W. Bromiley. Grand Rapids: Eerdmans, 1990.

Guthrie, Stewart. *Faces in the Clouds: A New Theory of Religion.* Oxford: Oxford University Press, 1995.

Hoggard Creegan, Nicola. *Animal Suffering and the Problem of Evil.* Oxford: Oxford University Press, 2013.

Johnson, Dominic, et al., "The Puzzle of Human Cooperation." *Nature* 421 (2003) 911–12.

Kant, Immanuel. *Critique of Practical Reason, in Practical Philosophy.* Translated by M. Gregor. Cambridge: Cambridge University Press, 1996.

Kelemen, D. "Why are Rocks Pointy? Children's Preference for Teleological Explanations of the Natural World." *Developmental Psychology* 35 (1999) 1440–52.

Lovelock, J. *Gaia: A New Look at Life on Earth.* Oxford: Oxford University Press, 1979.

Marion, Jean-Luc. *In Excess: Studies of Saturated Phenomena.* Translated by Robyn Horner and Vincent Berraud. New York: Fordham University Press, 2002

McGilchrist, Iain. *The Master and His Emissary: The Divided Brain and the Making of the Western World.* New Haven: Yale University Press, 2010.

Moltmann, Jürgen. *Theology of Hope: On the Ground and the Implications of a Christian Eschatology.* London: SCM, 1967.

Murray, Michael J. *Nature Red in Tooth and Claw: Theism and the Problem of Animal Suffering.* Oxford: Oxford University Press, 2008.

Norman, Russell, Address to the New Zealand Parliament, 21st Dec, 2011. No Pages. Online: http://inthehouse.co.nz/node/11148, accessed Oct 12, 2012.

Pannenberg, Wolfart. "God's Presence in History." *Christian Century* 98.8, March 11, 1981, 260–63.

Robinson, Andrew. *God and the World of Signs: Trinity, Evolution, and the Metaphysical Semiotics of C. S. Peirce.* Philosophical Studies in Science and Religion 2. Leiden: Brill, 2010.

Robinson, Marilynne. *Absence of Mind: The Dispelling of Inwardness from the Modern Myth of the Self.* Terry Lecture Series. New Haven: Yale University Press, 2010.

Schleiermacher, Friedrich. *On the Glaubenslehre: Two Letters to Dr Lücke.* Translated by James O. Duke and Francis Fiorenza. Chico, CA: Scholars, 1981.

———. *On Religion: Speeches to Its Cultured Despisers*. Cambridge: Cambridge University Press, 1988.

Scott, A. O. "Lives Lived at Monk's Pace Allow Life to Flourish." *New York Times*, Feb 28, 2007. Online: http://movies.nytimes.com/2007/02/28/movies/28sile.html?_r=0.

Southgate, Christopher. *The Groaning of Creation: God, Evolution, and the Problem of Evil*. Louisville: Westminster John Knox, 2008.

Suchocki, Marjorie. *God, Christ, Church: A Practical Guide to Process Theology*. New York: Crossroad, 1982.

Taylor, Charles. *A Secular Age*. Cambridge, MA: Belknap, 2007.

Van Huyssteen, J. Wentzel. *Alone in the World? Human Uniqueness in Science and Theology*. Gifford Lectures 2004. Grand Rapids: Eerdmans, 2006.

2

Face to Face with Violence

Hitchens & Religion, Hospitality, and Peace-Building

Andrew Shepherd

It is difficult to deny that we live in a world beset with violence. In his book, *God Is Not Great*,[1] British-born journalist, essayist and public intellectual Christopher Hitchens advances the case that fundamentally this violence stems from humanity's continuing fascination and allegiance to religion. Hitchens leaves little room for misunderstanding. Boldly, he nails his colors to the mast, to use a military metaphor, subtitling his book: "*How Religion Poisons Everything*." But what are we to make of Hitchens' claim? Does he really believe that religion poisons everything, or is he simply using hyperbole to state forcefully his case against religious belief? What, if any, validity is there to Hitchens' provocative assertion, and critically, what solution does Hitchens offer to this "religious violence"?

In commencing, it cannot be denied that Hitchens is not the first to find religion a likely candidate for blame when engaging in a finger-pointing exercise with regard to violence—and nor will he be the last. From the human sacrifices practiced by the Aztecs, the slavery of ancient Egyptian society, the ethnic cleansing seemingly condoned in Old Testament narratives, the religious crusades of the medieval period in which Christians waged war on Islam in a bid to reclaim the Holy Land, through to the contemporary violence of "fundamentalist" suicide bombers, there is no denying that violence is often closely related to religion. Indeed, to claim that religious adherents are always peace-loving and non-violent would be both untruthful and

1. Hitchens, *God Is Not Great*.

foolhardy. Nor, to Hitchens' credit, does his attack on religion hide a secret agenda. In the course of the book Hitchens openly criticizes Christianity, Islam, Judaism, Buddhism, Confucianism, and Hinduism. For Hitchens, there are no favorites. He asserts that religions, all and sundry, are violent by nature and therefore to be reviled.

However, while recognizing some validity to Hitchens' observations, and sharing his sense of outrage at violent actions committed in the name of religion, there are a number of major concerns I have with his argument. These concerns, regarding Hitchens' slippery and simplistic conceptions of both "religion" and "violence," will be rehearsed in the first part of this work. In contrast to Hitchens' scapegoating of religion, I will suggest that far from being a product of religious belief, violence appears to be embedded in our very nature as humans. In the second half of the work, drawing on the thought of twentieth-century philosophers Jacques Derrida and Emmanuel Levinas, I will propose that rather than poisoning everything, the practice of hospitality—a practice with a rich religious tradition—offers an ethical activity with the potential for both building and sustaining peace. I will conclude by reflecting on a specific example where such has been the case.

An Initial Response to Hitchens: Non-Definition, Binary Structuralism, and the Selective Readings of Sacred Texts

The first problematic feature of Hitchens' argument is that, as with other critics of religious belief, nowhere does Hitchens set out a clear definition of religion, instead, deeming this self-evident to his readers. Within scholarship there are two broad categories used to distinguish theories of religion: *substantivism* and *functionalism*. Substantivism or substantivists, as the terms suggests, are interested in studying the *substance* of the religion. The examining of the ideas and concepts entailed within a religion is done through the reading of religious texts, the listening to oral tradition and attention to what adherents have to say about their religion, and the visiting and observing of religious practices and rituals. While approaching the study of religion from different angles—phenomenology, theology, psychology, or hermeneutics—substantivists, essentialist by nature, have in common the belief that the religious experience is a genuine human experience. Thinkers such as Friedrich Schleiermacher and Paul Tillich (theologians), Gerardus van Der Leeuw and Emmanuel Levinas (phenomenologists), William James (psychologist), Mircea Eliade (historian), and Hans-Georg Gadamer (hermeneutical philosopher) all approach religion from a substantivist perspective.

In contrast, functionalists are not interested in religion *per se* but rather how religion functions in a person's life or in society as a whole. As the term suggests, they have a *functionalist* understanding of religion. Prominent functionalist accounts of religion are given by Emile Durkheim, Sigmund Freud, and Karl Marx. While beginning with religion, ultimately Durkheim, Freud, and Marx take a reductionist view and move from religion to speak about sociology, psychology, economics, and politics. Thus, for Durkheim—the father of modern sociology—religion is simply *an expression of social cohesion*; for Freud, religion is a *universal obsessional neurosis*—that is, an attempt to deal with our repressed feelings; while for Marx, religion is *an expression of material realities and economic injustice*—that is, religion is simply an *opiate* which helps the oppressed to feel better about the injustice and exploitation they are experiencing.

While never stated explicitly, Hitchens, shaped by his intellectual formation as part of the political left, appears similarly to hold to a functionalist and reductionist view of religion. Beginning with the presupposition that religion itself is merely a social phenomenon (Durkheim) or, at worst, a neurosis (Freud), Hitchens shows little interest in engaging in a close reading of sacred texts, interviewing the "faithful," or observing religious practices and rituals. Despite proclaiming loudly the merits of empirical research and his own allegiance to free-thinking, the analyst, in this case Hitchens, has a pre-determined interpretation of what he is viewing. Thus, Hitchens declares emphatically that religions are based upon historical figures who cannot be proved to exist, and sacred texts full of "contradictions and illiteracies."[2] Hitchens asserts that all religions are grounded upon a misrepresentation of the origins of man and the cosmos. This erroneous belief leads to a combination of servility and solipsism, which both results in and causes a dangerous sexual repression. Hitchens, following Freud's *The Future of an Illusion*, believes that all this self-loathing, fear, and self-deception ultimately stems from our fear of death and thus our tendency to wish-thinking.[3] Summarizing his view of Western religions, Hitchens declares:

> The three great monotheisms teach people to think abjectly of themselves, as miserable and guilty sinners prostrate before an angry and jealous god. . . . The positions for prayer are usually emulations of the supplicant serf before an ill-tempered monarch. The message is one of continual submission, gratitude, and fear.[4]

2. Ibid., 109–22, 115.
3. Ibid., 4.
4. Ibid., 73–74.

For Hitchens, organized religion, "violent, irrational, intolerant, allied to racism and tribalism and bigotry, invested in ignorance and hostile to free inquiry, contemptuous of women and coercive of children" most dangerously of all, "looks forward to the destruction of the world."[5] Stricken by fear of death and hostile to free-thought, the religious faithful have a "death-wish" which, at its worst, is manifested in a "wish for obliteration."[6] For Hitchens, the equation is simple and his argument can be summarized as a maxim: *Religion is inherently violent and thus any violence that exists stems from religion.*

By following this basic binary structure—religion is violent, irrational, and evil; secular atheism is non-violent, rational, and good—Hitchens releases himself from the more onerous task of acknowledging and coming to terms with the nuances, paradoxes, and complexities of religious belief and practice. Within this simplistic rubric, anything Hitchens deems "violent" is religious, while any action he considers appropriate is regarded as evidence of secular-humanist thought. Thus, having outlined a long history of violence committed with religious motivation or justification, Hitchens explains away the counter-evidence, writing:

> In all cases I have mentioned, there were those who protested in the name of religion and who tried to stand athwart the rising tide of fanaticism and the cult of death. I can think of a handful of priests and bishops and rabbis and imams who have put humanity ahead of their own sect or creed. . . . *But this is a compliment to humanism, not to religion.*[7]

Hitchens adheres to this binary logic throughout his book. By definition, religion is evil and life-destroying, so any action of religious people which is peace-loving must be evidence not of their religiosity, but of their still active humanism. It is on the basis of this supposed self-evident truism that Hitchens reaches some remarkable conclusions. Rich in his praise of Rev. Dr. Martin Luther King, the leader of the American Civil Rights movement, Hitchens contends that since King was non-violent and Christianity as a religion is violent, then accordingly, "In no real sense as opposed to nominal sense was he [King] a Christian."[8] Ignoring the explicit connection between King's non-violent approach exercised in his quest of justice and his Christian faith, Hitchens outlandishly declares that:

5. Ibid., 56.
6. Ibid., 59–60.
7. Ibid., 27. Emphasis added.
8. Ibid., 176.

> When Dr. King took a stand on the steps of Mr. Lincoln's memorial and changed history, he too adopted a position that had effectually been forced upon him. But he did so as a profound humanist and nobody could ever use his name to justify oppression or cruelty. He endures for that reason, and his legacy has very little to do with his professed theology.[9]

Likewise, it is this simple binary structure—in which violence is equated with religion—which is the basis on which Hitchens engages in a form of revisionist history, reinterpreting the violence done outside of religion. To the inevitable objection that secular-humanism/atheistic ideologies have as much blood on their hands as religions—particularly as evidenced in arguably the most irreligious and most violent century in human history, the twentieth century—Hitchens simply re-baptizes such violence as "religious."[10] Adhering to his broad functionalist definition of religion and following the thought of George Orwell,[11] Hitchens argues that "the object of perfecting the species—which is the very root and source of the totalitarian spirit—is in essence a religious one."[12] For Hitchens: "Totalitarian systems, whatever outward form they may take, are fundamental and, as we would now say, 'faith-based.'"[13] Accordingly, atheistic regimes such as the Soviet Union under Stalin, Nazi Germany, the Khmer Rouge in Cambodia, or modern-day North Korea under Kim Jong-Il, all fall under the banner of religion and any brutality committed by these regimes is therefore religious violence.

As well as the slippery definition of religion and a steadfast loyalty to a binary structuralism, another frustrating aspect of Hitchens' argument is his simplistic reading of the biblical text . For Hitchens, the Pentateuch and the Ten Commandments display their irrelevance and moral bankruptcy in giving no commandments about the "protection of children from cruelty, nothing about rape, nothing about slavery and nothing about genocide."[14] But is this really the case? How does Hitchens square such an assertion with the specific laws and practices contained within the Pentateuch designed to protect victims of such violence? For example, the Jubilee practice was

9. Ibid., 180.

10. See Hitchens, "An Objection Anticipated: The Last-Ditch "Case" against Secularism," 229–52.

11. Hitchens quotes from George Orwell's 1946 essay, "The Prevention of Literature," where he states: "A totalitarian state is in effect a theocracy, and its ruling caste, in order to keep its position, has to be thought of as infallible." See Hitchens, *God is not Great*, 232.

12. Hitchens, *God is not Great*, 232.

13. Ibid., 250.

14. Ibid., 100.

instituted to ensure that those who suffer misfortune are treated ethically and have a mechanism to guarantee they do not remain long-term victims of servitude (Lev 25). Additionally, limits were set for actions of retribution and cities of refuge established—both measures which, if observed, would ensure that the cycle of violence did not become an embedded feature of the society (Exod 21:24–25; Lev 24:19–20; and Num 35:15).

Indeed, a central feature of Israel's covenant relationship with Yahweh as narrated in the Hebrew Scriptures is the demand that they care for the most vulnerable—the widow, orphan, alien, and poor. As Exodus 22:21–27 states:

> You shall not wrong or oppress a resident alien, for you were aliens in the land of Egypt. You shall not abuse any widow or orphan. If you do abuse them, when they cry out to me, I will surely heed their cry; my wrath will burn, and I will kill you with the sword, and your wives shall become widows and your children orphans.
>
> If you lend money to my people, to the poor among you, you shall not deal with them as a creditor; you shall not exact interest from them. If you take your neighbor's cloak in pawn, you shall restore it before the sun goes down; for it may be your neighbor's only clothing to use as cover; in what else shall that person sleep? And if your neighbor cries out to me, I will listen, for I am compassionate.[15]

Stemming from their own experience as oppressed "aliens," and Yahweh's own impartiality (Deut 10:17–19) Israel's treatment of the alien, the Other, is not to be one of ignorance or mistreatment. Rather: "The alien who resides with you shall be to you as the citizen among you; you shall love the alien as yourself, for you were aliens in the land of Egypt: I am the Lord your God" (Lev 19:34). In fact, the call for the ethical treatment of the widow, the orphan, and the stranger, as evidence of true religion, is a constant refrain throughout the Hebrew Scriptures, featuring in its poetical writings and wisdom literature (Pss 68:1–5; 82:3–4; Prov 14:31; 22:22–23; 23:10–11) and through into the Prophets (Isa 1:16–18, 23; 10:1–2; Jer 7:4–16; 22:3). As the Prophet Zechariah states: "Thus says the Lord of hosts: Render true judgments, show kindness and mercy to one another; do not oppress the widow, the orphan, the alien, or the poor; and do not devise evil in your hearts against one another" (Zech 7:9–10).

15. See also Deut 27:19.

Hitchens' "New Enlightenment" and the Advocating of Secular Violence

My disquiet at Hitchens' argument does not rest merely with the fact that he offers a caricatured and crude rendering of religion. What causes greater alarm is the way in which failing to be consistent in applying his broad definition of religion, Hitchens overlooks certain forms of violence committed—particularly violence done in the name of militant secular nationalism.

If totalitarian communist states such as North Korea and secularist Iraq under Saddam Hussein fall under Hitchens' rubric of "religious," then what about American civil religion, comprising as it does the holy texts of the constitution, the religious symbol of the flag, the ex-cathedra statements issued from the "anointed one" in the Oval office of the White House, and the language of "sacrifice," "freedom," and "justice" used to describe and justify actions of violence committed by one's troops in the process of "liberating others"?

Then there are questions regarding what exactly one defines as "violence." Does only armed struggle or physical acts of aggression towards fellow humanity count as "violence"? What about the violence committed in the name of the "free-market"? Hitchens says nothing of the ongoing structural violence of liberalized global financial systems whereby vast populations are plunged into poverty due to currency speculation, nor of the fact that millions are held in essential slavery and forced to live lives of poverty due to the debts stemming from the excesses of their non-elected leaders, supported by Western powers. And what about the environmental and social catastrophes either caused by, or exacerbated by multi-national corporations such as Shell in Nigeria, Halliburton in Iraq, or BP in the Gulf of Mexico? Do the actions of these companies, in destroying existing ecosystems and social communities, in the name of shareholder profit, count as "violence"? All of these and other uncomfortable questions are ignored by Hitchens. Although for many years one of America's leading leftist intellectuals, in the wake of the events of 9/11 Hitchens broke ranks with other leftists for what he saw as their failure to stand up to "Islamo-fascism." Vociferous in his support of the campaigns in Iraq and Afghanistan and the "war against terror," Hitchens does not regard American style liberalism—political and economic—as "religious" and therefore, as a corollary, neither is the action of the US military in attempting to spread the benefits of this secular-liberalism to other countries an act of violence.

But if, for the sake of argument, one was to agree, at least partially, with the proposition that all violence is ultimately the fault of religion, then what solution does Hitchens offer? In the final chapter—"In Conclusion: The

Need for a New Enlightenment"—Hitchens begins to outline some sort of manifesto for the way forward. "Above all," Hitchens writes, "we are in need of a *renewed Enlightenment*, which will base itself on the proposition that the proper study of mankind is man, and woman. . . . The study of literature and poetry, both for its own sake and for the eternal ethical questions with which it deals, can now easily depose the scrutiny of sacred texts that have been found corrupt and confected."[16]

Ignoring the fact that the sacred texts of the world's religions are themselves pieces of great literature and poetry and that their being deemed "sacred" stems from the fact that over millennia millions of people have discovered in them answers about humanity (man and woman), our place in the world, the purpose of human life, and how therefore we should live (ethics), Hitchens seeks a new set of sacred texts to inspire a new Enlightenment. *But what literature and poetry would be part of this new canon of secular atheism which Hitchens would find acceptable?* While not made explicit, Hitchens offers enough hints of which texts and authors may fit the bill. For Hitchens, it is the finer tradition of the rational which supersedes the irrationality and superstition of religion. Beginning with Plato and Socrates, Epicurus, and Lucretius, Hitchens assembles a list of acceptable philosophers, those with the rationality to realize "that religion was the cause of hatred and conflict, and that its maintenance depended upon ignorance and superstition."[17] Hitchens' list includes David Hume, Pierre Bayle, René Descartes, Baruch Spinoza,[18] Voltaire, Immanuel Kant, Edward Gibbon, John Stuart Mill, Charles Darwin, Sigmund Freud, and predictably, moves through to the founding thinkers of American republicanism such as Thomas Paine, Thomas Jefferson, and Benjamin Franklin.

And what trajectory will this new Enlightenment take? Hitchens admits that "only the most naive utopian can believe that this new human civilization will develop, like some dream of 'progress' in a straight line."[19]

16. Hitchens, *God Is Not Great*, 283. Emphasis added.

17. Ibid., 255.

18. Here again, Hitchens re-baptizes the thought of those with whom he agrees. Acknowledging the ongoing debate regarding whether Spinoza was a pantheist or atheist, Hitchens states: "Spinoza's definition of a god made manifest throughout the natural world comes very close to defining a *religious* god out of existence" (ibid., 262). Ironically, having asserted that he has "no wish to repeat the gross mistake" of Christian apologists who reinterpreted the ancient philosophers as prefiguring Christ, and therefore "no right to claim past philosophers as putative ancestors of atheism," nevertheless, Hitchens does exactly this. As with his treatment of Martin Luther King, Hitchens casts aspersions on how meaningful Christian faith really was for those on his assembled list, such as Galileo and Newton, who had Christian convictions. See ibid., 254–55 & 259–60.

19. Ibid., 283.

Rather, for Hitchens, the progress will be a struggle. And thus, he concludes: "To clear the mind for this project, *it has become necessary to know the enemy, and to prepare to fight it.*"[20] These closing lines are both instructive and deeply disturbing. Hitchens' dualistically-ordered world ultimately consists of good peace-loving people (secular atheists) and an enemy (the religious) who for their sake, and the sake of the world, must be fought against and overcome. In a simple reversal of the rhetoric of those he most despises, Hitchens argues that the "religious" are the "enemy" to be vanquished.

While it may be easy to simply dismiss this choice of words as hyperbolic rhetoric employed to make his case, elsewhere Hitchens makes it explicitly clear that as far as he is concerned, the response to "religious violence" necessitates violence. For, despite Hitchens' praise of Martin Luther King and non-violence, ultimately Hitchens has very little room for religious practices such as forgiveness. In a public debate, Hitchens states:

> And I say to the Christians while I'm at it, "Go love your own enemies; by the way, don't be loving mine." . . . I think the enemies of civilization should be beaten and killed and defeated, and I don't make any apology for it. And I think it's sickly and stupid and suicidal to say that we should love those who hate us and try to kill us and our children and burn our libraries and destroy our society. I have no patience with this nonsense.[21]

Indeed, Hitchens' own dogmatic belief in his being absolutely right, his simplification and caricaturing of the "religious" Other with whom he disagrees, and his adamant resolution that those who possess the truth are called to triumph over the misguided and irrational, leads him to happily endorse violent actions. As William T. Cavanaugh points out, the most disturbing element of Hitchens' argument, therefore, is not only his inconsistency in failing to apprehend the violence done in the name of secular-liberal nationalism, but the fact that in the end, as with other proponents of the myth of religious violence, Hitchens both condones and legitimizes this form of secular violence.[22] Vocal in his support of the US invasion of Afghanistan and Iraq, Hitchens sees these conflicts as part of a broader war between secularism and Islamic radical fundamentalism, a war, as Cavanaugh suggests, that Hitchens seems to face "with a certain relish."[23] As Hitchens states in another interview:

20. Ibid., 283. Emphasis added.

21. Hitchens, from a public debate in San Francisco, quoted in Chris Hedges, *I Don't Believe in Atheists*, 23.

22. Cavanaugh, *The Myth of Religious Violence*.

23. Ibid., 219.

> We can't live on the same planet as them, and I'm glad because I don't want to. I don't want to breathe the same air as these psychopaths and murders [*sic*] and rapists and torturers and child abusers. It's them or me. I'm very happy about this because I know it will be them. It's a duty and a responsibility to defeat them. But it's also a pleasure. I don't regard it as a grim task at all.[24]

Ultimately, for Hitchens, the state of the current world is one in which a war is being waged between the religious and those committed to "the defense of secular pluralism and of the right *not* to believe or be compelled to believe."[25] While acknowledging that "religious faith is . . . ineradicable"[26] Hitchens nevertheless views the defeat of religion as "a matter of survival."[27] Employing the same logic as former President George W. Bush Jnr. in his declaration of a "war on terror," Hitchens therefore envisages and commits humanity to an endless and unwinnable war. Far from offering hope for a new world of peace, Hitchens' solution simply exacerbates our current predicament.

Levinas, Derrida, and an-Other "New Enlightenment" Project

But is there another way of looking at religion? Are the sacred texts of Judaism and Christianity which come under particularly vehement assault from Hitchens,[28] inherently violent texts, which thus provide the foundation for the violence committed by these two monotheistic religions? Is religion, as Hitchens argues, in and of itself, violent? Or, is there the possibility that texts and religious practices, rather than being the cause of all violence within the world, actually contain invaluable ethical resources which may assist in creating a more peaceful world?

Hitchens is not the only contemporary intellectual to call for a "new Enlightenment." French philosopher Jacques Derrida regards his own work as part of a "new Enlightenment." While "Jewish," neither Derrida, nor his close friend and fellow philosopher Emmanuel Levinas, regard their writings as explicit "religious" writing. Rather, they envisage their work as a continuation of the Enlightenment philosophical tradition of which Hitchens is also

24. Hitchens: "Moral and Political Collapse," quoted in Cavanaugh, *The Myth of Religious Violence*, 219.

25. Hitchens, *God Is Not Great*, 252.

26. Ibid., 12.

27. Ibid., 252.

28. Ibid., in particular, "Revelation: The Nightmare of the 'Old' Testament," 97–108; and "The 'New' Testament Exceeds the Evil of the 'Old' One," 109–22.

so fond. Nevertheless, while shaped by and indebted to Western philosophy, both Derrida and Levinas have concerns about this heritage of Western thought. It is Levinas' and Derrida's belief that the Western philosophical project—particularly post-Cartesian thought—has been of a unitary nature, prioritizing reason and consciousness over subjectivity and action, and giving primacy to ontological and epistemological questions over ethics. They argue that such philosophy, in the quest to possess a totalizing knowledge, and in giving primacy to the *cogito*, displays indifference to the Other and exhibits anti-humanist tendencies which inevitably lead to the horrors of events such as the Holocaust.[29]

In contrast to such philosophy—the *love of wisdom*—Levinas and Derrida propose a new way of doing philosophy—a *wisdom of love*—in which primacy is given not to the *cogito* but to the Other, and in which priority is given not to knowledge, but to ethics. And what are the resources that Levinas and Derrida draw upon in the formation of their new Enlightenment philosophy? Moving beyond the "pure reason" of Enlightenment thought, Derrida, Levinas, and other post-structuralist and postmodern thinkers, far from demeaning religion, give renewed attention to the role that faith plays in knowledge.[30] While both thinkers engage explicitly with the biblical narrative, Derrida is also deeply shaped by his reading of the works of prominent Christian theologians, in particular, St. Augustine and Søren Kierkegaard.[31] Further, particularly throughout his later work, Derrida displays a fascination with the concept of the "messianic."[32] Indeed, such is the religious import within their "new Enlightenment" project that it has been termed the "religious turn" in Continental philosophy.[33]

29. Called up to serve in the French Army during World War II, Levinas was captured by the German Army and spent the duration of the war as a prisoner of war. While his wife and daughter, with the assistance of fellow French philosopher Maurice Blanchot, found safe refuge in a French monastery, the rest of Levinas' extended family, including his mother-in-law, father and brothers, were victims of the holocaust. That such experiences of hostility and hospitality clearly shape Levinas' own philosophical thought, is made overt in his second major work *Autrement qu'être ou au-delà de l'essence / Otherwise Than Being or Beyond Essence* (1974) which Levinas dedicates: "To the memory of those who were closest among the six million assassinated by the National Socialists, and of the millions on millions of all confessions and all nations, victims of the same hatred of the other man, the same anti-semitism." See Levinas, *Otherwise Than Being or Beyond Essence.*

30. See, for example, Derrida, "Faith and Knowledge," 40–101.

31. See Derrida, *The Gift of Death*; and "Circumfession."

32. In particular, see Derrida, *Specters of Marx.*

33. de Vries, *Philosophy and the Turn to Religion.*

Below we will briefly engage with the thought of Derrida and Levinas, noting the way in which, in contrast to Hitchens, they offer not only a more positive perspective of the sacred texts of the Bible, but also a different diagnosis and solution to the question of violence in the world.

Sacred Texts, Tradition, and the Ubiquity of Interpretation

Both Levinas' and Derrida's philosophical work engages frequently with the biblical narrative. While Hitchens complains that the Bible contains "a warrant for trafficking humans, for ethnic cleansing, for slavery, for bride-price, and for indiscriminate massacre,"[34] and regards the text as inherently violent, Levinas regards the ethical significance of the Bible as critical to his philosophical thought. Referring to the Bible, Levinas states:

> in the entirety of the book, there is always a priority of the other in relation to me. This is the biblical contribution in its entirety. . . . The Bible is the priority of the other [*l'autre*] in relation to me. It is in another [*autrui]* that I always see the widow and the orphan. The other [*autrui*] always comes first. This is what I've called, in Greek language, the dissymmetry of the interpersonal relationship. If there is not this dissymmetry, then no line of what I've written can hold. And this is vulnerability. Only a vulnerable I can love his neighbor.[35]

While for Hitchens the Bible contains only texts of terror, Levinas, Derrida, and many "religious" believers see the biblical narrative as fundamentally concerned with the plight of the Other. *So, how does one account for this difference?* While there is no denying that the biblical text certainly describes such atrocities as those listed by Hitchens above, whether these acts are condoned and authorized, is, of course, *a matter of interpretation.* One might anticipate that as a self-confessed lover of literature and poetry Hitchens would be aware of the complexity of ancient texts such as the Bible, composed as it is of different historical documents, oral traditions, and genre, and likewise, the extent to which such texts can be interpreted in a myriad of ways. Alas, Hitchens presupposes a monolithic one-dimensional understanding of religious texts, one which both fails to take into account the multiple voices within a text, and also ignores the whole complex question of hermeneutics.

34. Hitchens, *God Is Not Great*, 102.

35. Levinas, *Of God Who Comes to Mind*, 91.

In contrast to Hitchens' reductionist reading of the biblical text, Derrida and Levinas display a clearer awareness of the complexity of the hermeneutical task and accordingly offer more nuanced readings of the Judeo-Christian Scriptures. Derrida's well-known, but often misunderstood statement: "*Il n'y a pas de hors-texte,*" "there is nothing outside the text"[36] points to Derrida's understanding of this complexity of texts and the issue of interpretation. Many critics—in particular many Christian scholars—see Derrida's phrase as evidence of the essential poverty of Derrida's thought, arguing that *deconstruction* suspends any reference between words and reality and is therefore inherently nihilistic, relativistic, and a-political. Such criticisms, however, fail to appreciate Derrida's point. Far from calling into question the very concept of reference, "*il n'y a pas de hors-texte*" literally reads "there is no outside-text" or, as Derrida paraphrases it in *Limited Inc*, "there is nothing outside context."[37] Derrida is not making the ridiculous claim that nothing exists outside of books, but rather is arguing that a text cannot be interpreted without a consideration of the various "external" factors—historical, biographical, material, ideological, etc.—that have contributed to its production. At the same time, according to Derrida, these allegedly "external" phenomena—e.g., "humanism," "the age of Enlightenment," "logic," and, perhaps most importantly, "human nature"—are not to be considered according to structuralist assumptions, as *essences* or *givens.* Rather, such phenomena are to be considered historical, contingent, and temporary. As such, these supposed "givens" are subject to contextualization and themselves are open to critical reading. For Derrida, therefore:

> It is totally false to suggest that deconstruction is a suspension of reference. Deconstruction is always deeply concerned with the "other" of language. I never cease to be surprised by critics who see my work as a declaration that there is nothing beyond language, that we are imprisoned in language; it is, in fact, saying the exact opposite. The critique of logocentrism is above all else the search for the "other" and the "other" of language.[38]

Derrida's work reminds us that any engagement with a text, even a "sacred text," is not an unadulterated, pure experience in which one has direct access to the writer's intention. Rather, the reading of all texts is always mediated through the process of interpretation. Such interpretation is however, unavoidably shaped by the position of the interpreter (their background—ethnicity, socio-economic status, sexuality, education, etc.—and the

36. Derrida, *Of Grammatology*, 158.

37. See Derrida, "Afterword," 136.

38. Derrida, "Deconstruction and the Other," 123.

presuppositions and assumptions that stem from this). Accordingly, starting from his pre-determined constrictive binary structure and the assumption that "religion" is illogical and violent, Hitchens discovers, unsurprisingly, texts full of inconsistencies and violence. Yet, in contrast, many within the Christian tradition would argue that while there are many *descriptions* of violence within the biblical text, this by no means authorizes such actions.

Despite his highly selective reading of the sacred texts, there are, at times, hints that Hitchens himself does recognize the issue of interpretation and thus is aware of the complexity of religious belief and the problematic nature of his caricature. Having recounted the obscene and threatening phones calls he has received from Muslims due to his support of the publishing of the Mohammed cartoons, Hitchens then narrates the story of the Sudanese taxi-driver who goes to the trouble of locating the Hitchens' residence and returning money that Hitchens' wife had inadvertently left in his taxi. Hitchens writes: "When I made the vulgar mistake of offering him 10 percent of the money, he made it quietly but firmly plain that he expected no recompense for performing his Islamic duty." In the face of such gracious action, Hitchens raises the profound question: "Which of these two versions of [Islamic] faith is the one to rely upon?"[39] To respond genuinely to such a question would require a substantivist approach—a need to engage with the two protagonists and hear how they justify their actions, particularly in light of their sacred texts. Yet, as quickly as Hitchens opens the door to the possibility that he recognizes such complexity, he slams it shut, stating: "The question is in some way ultimately undecideable."[40]

But is the question *ultimately undecideable*? Even Derrida, accused by his critics of being a purveyor of relativism and nihilism and one who praises "undecidability," recognizes that the issue here is one of interpretation. So how does one decide which of these "religious" actions—the death threats or return of another's property—is ethical? How does one determine which interpretation of a sacred text, providing justification for differing actions, is "true"? It is at this point that the congruence between the interpretation/practice offered/enacted by a particular individual or community and the broader history of interpretation/practice becomes important. While different communities may reach contrasting, and at times conflicting, interpretations of "sacred texts," ultimately a *tradition*, emerging from the history of interpretation, establishes the parameters of what constitutes appropriate interpretation. Thus, interpretative communities in reaching an agreement over what constitutes appropriate interpretation establish a context—and it

39. Hitchens, *God Is Not Great*, 188.

40. Ibid.

is this context which ultimately determines the meaning of texts.[41] Derrida does not decry the existence of such traditions, but importantly recognizes that these traditions themselves are not beyond question. Thus, through the process of reading and re-reading texts and a constant critical reflection upon tradition, religion is engaged in the continual process of deconstruction and thus remains open to the Other.[42] Therefore, while there exists considerable difference in interpretation, it could be argued persuasively that overwhelmingly the Christian tradition—based upon the Hebrew Scriptures and New Testament writings—has been one that emphasizes an ethic of peace.[43]

Ultimately, Derrida's observation of the ubiquity of interpretation reminds us that "sacred texts" are not in and of themselves violent, but rather it is those who interpret the text who are "violent." While Hitchens sees the "ineradicable"[44] existence of religion as the problem to be surmounted, I suspect Derrida may be closer to the mark when—in an utterance coming close to an affirmation of the Christian doctrine of original sin—he states: "I believe violence remains, in fact, (almost) ineradicable."[45] While Hitchens' "chief hope" lies in the "lives and minds of combatant known and unknown," in those secular atheists who will respond to his clarion call to fight

41. For a helpful discussion on this point, see: Smith, "Nothing Outside the Text?"

42. Hence the way that over the centuries interpretation on issues such as slavery, and the treatment and role of women, has been reinterpreted as the interpretative community of the tradition has re-read the biblical text and come to new understanding. (A particularly striking example of this, which pertains to our later discussion, is the action of the Dutch Reformed Church of South Africa in 1986, whose interpretation of Scripture had provided the moral legitimacy for the policy and practice of apartheid. Many argue that the Church's renouncing of such interpretation and their repentance for their failure to recognise apartheid as sin, marked the beginning of the end of apartheid in South Africa.) Rather than being problematic to Christians, Derrida's philosophical insight coheres with the Christian belief that revelation is not a static, one-off event, but rather a dynamic ongoing experience as the Spirit, through assisting the community of faith to read Scripture more faithfully, leads them into "truth" (John 16:12–15).

43. While the Catholic and Orthodox streams of Christianity place a greater emphasis on *tradition* in both their interpretation of Scripture and their sanctioned practice, even Protestantism, with its principle of *sola scriptura* still has an unwritten tradition which determines the rules for interpretation and fixes the parameters for what constitutes acceptable or unacceptable interpretations. While violence may sometime be perpetrated by those who call themselves "Christian" arguably, the overarching ethical injunction of the biblical narrative is for the religious faithful to seek "peace." Indeed, that non-violence is the normative Christian ethic thus explains the requirement for the difficult—and, I would argue, ultimately misguided—elaboration of just-war theory, necessary for justifying one's contravention of this norm. The classic statement that Christian discipleship involves commitment to an ethic of peace is Yoder, *The Politics of Jesus*.

44. See note 26.

45. Derrida, "Afterword," 112.

against religion, Derrida and Levinas summon their readers to a different approach to the question of violence and our future with the Other. Rather than responding aggressively to the violence committed against oneself, Derrida instead calls for a deeper analysis of violence itself, suggesting that an "analysis and the most refined, ingenious account of its conditions will be the least violent gestures, perhaps even non-violent, and in any case those which contribute most to transforming the legal-ethical-political rules."[46]

Such an analysis and account of the conditions of violence leads us from the domain of hermeneutics to that of anthropology.

The Levinasian-Derridean Ethic of Hospitality: Heteronomy and Hostility

As we have already noted, central to the projects of Levinas and Derrida is their challenging of the traditional Western approach to philosophy. Both Levinas and Derrida are concerned at the way in which the autonomous rational individual—*cogito*—is given primacy and ethics is reduced to a subset of philosophy. In contrast, for Levinas and Derrida, ethics is not a conception known *a priori*, grounded in ontological or metaphysical theories, but rather stems from our actual encounter with the Other. For Levinas, our ethical engagement with the Other is not an action of rational consciousness. Rather, for Levinas, the enacted and economic action of hospitality in the world of being is the direct consequence of the "irreducible structure"[47] in which "my welcoming of the other, is the ultimate fact."[48] The fact that "intentionality, consciousness . . . is attention to speech or welcome of the face, hospitality and not thematization"[49] means that "Metaphysics, or the relation with the other, is accomplished as service and as hospitality."[50]

Derrida concurs with Levinas that the underlying structure of human consciousness and subjectivity is alterity expressed in the act of welcome. For Derrida "[I]ntentionality opens, from its own threshold, in its most general structure, as hospitality, as welcoming of the face, as an ethics of hospitality, and, thus, as ethics in general. For hospitality is not simply some region of ethics[;] . . . it is ethicity itself, the whole and the principle of ethics."[51]

46. Ibid.
47. Levinas, *Totality and Infinity*, 79.
48. Ibid., 77.
49. Ibid., 299.
50. Ibid., 300.
51. Derrida, *Adieu to Emmanuel Levinas*, 50.

But what does Derrida mean by "hospitality"? Engaging in an etymological analysis characteristic of deconstruction, Derrida notes the inherent tensions and paradoxes within the word "hospitality," which derived from the Latin word *hospes*, combines the words of *hostis*—which originally meant stranger, but came to take on the meaning of "enemy" or "hostile" stranger—with *potis*, to have mastery or power. The multiple meanings of the Latin word *hostis* is paralleled by the polysemous nature of the French word *hôte* which means both the one who gives (*donne*) and the one who receives (*reçoit*).

Derrida's etymological analysis provides him with evidence for two important conclusions he makes regarding hospitality, and, as James K. A. Smith suggests, therefore also provides us with a statement of Derrida's philosophical anthropology.[52] Firstly, the interchangeability of ideas such as "host" and "guest" are, for Derrida, evidence of the law of heteronomy—the fact that "the other is my law."[53] For Derrida, as with Levinas, the offering of hospitality is not an act of autonomous, sovereign freedom, but rather is a response to the Other, who is already within us.[54] In stark contrast to the autonomous individual of post-Cartesian enlightenment thought, Levinas and Derrida suggest that human identity consists not of independence and rationality, but rather of a heteronomous relationship with the Other.

Secondly, while suggesting that human identity is inextricably tied up with the call issued from the face of the Other, Derrida is aware that our summons to respond to this call, to act in accordance with the "infinite responsibility" we have before the Other, is one that we can ignore. Derrida uses another neologism—"hostipitality"[55]—to express his understanding that inherent within hospitality is the potential for such violence.

Derrida's account of hospitality, and thus his understanding of the relationship of the self with the Other, is vastly different from that implied in the thought of Hitchens. For Hitchens, the religious Other appears to be conceived either as one to be explicitly feared—a violent Other whose religious beliefs threaten to destroy civilization and therefore one who is

52. Smith, *Jacques Derrida*, 69.

53. Derrida and Roudinesco, "Unforeseeable Freedom," 52.

54. As Derrida states elsewhere, "the other is in me before me: the ego . . . implies alterity as its own condition. There is no 'I' that ethically makes room for the other, but rather an 'I' that is structured by the alterity within it, an 'I' that is itself in a state of self-deconstruction, of dislocation. . . . [T]he other is there before me, that it comes before me (*previent*), precedes and anticipates me. . . . Which means that I am not proprietor of my 'I,' I am not a proprietor of the place open to hospitality." See Derrida and Ferraris, *A Taste for the Secret*, 84–85.

55. In particular see: Derrida, "Hospitality."

to be fought against—or is, at best, one to be "tolerated."[56] For Derrida, human relationships do contain the possibility of violence, but such hostility is overcome not through violence or toleration, but rather through a *face to face* engagement with the Other.

The Face to Face Encounter with the Other: True Religion?

The critical significance of "face to face" encounters, the fact that in such encounters generalized labels and claims to knowledge of the Other seem to evaporate, is a reality that again even Hitchens appears to appreciate. In *God Is Not Great* Hitchens recounts a visit to Uganda where he encounters both victims of the "Lord's Resistance Army" (LRA)—a militia set up by former altar boy Joseph Kony, with rites and rituals borrowed from Christianity—and a "fundamentalist Christian organization" that seeks to rehabilitate those affected by the terror of the LRA—fitting prosthetic limbs and providing shelter and "counseling." Faced with the stark contrasts between differing "religiously" motivated actions, Hitchens is led to ask the fundamentalist Christian missionary: "How did he know, which of them was the truest believer?" The man's response: "All that a missionary could do was to try to show people a different *face* of Christianity."[57]

Yet the question remains, which of these "faces" is the "true" expression of religion? Levinas, in his acclaimed work *Totality and Infinity*, states:

> To posit the transcendent as stranger and poor one is to prohibit the metaphysical relation with God from being accomplished in the ignorance of men and things. The dimension of the divine opens forth from the human face. A relation with the Transcendent free from all captivation by the Transcendent is a social relation. It is here that the Transcendent, infinitely other, solicits us and appeals to us. . . . Ethics is the

56. In contrast to the mutual reciprocity of hospitality in which each participant shares with and receives from Others, Hitchens seems to prefer a unilateral relationality. Hitchens hopes for a relationship with his "religious friends" in which his attendance at religious events, marvelling at religious architecture and "respect" and "interest" is met with the "reciprocal condition—which is *that they in turn leave me alone.*" See Hitchens, *God Is Not Great,* 12–13, emphasis added. Hitchens seeming refusal to accept that the Other may have gifts to offer him is arguably evidenced in his encounter with the Sudanese taxi-driver recounted above. It seems Hitchens would prefer the predictability of a Rawls-like social contract rather than the freedom and graceful encounters that comprise genuine friendships.

57. Hitchens, *God Is Not Great*, 189. Emphasis added.

> spiritual optics[;] . . . metaphysics is enacted where the social relation is enacted—in our relations with men. There can be no "knowledge" of God separated from the relationship with men. The Other is the very locus of metaphysical truth, and is indispensable for my relationship with God.[58]

For Levinas, "true" religion does not consist of the correctness of one's dogma, but rather is evidenced—and more than this—*experienced* in the social relation one has with the Other. For Levinas, it is the face to face ethical encounter with the human Other which is the genuine encounter with the Divine.

While with its emphasis on the ethical Levinas' work has strong affinities with the prophets of the Hebrew Scriptures, there are also rich resonances between his thought and that expressed throughout the New Testament. Indeed, for those from the Christian tradition, Levinas' and Derrida's emphasis on the face to face encounter with the Other—though expressed in dense philosophical texts—should sound strikingly familiar. In Matthew's Gospel, Jesus offers his own ethical manifesto, calling for his disciples to be a people who display a hunger and thirst for justice, who show mercy, who seek to build peace, who are non-judgmental, and who, in response to violence, do not retaliate but rather respond with love and forgiveness, engaging in radical actions of generous gift-giving.[59] For Matthew and other New Testament writers this practical love of one's neighbor, inextricably connected to and flowing from one's love of God, is the fulfillment of the Law (Matt 22:37–39; Rom 13:8–10; Gal 5:14; Jas 2:8). Similarly, Johnannine thought places a special emphasis on the fact that love of God will be evidenced in one's obedience to God commands to love the Other (John 14:15, 23–24; 15:9–13; 1 John 3:10–24; 4:7–21). Significantly, a hallmark of this love will be one's non-retaliation to violence committed against oneself (Matt 5:43–44; Rom 12:17–21) and the practicing of hospitality both to fellow-believers, but also, in particular, to strangers (Matt 25:31–40; Rom 12:13; Heb 13:1–3; 1 Pet 4:8–9). In the Christian tradition, faith does not consist of a rational assent to a set of doctrinal or dogmatic propositions, but rather is evidenced in one's willingness to walk in obedience to God

58. Levinas, *Totality and Infinity*, 78–79.

59. Such actions, to paraphrase the Sermon on the Mount (Matt 5–7), are just some examples of the conduct that Jesus envisages will characterize those who profess to follow him. Hitchens argues that "Many of the sayings and deeds of Jesus are innocuous, most especially the "beatitudes" which express such fanciful wish-thinking about the meek and peacemakers." See Hitchens, *God Is Not Great*, 117. From my own experience however, it is intriguing that, more often than not, where such "beatitudes" are in evidence, so too "peace"—while imperfect—can, in some form at least, be said to exist.

and to love the Other—a practical love whose archetypal demonstration is hospitality, the welcoming of the Other.

Such a practice of hospitality, the face to face encounter with the Other, will involve, of course, an element of risk. Derrida's awareness of and his advocating of ethical action which is inevitably excessive and risky, is made clear when he writes:

> Pure, unconditional or infinite hospitality cannot and must not be anything else but an acceptance of risk. If I am sure that the newcomer that I welcome is perfectly harmless, innocent, that (s)he will be beneficial to me . . . it is not hospitality. When I open my door I must be ready to take the greatest of risks.[60]

While the decision to welcome the Other regardless of the risk opens us to the potential for hostility and therefore to suffering, again such a reality is not foreign to Christian ethical thought. As Jim Fodor, referring to the first "Christians," observes: "Suffering certified the disciples' witness as Christians; it marked them as followers of Jesus." Accordingly, suffering remains "perhaps one of the most determinative, identifying marks of the church."[61]

Nevertheless, while there is the possibility of exposing ourselves to hostility and suffering, such a risk is worth taking. In encountering the Other face to face, in entering into the experience of hospitality, the stereotypes and prejudices that shape one's view of the Other are gradually dissipated as one listens to the Other speak for themselves. As mutual respect emerges, the binaries of host and guest, victim and oppressor, rational and irrational, secular and religious, give way to recognition of one's common humanity. Thus, hospitality opens the way to the developing of a future of mutual reciprocity in which all give and receive from one another.

Theory in Action: Hospitality and Peace-Building

But does the practice of hospitality, the face to face encounter with the Other, really overcome misunderstanding, develop trust, and thus offer a potential avenue for the building and sustaining of peace? Two brief examples—one historical and one contemporary—will suffice here to demonstrate the powerful peace-building potential in the practice of hospitality. The first example is drawn from the recent history of South Africa.

60. Derrida, "Debat: Une Hospitalité sans condition," 137, quoted in Rosello, *Postcolonial Hospitality*, 11–12.

61. Fodor, "Christian Discipleship as Participative Imitation," 250.

On February 2nd, 1990, South Africa State President F. W. de Klerk reversed the ban on the ANC and other anti-apartheid organizations and announced his intention to free Nelson Mandela from his twenty-seven year imprisonment. In doing so, he set in motion the beginning of the end of the apartheid regime that had existed in that country since 1948. The decision to release political prisoners and hold genuinely democratic elections does not, however, change a country overnight. As different factions sought to ensure that their voice and priorities would be taken account of in the new South Africa, mutual distrust and suspicion spilled over into open antagonism and then episodes of conflict. As the election drew ever closer, the country spiraled towards the brink of civil war. On April 14th, 1994, less than two weeks before election day, international mediators Henry Kissinger and Lord Carrington, having failed in their bid to resolve the differences between the major power-brokers—F. W. de Klerk, Mandela, and Chief Buthelezi—departed. The world waited and watched, voyeuristically preparing to witness South Africa's descent into turmoil, violence, and bloodshed, akin to what had taken place contemporaneously in Rwanda and Yugoslavia.

Predictably, Hitchens argues that, "It is to the credit of many secular Christians and Jews, and many atheist and agnostic militants of the African National Congress, that South African society was saved from complete barbarism and implosion."[62] But again, Hitchens' bold assertion ignores the facts. South Africa was a deeply "Christianized" country.[63] In the eyes of many South Africans and international commentators alike, what prevented South Africa from heading down the same road of destruction as being travelled by other significantly "Christianized" countries at the same time—Rwanda and Yugoslavia—was the phenomenal turn to prayer, but also, significantly, the groundwork of building relationships that many, in particular Christians, had invested their energy into during the time between de Klerk's 1990 announcement and the elections of April 1994.

Michael Cassidy, in *A Witness Forever*, recounts how during these troubled days Christian leaders such as Archbishop Desmond Tutu and Methodist Bishop Mmuthlanyane Mogoba worked tirelessly, facilitating face to face meetings between leaders of the opposing political factions. Of particular note is the endeavor of Cassidy's own evangelical organization African Enterprise, which over a period of a year from December 1992 ran six weekends in which over one hundred leaders from the differing

62. Hitchens, *God Is Not Great*, 251–52.

63. Church membership comprises close to 75 percent of South Africa's population.

political parties were brought together.[64] Based at an isolated lodge the weekends consisted of fun, food, and relationship-building. Central to the exercise was each person telling their own story. Cassidy writes: "the experience of hearing each other's autobiographies was the most magical and transforming experience. For myths explode and stereotypes shatter. Humanity shines through. Mercy and compassion are born along with the desire to reach out and accommodate."[65] Participants who historically had been sworn enemies would end weekends with their hands clasping, as they joined in reciting the Lord's Prayer: "Thy Kingdom Come, Thy Will Be Done." As Cassidy writes: "The company of strangers had become the fellowship of friends."[66]

That periods of close proximity with the Other have the potential for assisting previously antagonistic combatants to overcome their prejudices and to learn to respect one's differences, is the premise which lies behind other peace-building initiatives in religiously diverse regions. *The Abraham Path*,[67] an initiative of the Global Negotiation Project at Harvard University, seeks to build a route of cultural tourism following the footsteps of Abraham / Ibrahim through the countries of the Middle East. As everyday pilgrims from Judaism, Islam, and Christianity journey together, retracing the steps of their shared founding Patriarch Abraham[68]—and are hosted along the route by local families—Muslim, Jewish, or Christian—it is hoped that pilgrims will develop a greater understanding and mutual respect for one another.

Hitchens and the New Atheists see religion as a dangerous and volatile cocktail which *poisons* everything and therefore threatens human survival. Following a Derridean lead, it is perhaps appropriate to point out that the word "poison"—derived from the Latin *pōtiō*—is closely related etymologically to the word "potion." While Hitchens thinks a world drunk on religion faces catastrophe, Derrida and Levinas, suggest less dogmatically, but more persuasively, that sacred texts and religious practices are perhaps the "potion" that offer a remedy to the age-old question of

64. Participants at these weekends came from across the political spectrum—from extreme right-wing Afrikaan parties such as the Afrikaner Volksunie, the Conservative Party and the ruling National Party, through to groups such as the African National Congress, Inkatha Freedom Party, Pan Africanist Congress, and the South African Communist Party.

65. Cassidy, *A Witness For Ever*, 53–54.

66. Ibid., 66.

67. Global Negotiation Project.

68. Appropriately, Abraham is considered the patron saint of hospitality. See Gen 18.

violence. Hitchens' predilection for public debate where he could engage in verbal jousting with his opponents was perhaps symptomatic of his preference for a violent relationality. One wonders whether an extended dinner or weekend spent with his "religious friends" may have been more mutually beneficial. The invitation stands for us to welcome the Other and share this drink of peace together.

Bibliography

Cassidy, Michael. *A Witness For Ever: The Dawning of Democracy in South Africa—Stories behind the Story*. London: Hodder & Stoughton, 1995.

Cavanaugh, William T. *The Myth of Religious Violence: Secular Ideology and the Roots of Modern Conflict*. Oxford: Oxford University Press, 2009.

Derrida, Jacques. *Adieu to Emmanuel Levinas*. Translated by Pascale-Anne Brault and Michael Naas. Stanford, CA: Stanford University Press, 1999.

———. "Afterword: Toward an Ethic of Discussion." In *Limited Inc.*, translated by Samuel Weber, 111–60. Evanston, IL: Northwestern University Press, 1988.

———. "Circumfession: Fifty-nine Periods and Periphrases." In *Jacques Derrida*, by Jacques Derrida and Geoffrey Bennington, translated by Geoffrey Bennington, 114–316 Chicago: The University of Chicago Press, 1993.

———. "Deconstruction and the Other: An Interview with Derrida." In *Dialogues with Contemporary Continental Thinkers: The Phenomenological Heritage*, edited by Richard Kearney, 107–26. Manchester: Manchester University Press, 1984.

———. "Faith and Knowledge: The Two Sources of 'Religion' at the Limits of Reason Alone." In *Acts of Religion*, edited by Gil Anidjar, 40–101. London: Routledge, 2002.

———. *The Gift of Death*. Translated by David Wills. Chicago: Chicago University Press, 1995.

———. *Of Grammatology*. Translated by Gayatri Chakravorty Spivak. 11 ed. Baltimore, MD: John Hopkins University Press, 1992.

———. "Hospitality." In *Acts of Religion*, edited by Gil Anidjar, 356–420. London: Routledge, 2002.

———. *Specters of Marx: The State of Debt, the World of Mourning, and the New International*. Translated by Peggy Kamuf. New York: Routledge, 1994.

Derrida, Jacques, and Maurizio Ferraris. *A Taste for the Secret*. Translated by Giacomo Donis. Edited by Giacomo Donis and David Webb. Cambridge: Polity, 2001.

Derrida, Jacques, and Elisabeth Roudinesco. "Unforeseeable Freedom." In *For What Tomorrow . . . A Dialogue*, 47–61. Stanford, CA: Stanford University Press, 2004.

Fodor, Jim. "Christian Discipleship as Participative Imitation: Theological Reflections on Girardian Themes." In *Violence Renounced: René Girard, Biblical Studies and Peacemaking*, edited by Willard M. Swartley, 246–76. Telford, PA: Pandora, 2000.

Hitchens, Christopher. *God Is Not Great: How Religion Poisons Everything*. Crows Nest, NSW: Allen & Unwin, 2007.

Hedges, Chris. *I Don't Believe in Atheists*. New York: Free, 2008.

Levinas, Emmanuel. *Of God Who Comes to Mind*. Translated by Bettina Bergo. Stanford, CA: Stanford University Press, 1998.

———. *Otherwise Than Being or Beyond Essence*. Translated by Alphonso Lingis. 5th ed. Reprint. Dordrecht, The Netherlands: Kluwer Academic, 1991.

———. *Totality and Infinity: An Essay in Exteriority*. Translated by Alphonso Lingis. Pittsburgh, PA: Duquesne University Press, 1969.

Rosello, Mireille. *Postcolonial Hospitality: The Immigrant as Guest*. Stanford, CA: Stanford University Press, 2001.

Smith, James K. A. *Jacques Derrida: Live Theory*. New York: Continuum, 2005.

———. "Nothing Outside the Text? Taking Derrida to Church." *Perspectives: A Journal of Reformed Thought* (2006). Online: http://www.rca.org/page.aspx?pid=3003.

Yoder, John Howard. *The Politics of Jesus*. Grand Rapids: Eerdmans, 1972.

History:
Atheism in Aotearoa

3

Perspective on the History of Atheism from Hammond to Dawkins and the Antipodes

PETER LINEHAM

Introduction

AS A RESEARCHER INTO religiosity, I find atheism a very intriguing phenomenon. It is common to treat it as the absence of religion, and therefore unsuitable for analysis as a distinct phenomenon. Perhaps on these grounds, and perhaps because atheism is of particular interest, or should one say distaste, to scholars of religion, there has been a curious lack of research into atheism as a social phenomenon.[1] There may be 500 to 900 million non-believers in the world. They deserve rather more attention than this.

Christian believers do not like atheism, and rarely give it much consideration. Alister McGrath's book *The Twilight of Atheism* (2004) looks on first appearance to be the exception, but it proves to be a slick but highly jaundiced account of its development and alleged decline. More than this is essential if we are to understand such a significant force in the modern Western world.

The British scholar and prominent defender of the secularization thesis, Steve Bruce, shrewdly describes atheism as a feature of a religious culture.[2] If this association is valid, then research into atheism may prove an alternative method to explore the changing patterns of belief. Such a study

1. Bullivant, "Research Note," 363.

2. Bruce, *God is Dead*, 42.

is difficult to focus, however. Atheism makes little sense as an independent phenomenon. It is a curious assemblage of ideas and adherents. There is a risk in focusing on the elite organizations of unbelief. While they have some influence, it is far more limited than the influence of church hierarchies over believers. It is possible to survey the attitudes and values that accompany atheism, but this too has limited value, since self-identified atheists do seem to come in different tribes. What do people mean when they describe themselves as atheists? How have changing definitions of God affected atheist culture? This paper seeks to ascertain whether Atheism is set in a vigorous culture, and how far its fortunes have changed in recent years. Conservatives have often claimed that Protestantism especially in its liberal form leads to atheism. Unitarians were frequently accused of this.[3] It is probably true that there is a continuity between liberal Christianity and liberal unbelief, but there is also a history of "flipping" from extreme Catholicism or Fundamentalism into atheism, and from atheism to conservative faith. Understanding atheism in its social setting may help us to understand this.

Stage One: Paine's Friends

Atheism is a very old religious position, although the Greek term may simply mean living without religion rather than disbelief in the gods. For our purposes it is necessary to eliminate this ambiguity wherever possible. Michael Martin distinguishes negative atheism from positive atheism, and for a while the New Zealand census distinguished "no religion" from atheism.[4] Distinctions like this are helpful for my purpose of understanding the phenomenon. Since Thomas Huxley coined the term agnosticism in the late nineteenth century, atheism has generally meant a belief that there are no gods, and it is this meaning that is assumed in this paper. Consequently this paper will set aside the questions of the Sophists and the Cynics and atomist ideas from the classical period, and not equate the so-called atheists of the Renaissance age with the modern meaning of the word. It may be an exaggeration to say that atheism in the modern sense was inconceivable in the sixteenth century, but it was certainly difficult given the common cosmology of the age.[5] David Berman has suggested that in the seventeenth century the Boyle lectures of Bentley and Cudworth were based on a distinction between practical and theoretical atheism, and the latter category existed only

3. See Wood's comments in *Daily Southern Cross*, 4.
4. Martin, *The Cambridge Companion to Atheism*, 1–2.
5. Febvre, *The Problem of Unbelief*.

in theory.[6] Cartesian theory did lend itself to a mood of skepticism, and thus Pierre Bayle's famous dictionary describes skepticism as a methodology. So Henry More wrote an antidote to Atheism, but the most notorious unbelievers of the century, Hobbes and Spinoza, never used the term atheism.[7] Attacking theoretical atheism was thus essentially an intellectual exercise. The opposition to the allegedly atheistical theology of Samuel Clarke for example, was largely a rhetorical game. Paul Hazard viewed the "crisis of conscience" as a corrosive tone in European philosophy but this was largely an eighteenth-century development.[8]

It was in the eighteenth century that scholarly atheism became a personal appellation. We can point to the French philosopher d'Holbach and his *Systeme de Nature* and La Mettrie's *L'Homme Machine* (1748), which did much to stimulate an understanding of a mechanistic universe in which there was no space for rational belief in a transcendent God. The first openly atheist English publication was *Answer to Priestley* published by Hammond in 1782.[9] A generation later, the poet Shelley was expelled from Oxford for his atheism. Bentham's project to extirpate religion might suggest that he be added to this list, although he made no public avowal of atheism.[10]

At the time of the French Revolution a popular atheist movement emerged on both sides of the Channel, and this has left a very deep mark on subsequent patterns of atheism and reactions to it. Some French Jacobin radicals convinced themselves that open rejection of religion was a necessary tool for the transformation of humankind. The extreme events of the Reign of Terror were often interpreted as a product of atheism, and opponents of French and Italian republicanism usually adopted a religious tone. This division was revived by the Communards of 1848–49 and the radicals of Paris in 1980–71. As far away as New Zealand this association of atheism and revolution was recognized a century after the events.[11]

These innuendoes influenced English radicalism. Thus although Paine was a deist rather than an atheist, his powerful criticism of organized religion in *The Age of Reason* nurtured atheism in some parts of the working class radical tradition. Such atheism was not "popular" in the sense of being widely adopted, but some working class leaders profoundly rejected

6. Berman, *A History of Atheism in Britain*, 1.

7. Force, "The Origins of Modern Atheism," 54.

8. Hazard, *The European Mind 1680–1715*.

9. Berman, *A History of Atheism*.

10. Crimmins, "Bentham on Religion," 95, 98.

11. *Daily Southern Cross*, 3. (These and other NZ Newspapers quoted are in National Papers online).

religion, and were extremely cynical not only of the churches but of Christian apologetics. The most extreme was the case of the Devil's Chaplain, Robert Taylor and his supporter Richard Carlile, who operated a pseudo church in London in the 1820s.[12] The Owenite Movement with its distinctive socialist views was imbued with a freethinking and atheist tone. Charles Southwell, the Chartist who moved to New Zealand in the 1850s, was renowned as an Owenist and therefore an atheist, although he rather hastily rejected atheism when he arrived in New Zealand.[13]

In that period the deniers of the existence of God endured very substantial legal disadvantages. J. G. Holyoake was hounded by theistic persecutors.[14] The New Zealand press noted that atheists could not present evidence in court.[15] Most settlers seem to have feared atheism as a pernicious social disease. One of the most repeated stories in colonial newspapers in the 1870s played on the horrors that atheism awakened:

> "What keeps our friend farmer B-r away from us?" was the anxious question proposed by a vigilant minister to his clerk; "I have not seen him amongst us," he continued, "for these three weeks; I hope it is not Socinianism that keeps him away." "No, your honor," replied the clerk, "it is something worse than that." "Worse than Socinianism! Heaven forbid that it should be Deism." "Worse than Deism." "Good Heavens! I hope it is not Atheism." "No, your honor; it is something worse than Atheism." "Worse than Atheism impossible! Nothing can be worse than Atheism." "Yes it is, sir—it is Rheumatism."[16]

The story demonstrates that atheism awakened paranoia. Before the 1880s it is impossible to find a single reference in New Zealand newspapers which uses atheism as a neutral or descriptive term. Unpleasant epithets were typically given to it. It was not just "godless atheism" but also associated with "chill and gloom."[17] There was a common view that Atheism was coupled with immorality. As the Vicar of St Matthew's in Auckland told those attending a Sunday School Anniversary, "Erase the thought of God from the human mind, and sordid self-interest would supplant every other feeling, and man would become what the principles of atheism represented

12. Aldred, *Richard* Carlile; Rowland, *Detroisier Williams.*
13. *Daily Southern Cross*, 3.
14. McCabe, *Life and Letters of George Jacob Holyoake.*
15. *New Zealand Colonist*, 4.
16. *Otago Witness* (10 June 1871), 21.
17. Peebles, cited in *Otago Witness* (15 February 1873).

him—fitted to be a companion for brutes."[18] These attitudes are very interesting for supposedly secular New Zealand. Although the colonial legislature had firmly resisted giving the Church of England a special status and rejected religious education in schools, its cultural and intellectual options were overwhelmingly Christian. The original meaning of secularism in New Zealand was voluntarism in religion, for the *bête noir* of colonial society was religious coercion. This explains the strength of anti-clericalism in the colony, particularly in Otago with its strong religious roots.[19] Judge Richmond, the Unitarian gained some public notoriety because his liberal views were regarded as likely to undermine traditional faith.[20]

The Emerging Modern and Atheism

In many parts of the Western world there was a significant change of tone in the 1880s, and New Zealand attitudes followed this trend. When Charles Bradlaugh fought his way into the English Parliament as elected Member of Parliament for Northampton, he pioneered a new respect for atheism. His stance was more acceptable because he was a middle class reformer, not a working class revolutionary. Bradlaugh was still notorious in the eyes of many people and the New Zealand press described him as the scum of London and parallel to the French communards.[21] In New Zealand, there were, as it happens, two prominent political sympathizers with Bradlaugh, Robert Stout and John Ballance, each of whom served a term as Premier of the colony in the late nineteenth century. They seemed to be associated with a more radical liberal grouping in parliament, and they formed a Freethought Association which gained quite a following in New Zealand in the 1880s. The name "Freethought" should be noted; although their personal views may have been atheist, their public argument in essence was a criticism of the institutional stasis of Christianity. In later years Stout attended the Unitarian church.[22] The numbers identifying themselves as atheist or allied professions were modest yet significant. The census reports first listed Atheist

18. *Daily Southern Cross* (31 December 1868), 3.

19. See for example *Nelson Examiner and New Zealand Chronicle* (11 August 1849), 95; *Wellington Independent* (9 January 1873), 2; *Tuapeka Times* (16 November 1871); *Star*, Christchurch (16 April 1872), 3.

20. See review of his book in *Nelson Examiner and New Zealand Chronicle* (18 August 1869), 3.

21. *Star* (25 July 1871), 2.

22. See Lineham, "Freethinkers in Nineteenth Century New Zealand" and Lineham, "Christian Reaction to Freethought and Rationalism."

as an identity in 1874 although three "Owenites etc." were counted in 1848, and the general category of "No religion" was first listed in 1874. In the report of that census, 4 male atheists were listed along with heathens, infidels, materialists, no creed, nothing, skeptics, utilitarians and unbelievers and the two large categories, secularists (33 males, 18 females) and No Religion (65 males, 12 females).[23] There were 26 male and 4 female atheists in New Zealand in 1878 along with 7 materialists, 49 No Religionists, 94 secularists and 22 others.[24] In 1881 there were 47 atheists, 39 of them male. In 1886 there were 105 atheists (74 men and 31 women) along with 189 secularists and 11 materialists and 668 people of no religion.[25] By 1891 the term Freethinker was in use as was agnostic (4,475 of the former, 322 of the latter) but the number of atheists had dropped to 123 (92 males and an identical 31 women) and secularists were just 65.[26] The term was in decline. There were 117 atheists (88 men, 29 women) in 1896, along with 153 secularists, 1,490 of no religion and 115 others, but the "no denomination" category had declined to 3,983 freethinkers, 562 agnostics, 46 Deists, 3,898 of no denomination and 46 doubtful.[27] Some observers saw the various secular aspects of the colony as integral to New Zealand's reputation as a "social laboratory," but the link does not seem to be a tidy one.

The heart of the appeal of atheism lay in its alliance with secularism. Even in secular New Zealand almost all Christians in the nineteenth and early twentieth century believed that the state ought to protect and preserve Christianity in order to retain the ethical authority of the state. Atheists were enthusiastic supporters of the Enlightenment belief that the modern state could not be constructed on Christian grounds. The late twentieth century saw almost the complete triumph of this viewpoint, for example in debates on ethical issues, such as abortion, marriage, and euthanasia. Christian interventions in those issues were most effective when they offered secular arguments for Christian positions. When Gordon Brown, former Labour Prime Minister of Great Britain commented that "we don't do God" he was talking of his public position, for in private he was a Christian believer and churchgoer. His predecessor, Tony Blair, found the safest way to project Christianity into public issues was by way of an appeal to all religions without privileging any one.

23. *New Zealand Government, 1874 Census*, 57.
24. *New Zealand Government, 1878 Census*, 255.
25. *New Zealand Government, 1886 Census*, 105.
26. *New Zealand Government, 1891 Census*, 111.
27. *New Zealand Government, 1896 Census*, 86.

In the early twentieth century, there was a brief rise in the number of atheists. Atheists and agnostics jumped to 679 by 1896, and then in 1897 they climbed to 4967. In 1916 the figure reached 5213, but thereafter there was a sharp decline, and it did not reach such numbers again until 1956. The New Zealand census from 1921 to 1936 distinguished the category of None/Undenominational which reached 1542 in 1936, from None/Freethought, which peaked at 8712 in 1911.[28]

The heart of the atheist movement in New Zealand probably lay in the militant unions. The leading Freethinker after 1890 was William Whitehouse Collins, a Christchurch Member of Parliament with a very left leaning socialist orientation, and among the early members of the various industrial political groups this was a prominent feature. Gradually atheist organizations came and went but the Rationalist Society of Auckland was the one that survived, with a strong magazine, the *Truth Seeker*, and a passionate determination to battle against the religious elements in the city. Auckland had strong Nonconformist Protestant churches and Joseph Kemp in the 1920s gave expression to the latest trends of revivalist or fundamentalist Protestantism. Atheist organizations reveled in this kind of opposition. In Auckland there were hot issues about the opening of the Museum, the Library and public transport provision on Sunday. These motivated figures like Dove Myer-Robinson into politics, and he was a life member of the Rationalists.

Yet this viewpoint remained that of a minority. Hence Liggins, writing in response to correspondence wanting more freedoms for trains to run on Sunday saw the dark truth of the situation:

> The true secret of so much Sunday desecration is to be found in a growing impatience of divine control[;] . . . a whirlpool on the surface caused by a deep dark current of practical atheism below. . . . The prevailing Sunday desecration cannot, we think be rightly understood if isolated from the various movements around us, viewed from this standpoint, we do not see much to encourage the hope that the desecration we deplore is soon to cease. The godless tendency indicated has not yet reached a climax, nor is it likely to do so for some time to come. We hope, however, when the practical atheism that abounds shall have produced its appropriate fruits, and men are awakened to a sense of their danger, we hope that there shall be a return to God, and with that a return to the ordinances and appointments of religion. Meantime, the authority of God is not felt, and herein lies the gist of the whole matter. This want of spiritual feeling is seen in the conduct of the public men to whom reference has been made; it is seen in the

28. Department of Statistics, *Census of New Zealand Population* for the listed years.

> characters of members of the higher legislatures, in magistrates, &c. We are a professing Christian people, and yet no respect is paid to directly Christian obligations.[29]

Yet the change in the mood towards atheism is evident in the first positive references to atheism in the New Zealand press, which view it as better than sectarian Christianity. These were voiced by the early spiritualists who flourished in Dunedin the early 1870s. Thomas Redmayne, President of the Society for Investigating Spiritualism in Dunedin, remarked publicly in 1872 that atheism was better than hypocrisy and J. M. Peebles contrasted spiritualism with sectarianism, and said that atheism was better than sectarianism.[30]

The most intense opposition to atheism sometimes came from more evangelical forms of Christianity. Probably this was because atheists and sectarian forms of Christianity were each seeking to convert the working class community. While there was relatively little infiltration of upper levels of society, there was a lively debate in the popular world. There is evidence that the Salvation Army in particular thrived on its antagonism to working class atheism. The following account is from the point of view of an early Freethinker in Taranaki:

> About six or eight weeks ago a few friends and myself, being aware that there were many avowed and unavowed Freethinkers in the neighbourhood, thought it desirable to organise an Association, knowing that unity is strength and that a dis-organised body of Freethinkers possesses no more strength than a dis-organised army would, disbanded and spread abroad amongst the people without a leader or place of rendezvous. We therefore entered into negotiations for the purchase of the empty Primitive Methodist Chapel and section, in Inglewood Town, but these negotiations fell through and the Wesleyans rushed to the front and bought the building, evidently to keep Freethought from having a prominent position and footing, but alas! no sooner had the "dearly beloveds" completed their purchase, than Freethought hammers and paint brushes were at work converting a four-roomed cottage into a meeting room and reading room, which it is proposed to open to members and the public formally on Sunday afternoon, the 30th inst., at 2.30 p.m. sharp, when short addresses explanatory of the objects and reasons for what has been done will be delivered by three gentlemen who are on the committee. There is no doubt that it is high time that Freethought made some effort to assert itself and let the world know that it is not the mean, vile

29. Bruce *Herald* (9 August 1871), 5.

30. *Otago Witness* (6 July 1872); *Otago Witness* (8 February 1873), 5.

> thing some of the preachers of the whale story, the snake story, and other similar gullet-stretching narratives assert that it is. We are often defamed publicly from the pulpit, and no doubt privately during the house to house visitations of "those gentlemen," and in our present unorganised state, not one word can be heard from us in reply.[31]

The attitude towards atheism was different for Catholics than for Protestants. Catholics viewed the Protestant spirit of the modern age as heading inevitably towards secularism and its ally, atheism. The Catholic newspaper, the *Tablet*, frequently commented darkly that Protestantism had no faith left in it. Catholic opinion took a polar view of the tensions between Catholicism and infidelity: "The spirit of the age will force them either into Catholicism or Atheism in the end—there is no middle course."[32] And certainly atheism was a kind of ultra- Protestantism, fostered to some extent by the apparatus of Rationalism, which functioned like a sectarian church.

High Noon of Atheism 1945–90

By the late 1940s, the status of Atheism began to change. During the Cold War there was much talk about the Christian West opposing godless communism but this was an era in which atheism and agnosticism steadily grew. The turning point within census data seems to be 1966 when the number of atheists nearly doubled to 10,434; they then rose dramatically in each subsequent census and reached a peak of 45,729 in 1981. At the same time the "none" category also grew from 17,486 in 1961 to 32,780 in 1966, and then to 167,814 in 1981. Then in the 1986 census a set of standardized options were provided for the religious question, including "none," and an astonishing 533,766 chose this option. This religious option has grown rapidly since then, reaching 1,297,104 in 2006. There are also increasingly significant numbers who do not answer the religious question (293,052 in 2006) and others continue to object to reply (242,610 in 2006). The consequence, however, is that explicit atheist numbers collapsed dramatically, to 2,940 in 1986 and to 1,542 in 1991, and since then they have not been reported. The age structure of atheists is also curious. The median age in 1961 was thirty to thirty-four, and was overwhelmingly male; in 1966, however, it was twenty to twenty-four and the proportion of males to females 4,063/1,411. In 1981 it was again the twenty to twenty-four year olds who were the strongest

31. Cited in Davidson and Lineham, *Transplanted Christianity*, 200–201.
32. *New Zealand Tablet* (20 June 1874), 9.

atheist group, but the male/female ratio was much more balanced with 14,109 male atheists to 7,419 females.

The 1960s to 1980s were a period laced with religious debate. The loudest voices were the defenders of traditional Christianity, as the Geering dispute showed.[33] Nevertheless a significant change in religious opinion was occurring. By the 1990s there was an impression that quite a wide variety of prominent New Zealand people were openly avowing and advocating atheism, while the public acknowledgement of church-going sharply retreated. Ironically the atheist organizations were in sharp decline at the time. In the late 1960s the Rationalist Association experienced schism between its rationalist and humanist members and the organization struggled thereafter to recruit new members. Meanwhile the Wellington-based Humanist movement only attracted a small circle of supporters.[34]

Today the proportion of unbelievers is about 45 percent of NZ society. This is one of the highest proportions in Western society. Their average age is much lower than believers, and therefore it seems likely that it will continue to grow. This "no religion" position is rather different from atheism, however; in many cases it simply dismisses the religious issue as of no account. The passionate belief in atheism is perhaps as unusual as ardent Christian faith in the contemporary world. The post-modern turn with its skepticism of ideology made atheism seem a curious and old-fashioned phenomenon.

Alister McGrath assumes that atheism had a heyday during the French revolutionary era. Even then atheism was not a majority position. "No Religion" is certainly not the same as atheism. Atheism is not the same as secularism. While secularism appeals to atheists it also appeals to some Christians.[35]

Perspectives on the New Atheism

From the early twenty-first century, however, the situation changed again. The flourishing of the so-called New Atheism is an interesting phenomenon of the last ten years. Christopher Hitchens' provocative book, *God Is Not Great* (2007) and *The God Delusion* (2006) by the scientist Richard Dawkins, have gained a great deal of attention. There are many other works in the same genre including Daniel Dennett's *Breaking the Spell: Religion as a Natural Phenomenon* (2006). A host of debates and discussions have occurred in England and America. The website "The Brights" expresses the new confidence of the "Bible bashers."

33. See Grimshaw, *The Moulding of Opinion.*
34. Cooke, *Heathen in Godzone,* 128–41.
35. See Baggini, "The Rise, Fall and Rise Again of Secularism."

Why the burst of new atheism in the West, at a time when the exact opposite has happened in some parts of the world? There has been a huge decline of atheism in the Soviet Union.[36] Anti-religious polemics have reacted to the religious inclusivism of governments after the 9/11 terrorist attacks. While governments urge a careful recognition of religion, fundamentalist atheism offers a cultural critique of religion's damaging effects, which are now as apparent in Afghanistan as in middle America.[37] The rise of the various types of "fundamentalism" is so evident that religion is reduced to no more than this in the eyes of many. One may wonder whether it would have happened if terrorism had not become cognate with "Islamic extremism." The sudden reversal in secularity in Western countries is very striking. The Statement on Religious Diversity was produced by the rather secular Labour Government in New Zealand and similar attempts to appease religious bodies have taken place in other states. Atheists who thought that their position was becoming widely supported by the social environment have suddenly found Islam and other forms of religion the subject of especial sensitivity from governments.

The unexpected growth of new religions and religious substitutes in Western countries is surely a factor in the growth of atheism. In these days, the forms of religion are increasingly diverse and the old religious mainstream is in profound decline. Some have suggested that there is a certain desperation in this New Atheism in the face of the new religiosity. Certainly they feel provoked. Thus the Skeptics Society found energy in its abhorrence of the new respect for Maori religiosity by agencies of the state anxious to appease appeals to *taniwha* and traditional Maori values.[38] In the past Christian missionaries played a key role in opposing this mythology, but now the role has fallen to the secular rationalist, further confirming their suspicion of religion.

The popularity of the New Atheism is far from clear. There is something rather highbrow about its attempts to engage with ordinary people. There is a condescending tone in the approach of Hitchens and Dawkins, an odd amalgam of Oxford and *Vanity Fair*. The educated elite is discomforted by sensitivity to minorities and their religious values. It is a significant force, but it lacks the vigor of the tradition of working class atheism. Oxford does not produce many martyrs.

36. Froese, "After Atheism," 63.

37. Nall, "Fundamentalist Atheism," 264R.

38. See Hardy, "The Return of the Taniwha"; Corbett, "Transit and the Taniwha," *New Zealand Herald* (9 November 2002). Online: http://www.nzherald.co.nz/nz/news/article.cfm?c_id=1&objectid=3003401

The strongest support for atheism tends to be among the young. A most interesting survey of 728 students at Oxford University found that 49.6 percent chose "none" to describe their religion. A follow-up question asked for more detail, and 32.9 percent chose atheist and 24.4 percent agnostic so more people chose these options than chose none.[39] These figures are much higher than in broader English society. Smart young people may shape their values around hostility to fundamentalism and the religious currents that swirl more strongly among the young than among the older.

Researchers into English religiosity suggest that atheists tend to be more independent and have weaker social links. This is not altogether surprising; traditionally atheists were distinctly outsiders. However they are not the only outsiders in society. Evangelical Protestants can also be outsiders who have an abrasive attitude towards the evils in their community, and seek to convert it rather than influence it. Perhaps then the New Atheists are actually copying the evangelicals. Cimino and Smith write about "the evangelicalization of secular humanism and atheism."[40] Just as the evangelicals formed strong units committed to evangelization, similarly working class atheists in the nineteenth century focused on spreading enlightenment among fellow workers. In certain respects the New Atheists are very like an evangelical agency, or perhaps even more aptly, like Moral Rearmament, which was a similarly elite organization using evangelical methodologies for different ends. Although they feel alienated from wider society, their intense bonds with each other are as tight as any evangelical group or their Rationalist predecessors.

One factor which has long assisted atheism is the triumph of a scientific worldview in the popular imagination. Many nineteenth-century atheists were well read in Darwin's theories and their implicit abandonment of a religious interpretation of natural phenomena. Thomas Huxley's lectures expounded this viewpoint. There are many examples of colonial New Zealanders reacting to Huxley's approach.[41] This is a very strong theme among the New Atheists. The environment in which they expound their views has changed remarkably. No longer is science viewed as the only source of true knowledge. Suspicion of the scientific worldview is very common within both traditional and new outlooks today.

The New Atheism has thrived in opposition to this trend. It has particularly focused on the revival of Young Earth Creationism among many

39. Bullivant, "Research Note," 364.

40. Cimino & Smith, "Secular Humanism and Atheism beyond Progressive Secularism," 415, 417.

41. *Nelson Examiner and New Zealand Chronicle* (28 April 1866), 3.

fundamentalist Christians. This position, which was once a minority position now is widely held in the Christian community. The attitude of high suspicion of science feeds directly into the war between atheism and fundamentalism.

Is the New Atheism more sympathetic to liberal religion? What view does it take of the broad Protestant position? Certainly it focuses on the new fundamentalism, and scarcely knows anything to say to the new spiritualities and the rather weak social phenomena of liberal theologies. But there is little evidence that religious liberalism has much momentum in the contemporary world. Hitchens is insistent that the moderate position is not good enough.

Conclusion

Atheism has a long and distinguished history which deserves respect from Christians. But like every religious movement it is continually evolving. So the atheism of the moment represents a distinct evolution from its forerunners.

We must be careful how we speak. We have a weight of history behind us and this makes the situation more defensive. So we face many attacks on what we have done and yet we must resist the *argumentum ad hominem*. This is frustrating because these New Atheists often seem to have an autobiographical basis in abandoned belief, often of a rather fundamentalist kind. Moreover, the grand generalizations about the effects of belief tempt us to make the same statements about atheists. Hitchens accuses the church as complicit in fascism—and misses the risk that by the same logic atheism is complicit with Stalinism and Maoism. But perhaps we need to show some restraint before we lay such charges.

In certain respects the history of Christianity and the history of atheism have moved somewhat in tandem. Whether atheism can discover spirituality in this new phase, as Alain de Botton has proposed, may seem unlikely, but in the same way Christianity has readjusted in the face of changing concepts of identity and community. But this shift is very difficult for atheism, which is so profoundly shaped by its Enlightenment heritage. Christianity draws on a richer range of values and traditions which gives it a deeper set of resources for its renewal.

Bibliography

Aldred, Guy A. *Richard Carlile, Agitator*. Glasgow: Strickland, 1941.

Baggini, Julian. "The Rise, Fall and Rise Again of Secularism." *Public Policy Research* 12.4 (2005–6) 204–12.

Berman, David. *A History of Atheism in Britain from Hobbes to Russell.* London: Croom Helm, 1988.

Bruce, Steve. *God is Dead: Secularization in the West.* Oxford: Blackwell, 2002.

Bullivant, Stephen. "Research Note: Sociology and the Study of Atheism." *Journal of Contemporary Religion* 23.3 (2008) 363–68.

Martin, Michael, editor. *The Cambridge Companion to Atheism.* Cambridge: Cambridge University Press, 2007.

Cimino, Richard, and Christopher Smith. "Secular Humanism and Atheism beyond Progressive Secularism." *Sociology of Religion* 68.4 (2007) 407–24.

Cooke, Bill. *Heathen in Godzone: 70 years of Rationalism in New Zealand.* Auckland: New Zealand Association of Rationalists and Humanists, 2008.

Corbett, Jan. "Transit and the Taniwha." *New Zealand Herald* (9 November 2002). Online: http://www.nzherald.co.nz/nz/news/article.cfm?c_id=1&objectid=3003401, accessed Oct 16, 2012.

Crimmins, James. "Bentham on Religion: Atheism and the Secular Society." *Journal of the History of Ideas* 47.1 (1986) 95–111.

Davidson, Allan K., and Peter J. Lineham. *Transplanted Christianity: Documents Illustrating Aspects of New Zealand Church History.* 2nd ed. Palmerston North, NZ: Dunmore, 1989.

Dawkins, Richard. *The God Delusion.* Boston: Houghton Mifflin, 2006.

Dennett, Daniel C. *Breaking the Spell: Religion as a Natural Phenomenon.* London: Penguin, 2007.

Dooley, Brendan. *The Social History of Skepticism: Experience and Doubt in Early Modern Culture.* Johns Hopkins University Press, 1999.

Febvre, Lucien. *The Problem of Unbelief in the Sixteenth Century: The Religion of Rabelais.* Translated by Beatrice Gottlieb. Cambridge: Harvard University Press, 1982.

Force, James E. "The Origins of Modern Atheism." *Journal of the History of Ideas* 50.1 (1989) 153–62.

Froese, Paul. "After Atheism: An Analysis of Religious Monopolies in the Post-Communist World." *Sociology of Religion* 65.1 (2004) 57–75.

Grimshaw, Michael. "The Moulding of Opinion: The Geering Controversy and the Printed Media 1966–67." University of Otago B.A. Hons. Dissertation in History, 1988.

Hardy, Ann. "The Return of the Taniwha: The Re-spiritualisation of Land and Film in New Zealand." *British Journal of New Zealand Studies* 14 (2003) 84–104.

Hazard, Paul. *The European Mind 1680–1715.* English translation by J. Lewis May. London: Penguin, 1953.

Hitchens, Christopher. *God Is Not Great: How Religion Poisons Everything.* Sydney: Allen & Unwin, 2007.

Jacoby, Susan. *Freethinkers: A History of American Secularism.* New York: Metropolitan/Owl 2004.

Lineham, P. J. "Christian Reaction to Freethought and Rationalism in New Zealand." *Journal of Religious History* 15.2 (1988) 236–50.

———. "Freethinkers in Nineteenth-century New Zealand." *New Zealand Journal of History* 19.1 (1985) 61–68.

McCabe, Joseph. *Life and letters of George Jacob Holyoake.* London: Watts, 1908.

McGrath, Alister. *The Twilight of Atheism: The Rise and Fall of Disbelief in the Modern World*. Grand Rapids: Eerdmans, 2004.

Nall, Jeff. "Fundamentalist Atheism and Its Intellectual Failures." *Humanity & Society* 32.3 (2008) 263–80.

National Library of New Zealand. "Papers past." Online: http://www.paperspast.natlib.govt.nz

New Zealand Government, Department of Statistics. *Census of New Zealand Population 1874–2006*.

Thrower, James. *Western Atheism: A Short History*. 2nd ed. New York: Prometheus, 2000.

Williams, Gwyn A. *Rowland Detroisier, A Working Class Infidel 1800–1834*. York, UK: Borthwick Publications No 28, 1965.

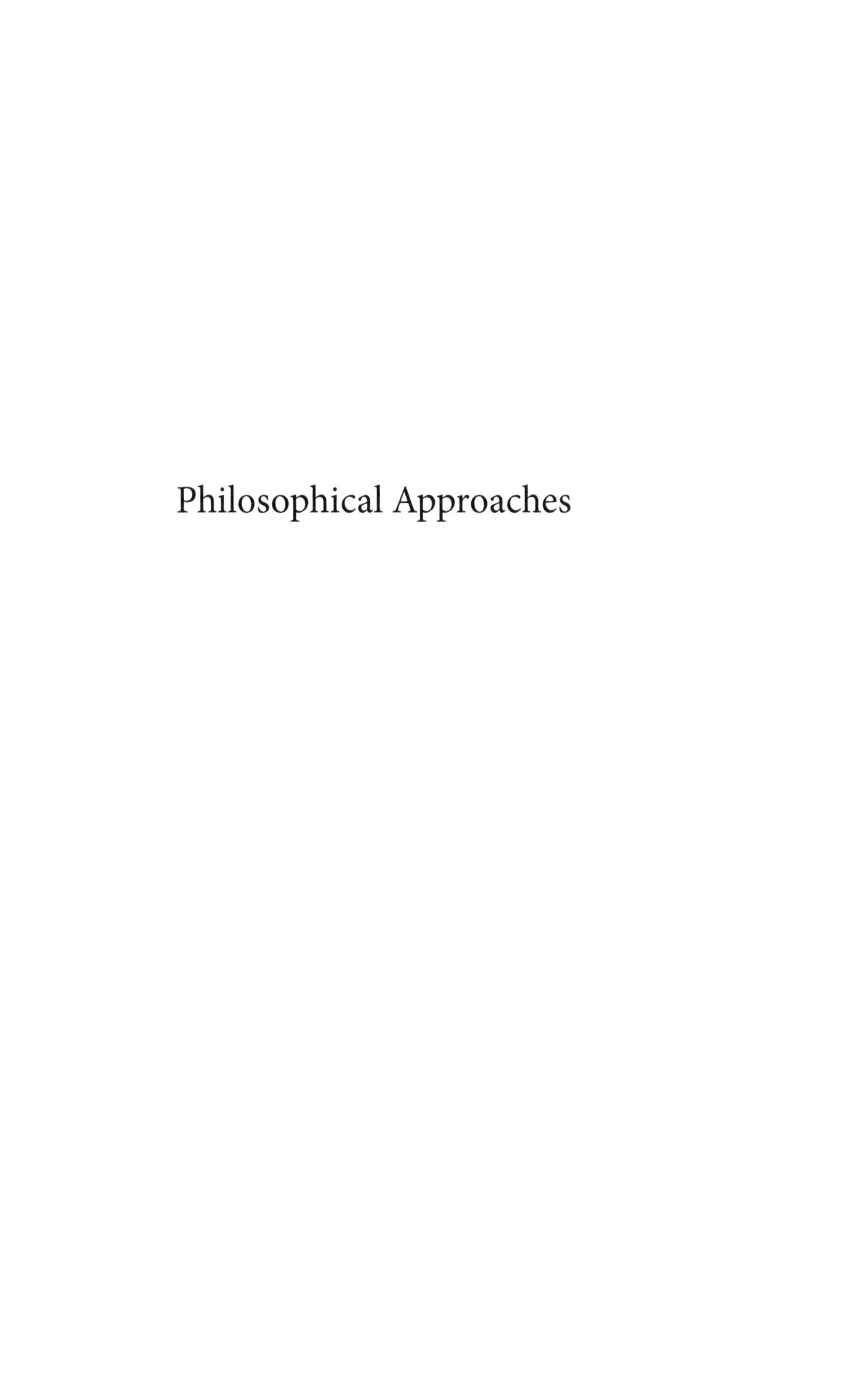

Philosophical Approaches

4

Some Thoughts on an Alternative to "Personal OmniGod" Theism[1]

John Bishop

"Does God exist?"

"It depends what you mean by God!"

This reply fits the caricature of the "analytical" philosopher as someone who dodges questions about reality and replaces them with puzzles about linguistic meaning. In this context, however, this response is entirely fitting. We ordinarily think it clear enough what it means to believe in God, and that the important question is whether we are *justified* in making such a commitment—a question that analytical philosophers, perhaps a little too rapidly, convert into the question whether there is adequate evidence to support the truth of the assertion that God exists. In fact, however, believing in God is always something of a mystery, as much to believers themselves as to outsiders who observe, criticize, and sometimes even envy them. Yet believing in God must have *some* cognitive component—in other words, it must be the case that believers have *some concept* of the God in whom they put their trust. But there can be—and surely there are—different concepts of God. So what it is to believe in God ("theism," as philosophers refer to it) must be *relativized* to the specific concept of God assumed in the faith-stance of each particular believer or group of believers. There are thus

1. This paper originated as a presentation under the same title for a workshop on "God in Light of the Critics," sponsored jointly by TANSA and the Vaughan Park Retreat Centre, held at that Centre on 29 May 2010.

conceptual varieties of theism—and, therefore, correspondingly, conceptual varieties of atheism.

The Atheism of a Believer

It follows that a believer may cheerfully accept *some conceptual varieties* of atheism. That is, a believer may affirm the reality of God according to one specific concept, while rejecting God's existence according to a different specific concept. Many believers will report that they had to reject belief in God according to some earlier held or inherited concept in order to clear the way for what they now regard as a more mature and authentic faith. A salient case in point is the *agreement* many believers have with the "new" atheism as found, for example, in the work of Richard Dawkins.[2] Dawkins rejects the hypothesis of a supernatural Divine Creator who brings the world into existence *ex nihilo*. Dawkins rejects "Creationist" explanations of our existence that compete with our best scientific explanations, which are, of course, Darwinian and evolutionary. Many believers in the theistic traditions agree: *they too* reject belief in God *relative to* this Creationist concept of what God is.

Belief in God Unlike Believing a Scientific Theory

Here is one reason why believers may agree with Dawkins in rejecting the Creationist God. Belief in God does not seem to be *in the same category as* attachment to a scientific hypothesis or theory. Indeed, belief in God *could not* be something that competes with our best, empirically well confirmed, scientific theories. Rather, belief in God functions to provide a *total interpretation* of all our experience—a way of organizing it into a coherent and meaningful whole. So theistic belief is not the kind of belief that could possibly be confirmed or disconfirmed by evidence, as a scientific belief can. It is the kind of belief that has to be committed to *by faith*—by a venture that takes to be true a particular way of understanding the world *beyond*, though not against, our total available evidence. (And it is worth adding that commitment to the "scientific naturalist" belief that there is no more to reality than science will in principle be able to discover *also* requires just such a faith-venture.)[3]

2. See Dawkins, *The God Delusion*. An earlier impressive defence of Darwinianism is to be found in Dawkins' *The Blind Watchmaker*.

3. I have discussed the question whether it can be justifiable to make faith commitments beyond the evidence—and, if so, under what conditions—in Bishop, *Believing by Faith*.

Many theistic believers, then, will agree that an evolutionary scientific cosmology is to be accepted, and that there is no such thing as the Creationist God. It is unfortunate that, although Dawkins is certainly aware of this point, he gives little weight to it. His public stance is very much that of the *outright atheist*—that is, someone who rejects, not only belief in a Creationist God, but belief in God *altogether*.

Dawkins' "Eucharistic Turn"

There are some chinks in Dawkins' atheist armor, however. When I heard him lecture in Auckland recently,[4] I was struck by his emphasizing that the proper attitude an evolutionary naturalist should have towards his own existence is *to give thanks*! Though it is predictable that, once life originates, there will be some evolutionary process in which organisms come to be increasingly well adapted to their environments, the fact that *we* are part of this process depends on a myriad of chances piled upon chances. We should thus be grateful, Dawkins thinks, for the astonishing contingency of our own existence.

Of course, Dawkins made it clear that he does not think there is Anyone to whom such thanks are due—though one might wonder whether it is fully coherent to believe that gratitude for our existence is a proper response to reality without accepting that there really is One who is the giver of existence and the fit object of such gratitude. My present point, though, is just that—rather to my amazement—Dawkins and the theists to whom he is opposed turn out actually to be *on the same side* of a significant divide between those who find thankfulness a proper response to reality and those who find it pointless or absurd. I like to think of this—perhaps somewhat wistfully—as "Dawkins' eucharistic turn"!

Tradition-Mediated and Philosophical Conceptions of God

If, as I have been suggesting, we complain against Dawkins that, in railing against the Creationist God, he hardly makes an entire case against theism, since *we* theists (at least) do not believe in *that* God, no doubt Dawkins will want to know what sort of a God we *do* believe in. And fair enough!

We could become coy, and emphasize the mysteriousness of the divine to the extent of holding that we are unable to grasp positively who or what God truly is. To treat God as wholly beyond our comprehension is

4. Under the auspices of the University of Auckland Alumni Association, on his way through Auckland after Writers and Readers Week at the Wellington Arts Festival (Saturday, 13 March 2010).

to overshoot the mark, however. This is because theists believe in a God *who reveals himself*—or, better to say, who reveals *Godself* . . . although that terminology still suggests that God is a "self," and that may be something we need to question. Theists must therefore certainly be able to say quite a bit about who God is *in so far as, according to their belief, God relates to them*: for theistic believers, God is the one who speaks and acts *thus and so*, and rich and deep and varied are the stories that fill out this "thus and so."

It is clear, then, that theists have various *tradition-mediated* conceptions of God as relating to them through great divine acts—such as, for example, the exodus, the incarnation, or the revealing of the Qur'an to the Prophet. These conceptions of who God is (as the one who has acted in these ways) may be sufficient for faith; but they are not sufficient for a *faith that seeks understanding*. If we are to debate with naturalist or scientific atheism, it is faith with understanding that we shall need: we shall need, that is, to give *some conception* of who or what it is that acts in relation to us in the ways related in our theistic religious traditions. And this is where philosophical reflection has a role to play: so far as we seek to understand our faith, we do need some positive philosophical conception of who or what God is.

Apophaticism and Its Limitations

So how do we understand the nature of the God in whom believe? There is a venerable tradition of *apophatic* theology according to which all we can say about who this God is in himself (in Godself) is negative: we can say what God *is not*, not what God positively *is*. The classical theism of Thomas Aquinas may be interpreted in this way: for Thomas, God is atemporal (= not in time), immutable (= not subject to change), impassable (= not subject to undergoing or suffering), necessary (= not contingent), and simple (= not composite or complex).

But this apophatic approach will not help when we are faced with the outright atheist who insists that God is nothing *at all*: to differentiate our acceptance of all that God is not from the outright atheist's perspective, we must have some view, however limited, of what *positively* constitutes divine reality. (It is important to acknowledge, however, that there may be some ways of interpreting the claim that God is nothing that are consistent with, or even required by, authentic theistic belief. For example, for the avoidance of idolatry it is necessary to accept that God is "no-thing," in the sense that God must not be identified with any item in the realm of things we encounter in our experience. Whatever divine reality is, it must somehow transcend the reality of things-in-space-and-time.)

A Dominant Conception: Personal OmniGod Theism

In the Philosophy of Religion—as conducted, anyway, within the "analytical" tradition over the past sixty years or so—there has been a confident degree of consensus about how to formulate a positive characterization of the nature of the theist God. Alvin Plantinga's formulation is typical:

> Classical Christian belief includes . . . the belief that there is such a person as God. God is a person: that is, a being with intellect and will. A person has (or can have) knowledge and belief, but also affections, loves and hates; a person, furthermore, also has or can have intentions, and can act so as to fulfil them. God has all of these qualities and has some (knowledge, power and love, for example) to a maximal degree. God is thus all-knowing and all-powerful; he is also perfectly good and wholly loving. Still further, he has created the universe and constantly upholds and providentially guides it.[5]

I will call this conception of God "the personal omniGod": and those who believe in God according to this conception, *personal omniGod theists.*

Theistic Doubts about the Personal OmniGod: The Problem of Evil

A good number of reflective theistic believers reject—or, anyway, are not comfortable with—this conception of God. There are many reasons for this, and I shall not here try to rehearse them. But I will mention one of the most significant of them, namely, the difficulty of dealing with the problem of evil on the personal omniGod conception of God. To explain why evil does not contradict the existence of a perfectly loving and all-powerful supernatural creator, we need at least a speculative account of what God's morally adequate reason for causing or permitting evil could be—an account known as a *theodicy*. Many theodicies have been proposed. Yet, on the most sophisticated theodicies, it remains the case that God first sustains his creatures in sometimes horrific suffering, and then wonderfully redeems them in eternal fellowship with him. But one may have doubts about whether the overall kind of relationship that a personal God would then have with his creatures could count as consistent with God's perfect goodness. Certainly, any human person who deliberately caused suffering in order eventually to save those same sufferers would be regarded as morally perverse.[6]

5. Plantinga, *Warranted Christian Belief*, vii.

6. For an elaboration of this way of formulating the Argument from Evil, see Bishop

Much philosophical industry has been directed at defending the reasonableness of personal omniGod theism in response to objections such as this. Alvin Plantinga, already mentioned, is a distinguished contributor to this project; Richard Swinburne is another.[7] There are many reflective theists who are satisfied with the results of the labors of philosopher-theists such as these. But there are also many who are not—and they are the ones with whom I shall now be concerned. I want to consider the situation of those who, like myself, cannot share the conception of God as a "grand cosmic controller," an all-powerful and morally perfect supernatural personal agent. For these reflective theists the question arises: if personal omniGod theism is found to be inadequate, what alternative conception of God might prove more adequate?

In Search of a More Satisfactory Conception of God

This is a large topic: my immediate aim is merely to sketch some ideas which I believe are worth following up in the search for a viable alternative to personal omniGod theism. It is worth remembering the spirit in which such a search needs to be conducted: God's positive nature *is* "incomprehensible" in the sense that it cannot be *fully* grasped, so any positive conception of the divine will be bound to have some limitations. There is no question of achieving a fully adequate conception of God—the interesting issue is whether there is a conception of God that, though limited, is more religiously and philosophically satisfactory for us than the personal omniGod conception.

God as Relational: "God Is Love"

I have three main ideas to put forward. The first is that we should understand God to be primarily *relational*, rather than primarily individual. Personal omniGod theism understands God to be "a" person, albeit a uniquely supreme one. But could an individual, however great "his" power and knowledge, really be "that than which a greater cannot be thought"—to cite Anselm's famous formula for a God worthy of worship? Is there not something potentially "greater" than personal individuality, namely interpersonal relationship into which individual persons enter?

---

and Perszyk, "The Normatively Relativised Argument from Evil."

7. Both Plantinga and Swinburne have extensive publications. Of particular interest for their treatment of the problem of evil are Plantinga, *God, Freedom, and Evil* and his "Supralapsarianism or '*O felix culpa*.'" See also Swinburne, *Providence and the Problem of Evil*.

To think of God, not as "a" supreme person, but as a supreme relationship amongst persons, is consistent with an important way of interpreting the Christian doctrine of the Trinity, namely the "social" doctrine of the Trinity. On this doctrine, what is divine in the primary sense are the bonds of relationship that unite Father, Son, and Spirit, each being equally divine in the secondary sense that each participates equally in, and individually contributes equally to, the dynamic relationship that unites them.

A relational understanding of the divine is also what seems required if we take seriously another Christian claim—namely, that God *is* love. Being lov*ing* is a property of an individual, but love itself is concretely realized only in relationship amongst individuals who are loving. If the divine is a kind of concretely realized relationship amongst persons, then it will be important to characterize *what kind* of relationship it is. We may *say* easily enough that it is the kind of relationship that counts as love, but it is a major task (the task of theological ethics) to grasp—and to grasp not merely intellectually but "existentially," in active living—what love truly is. Whatever we may think of the metaphysics of trinitarianism, the idea that the kind of relationship that unites the persons of the Trinity will be the paradigm of true love is a useful guide to theological ethics. For example, the tradition that characterizes the relationship of the persons in terms of *perichoresis*—which means "going round giving way to, or making place for, the other"—may help us to grasp the radical hospitality that characterizes agape love.

Some may fear that any move away from thinking of God as a person will "depersonalize" the divine, when surely it is vital to the Christian tradition that God be one to whom we relate as person-to-person. Did not Jesus teach us, after all, to address God as "our Father"? A relational conception of God is not depersonalizing. In rejecting the claim that the divine consists in "a" supreme individual, the conception of God as supremely real interpersonal love does not reduce God to something less than a person, but rather accepts the revelation that God is more than "a" person. We might express this by saying that this idea "transpersonalizes" God. And there need be no barrier to our continuing to relate in our prayer and liturgy to God as a loving parent—this may be psychologically helpful or even essential in our relationship with God. But it does not follow that our psychological limitations must constrain our understanding of what God is: what we psychologically relate to as a person, as "our Father," may be understood as altogether much more than these categories suggest. And the relational account of the divine gives us a hint as to what that "much more" may involve.

Certainly, there will be challenges in thinking of God as primarily relational rather than individual—how, for example, are we to understand divine action on this view? Is it coherent to think of the divine love as active in creating, sustaining and providentially ordering the world? Nevertheless, the philosophical and religious value of understanding God as supremely good relationship (Love) at work in the world may convince us not to be daunted by the intellectual challenges posed by this conception of the divine.

"De-Supernaturalizing" God

My second proposal is that we should try rejecting the traditional contrast between God as a supernatural being and the natural world which is God's creation and in which God's purposes are achieved. As already emphasized, God is not to be identified with any item within the world—but this suggestion goes further by insisting that God cannot be a supernatural item either, an item outside the world. Locating divine reality within the one Universe of Being will remove or reduce all those problems that arise for personal omniGod theism from thinking of God as operating on or controlling the Universe from outside it. This proposal might be supported for Christians by a radical interpretation of the doctrine of the incarnation, understood not merely as a christological doctrine (i.e., a teaching about the unique status of Christ), but as revealing the very nature of the divine itself: God's being is essentially "enfleshed," realized within the natural Universe.

This proposal will attract even more challenges, perhaps, than my first. It will no doubt invite the accusation of pantheism. Yet there need be no implication that God is simply to be identified with the whole natural Universe conceived overall as an organic and dynamic unity. There may be something to be said for such a pantheistic conception of divinity, but the present proposal may perhaps be better described as "pan*en*theistic," understanding God's being not as the being of the Universe but as "in and through" the Universe. The etymology may suggest, however, that a panentheist holds that "all is *in* God"(rather than that all simply *is* God), which carries the implicature that God's being is somehow more than the being of the Universe as a whole. My proposal here, however, might better be described as "the-en-pan-ism," since it suggests that, so to speak, the only place for God's reality to be is within the being of the Universe—and if God is not identical with the whole, it seems to follow that God must "only" be part of the Universe.

That implication may seem problematic, however, making God much too "small." If God is somehow *within* the Universe, then God's existence will presumably be contingent, and dependent on the existence of other things: yet a proper conception of the divine must ascribe to God an ontological priority fit for "that than which a greater cannot be conceived." Furthermore—and along the same line of objection—God must be Creator. We may reject the Creation*ist* God, but we surely cannot abandon the key theistic idea that God is the Source of all that is—and this key idea seems to put paid decisively to any location of full divinity within the natural Universe. (But, then, what do we Christians really believe about the incarnation? Do we not hold that divinity *in all its fullness* is to be encountered in the humanity of Christ?)

God as the Goal of the Universe

My third proposal is to emphasize the importance of God's being the Goal (or *telos*) of the Universe—that purpose for the sake of which the Universe exists. This fits nicely with my first proposal, if we allow that a Christian theism holds that the Universe's *telos* is precisely the existence of Love, supremely good relationship. Taking God to be the Universe's end or point also helps meet the challenge I have just been rehearsing to the second proposal to locate God wholly within the one Universe. This teleological conception of the divine offers a way of reinterpreting the idea that God is Creator, which there seemed under threat. Under this reinterpretation, we take the claim that the Universe is a creation *ex nihilo* absolutely strictly: *nothing*, not even a supernatural immaterial supreme being, is the efficient or productive cause of the Universe as a whole. The Universe as a whole has no productive cause. It does count as a Creation, however, because it has an ultimate point (*telos*), for the sake of which it exists and which explains why it exists. There is thus a uniquely irreducible teleological explanation for the existence of the Universe: we can explain why it exists, not by positing something somehow prior to it from which it is derived, but by showing what the point, end, or purpose of the Universe's existence is—by exhibiting the Good for the sake of which all that is, is. Theism then identifies this Good—the ultimate *telos* of the Universe—with God—or, more strictly, theism identifies God's reality *with all reality's existing for the sake of realizing, and because it actually does realize, the Good.* This identification then allows us to understand God to be Source as well as Goal ("I am the alpha and the omega")—but God is Source *because* God is the Goal (alpha because omega, and because it is only in terms of its omega that what is can be ultimately explained).

This proposal may seem to risk reducing God to an ideal: there may be something wonderful that is the purpose of the Universe, but maybe this purpose is no more than potential? It needs to be emphasized, therefore, that the proposal requires that the ideal divine purpose of the Universe be *actually* realized. Nothing that lacks concrete existence (such as a *mere* ideal) could possibly be God, given the ontological priority God must have as that than which a greater cannot be conceived (that, I think, is the useful lesson to be learnt from the famous Ontological Argument). What theism claims, on this proposal, is that the Universe is ultimately explicable in terms of the *actually achieved* Good for the sake of which it exists—and that God is manifest in this concretely real Good. Furthermore, for Christians, the concretely realized divine is not something purely eschatological (achieved only at a notional limiting point when the Universe reaches its final consummation). Christian eschatology is *realized* eschatology, with the divine purpose *achieved already* in human history and made fully manifest in Christ, crucified and risen. Nevertheless—it is important to add—the reality of God is not exhausted by the sum total of actual manifestations of the Good whose status as telos explains the Universe's existence: God's reality transcends those manifestations as the real ground of the possibility of unlimitedly many of them. For Christians, the incarnation of the divine in Christ is but the template for indefinitely many "incarnations": as we read in 1 John 4:16, "Whoever lives in love lives in God, and God in them."

Some Challenges . . .

These three ideas about how to generate a potentially helpful alternative to personal omniGod theism can evidently be put together. If we identify God as Creator with the Universe's having an actually achieved ultimate purpose, then divinity belongs to the Universe itself (rather than operating on it from "outside"). Divinity may then be identified as manifested in concretely real Love, understood as supremely good relationship amongst whatever participates in those relationships. In efficient causal terms, manifestations of the divine emerge, dependently, within the evolving Universe; but in teleological terms, the divine purpose and the fact that it is manifested is the Universe's ultimate explanation, the reason why contingent beings come into being, persist in being, and cease to be.

Two key challenges confront this conception of God.

First, it may seem that this conception is too naturalistic. God is Love, yes, but this understanding might appear to get it the other way round and make Love God. A vital ingredient in what is truly divine is its *transcendence*. The supernatural status of the personal omniGod readily accommodates that transcendence, surely: how could my suggested "de-supernaturalized" conception of God manage to do so?

Second, the God whom we worship is a God of dynamic *agency*, graciously dealing with us, forgiving, healing, and strengthening. But, as already noted, my proposed "God is Love" conception places God in the category of relation rather than agent. Personal omniGod theism makes it plain that God is a supreme agent. How could supremely good and supremely powerful *agency* belong to God—as surely it must—other than God's actually being a supreme and powerful *agent*?

. . . and a Possible Response?

I shall conclude in open-ended fashion by recording some current thoughts about how these challenges might be met.

The sum total of loving relationships achieved in the Universe is undoubtedly a remarkably valuable composite entity—but I agree that, as such, it lacks the transcendence needed for an authentic concept of God. My proposal is not, however, to make so straightforward an identification of Love (in this concrete sense) with the divine. Rather, my teleological proposal is that the divine is that most profound feature of reality that explains its existence in terms of its achieving a supremely good purpose, and, as I have emphasized above, though the divine in this sense must be really manifested in the world, the manifestations do not exhaust it. So there is that much transcendence to the divine.

A further aspect of divine transcendence may be developed on my proposal, however, in answer to the second challenge about how the agency of God, not just in original creation but also within history, is to be understood if God is not a supremely powerful supernatural agent. On my suggested conception, God is fully manifested in concrete loving relationships. Now, it does not seem impossible that a concrete relationship might itself be dynamic, might itself possess agency. Assuredly, as well as the action of individuals, there is also group and institutional action, the action of collectives. It is more controversial to maintain that group or collective action does not simply reduce to the sum total of the actions of the individuals who make up the group (we will need to confront those who endorse Mrs. Thatcher's notorious claim to the Conservative Party Conference in 1987 that "there is no such thing as society"!). Nevertheless, the idea that we can act more powerfully—both for good and for ill—when we come together in collectives and institutions is a perfectly intelligible and defensible one. Through the right kinds of relationships amongst individuals, a capacity for higher-order enhanced effective agency can emerge. (I think of political philosophy as inquiring into how we can best ensure that this collective agency is directed towards the good.)

But, now, if the phenomenon of "higher-order" agency emerging out of relationships in groups and collectives is well founded, there is surely conceptual space for the idea of agency of a *transcendentally* higher-order emerging out of the right kind of relationships? Understanding the divine as concretely realized in relationships of authentic agape love may then be consistent with ascribing to the divine the greatest conceivable power within history for bringing about the good, transforming a broken world, "making all things new."

Such a claim does, of course, go beyond anything that could be empirically established according to criteria for scientifically held knowledge. But that's just what we want! The kind of naturalism, or anti-supernaturalism, I have recommended is not *scientism*—it is not the claim that there can be no more to the Universe than a completed natural science could discover. Theism absolutely rejects this kind of scientistic naturalism—but, as it has been the main burden of the present discussion to show, in order to do so it need not appeal to a separate ontological realm whose inhabitant is a supreme monarchical individual person. Divine transcendence can consist in reality's existing because it realizes Love as its ultimate purpose, and, furthermore, in the transcendent power of that Love within the one natural Universe. Christian theists may then see themselves as children (of a "heavenly Father") who are born "anew" by this power, and whose inheritance is to participate in and contribute to fully loving relationships ("the kingdom of heaven amongst us"). The transformative potential of living this new life may be vastly beyond our imagining: when we believe in practice in the God who calls us to this way of living, we may be "doing the universe the deepest service we can."[8]

Bibliography

Bishop, John. *Believing by Faith: An Essay in the Epistemology and Ethics of Religious Belief.* Oxford: Oxford University Press, 2007.

Bishop, John, and Ken Perszyk. "The Normatively Relativised Argument from Evil." *International Journal for Philosophy of Religion* 70.2 (2011) 109–26.

Dawkins, Richard. *The Blind Watchmaker.* Harlow: Longman, 1986.

———. *The God Delusion.* Boston: Houghton Mifflin, 2008.

James, William. "The Will to Believe." In *The Will to Believe and Other Essays in Popular Philosophy,* edited by William James, 1–31. New York: Dover, 1956.

Plantinga, Alvin. *God, Freedom, and Evil.* Grand Rapids: Eerdmans, 1974.

———. "Supralapsarianism or '*O felix culpa*.'" In *Christian Faith and the Problem of Evil,* edited by Peter van Inwagen, 1–25. Grand Rapids: Eerdmans, 2004.

———. *Warranted Christian Belief.* Oxford: Oxford University Press, 2000.

Swinburne, Richard. *Providence and the Problem of Evil.* Oxford: Clarendon, 1998.

8. I borrow this phrase from James, "The Will to Believe," 28.

5

Recycling the Soul

Nancey Murphy's Physicalist Anthropology

John Owens

Introduction

Can religion accept a naturalist or physicalist view of the human being and still address its core business, or does it need something more, like a soul or spirit, or at least a spark of freedom, some concept invisible to the scientific eye, which has been traditionally drawn from metaphysics? The idea that we need to appeal to something beyond the reach of science, if we are to explain human things, goes back a good way in Western history. In Plato's *Phaedo*, Socrates records his disappointment with those who want to explain human realities through the workings of "sound and air and hearing," and his excitement on discovering Anaxagoras, who appeals to mind and soul, and explains the behavior of a thing by noting what is "best" for it.[1] Aspiration towards a good, the typical activity of soul or mind, seems to point to mysterious depths that go beyond anything explainable by combinations of materials. It reflects perhaps an attraction towards a fullness of life which transcends mere current physical states. Aristotle says that "the goal towards which all things strive" is that they may "partake in the eternal and divine."[2] Modern science, in the person of programmatic figures like Bacon and Descartes, set out to banish any sense of aspiration from the

1. Plato, *Phaedo*, 79.

2. Aristotle, *De Anima*, 661.

workings of the new scientific method. Sometimes there were hesitations when it came to the human being. Along with a materialist notion of nature, Descartes offered a well-developed doctrine of the soul. Nancey Murphy's position on such questions is however straightforward: "My central thesis is, first that we are our bodies—there is no additional metaphysical element such as a mind or soul or spirit."[3] Religion can make do with the physical explanations offered by the sciences, and needs no deeper mysteries than these. With suitable adjustments, a physicalist outlook can accommodate intelligence, morality, and spirituality, qualities that were once thought to require a base of a thoroughly different sort. I want to suggest in this paper that it is not so easy. The concepts developed in the tradition of philosophical anthropology are peculiarly tenacious, and cannot be dismissed without further ado. Sometimes even the very reflections which are meant to dispose of them, in fact unwittingly assume their validity. I will argue that this is the case with Nancey Murphy. In particular, the notion of life itself, with its associated idea of end-directedness or teleology, is assumed by the very reflections that want to insist that modern "scientific" concepts are enough. The human order clings to fundamental mysteries, however much we try to rid ourselves of them.

Non-Reductive Physicalism

In an article that is some decades old, Richard Taylor sets out the basic lines of the program that Murphy adopts for understanding the human being.[4] Taylor asks why I do not see myself as the totality of my bodily parts, in roughly the way that I see a table as four legs and a top, or a bicycle as wheels, frame, seat, and handlebars. He answers that it is because some of the things which are true of me, do not seem to be true of the connected parts of my physical body. I can be morally blameworthy or praiseworthy for example, while it seems strange to regard my body or its parts (e.g., my brain) in this way. Similarly, it seems odd to say that my body, or some part of it, wishes it were somewhere else, or has thoughts of the gods, or loves God and neighbor.[5] Since these things can be said of me, and not of my body, it seems I cannot describe myself simply as my body.[6] After rejecting

3. Murphy, *Bodies and Souls*, ix.

4. Taylor, "The Case for Materialism," 179–89.

5. Socrates relies on this sense of oddity when he make his famous joke that if it had been left to his bones or sinews, they would not have remained in prison but would have taken themselves to Megara or Boeotia. Cf. *Phaedo* 99a.

6. Taylor, "The Case for Materialism," 181–83.

a dualist option, Taylor makes a simple suggestion for settling the quandary, one which perhaps frees us from a case of what Wittgenstein would have seen as bewitchment of our intelligence by means of language.[7] Taylor points out that when we form an idea of a body or physical object, we tend to think of a stone or a piece of marble, rather than of a human or an animal. We then ask if *something like that* could be blameworthy or praiseworthy or religious, and conclude that it is impossible. Taylor suggests that if we begin with a wider set of core examples, the question changes its nature. If someone points to a human and a stone, and asks whether at least one of these might be able to think, choose, and deliberate, we have no problem in giving an affirmative reply. If someone then objects that a "mere physical object" cannot do these things, we answer that we are talking about a physical object of a certain kind, one equipped with a complex nervous system and so on. With this, the hesitation vanishes.[8]

Murphy is keen to fill in the detail of this sort of proposal, showing that there is no contradiction in our thinking of certain configurations of materials as acting freely, or pursuing a spirituality. They will be complex bodies of a special sort, which contain feedback loops and representations of other entities and of their own states, as part of their workings. But they will be bodies for all that, in full continuity with the simplest types of natural things. Murphy discusses several common examples of complex systems, including one which we will take as representative, a thermostat heater.[9] Such a heater registers the temperature of the air in the room, compares it with a pre-set norm, and gives instructions to its output mechanisms to change the room temperature until it corresponds to what is pre-set. We could take the example a step further and imagine a heater that could tell when an apartment was empty for a significant time, and would move to shut off the whole system during this time. This would be an example of a meta-function, in that the entire previous operation is registered as an object, and compared in turn with the wider system within which the heater is embedded (the economics of running the apartment), giving rise to a further level of output. Murphy thinks that if we imagine increasingly complex examples of such things, which include numerous meta-levels, we eventually arrive at bodies that we describe as acting freely, and having a spiritual dimension. Perhaps we can even talk about them as having "souls" if we want, though Murphy would prefer to do without such an expression.[10]

7. Wittgenstein, *Philosophical Investigations* n.109, 47e.

8. Taylor, "The Case for Materialism," 187.

9. Murphy, *Bodies and Souls, or Spirited Bodies?*, 86.

10. She recounts her reply to a reporter who thought that clones were zombies, and

Such "spiritual" functions can therefore be seen as dimensions of a body which has reached a certain level of complexity. Murphy wants to oppose any suggestion that the spiritual side of the human being goes back to a particular *part*, a spiritual soul or whatever, which has to be added to the other parts, as if along with receptors and comparators, the body needed something further of a different "spiritual" kind. Those who believe that something additional is necessary, perhaps because they remain bewitched by a picture of bodies as always being like heaps of stone, fall easily into a dualist position. Dualism is of course a main target of Murphy's program. She holds that talk of the soul or of the freedom of humans is not talk about a particular non-material part, but rather talk about an *aspect* of a type of natural body. She quotes with approval James D. G. Dunn, who holds that the Greeks saw humans "partitively," as made up of distinct parts, while the Hebrews saw humans "aspectively," as organic units which have different dimensions, one of which might be described by the word "spiritual."[11]

She realizes that conflicts between fundamental approaches will not be resolved by an appeal to the facts, since each approach can account for the facts in its own way. She encourages us rather to regard the conflict between naturalists and dualists as if it concerned competing research programs or hypotheses, proposals which are to be judged by their fruitfulness for further discovery and research.[12] To adopt the "aspective" view is to see the question of the soul as coming down to the question of whether we want to use this expression to describe particular aspects of the human person. Once we see the question in this way, we will quickly conclude there is not much reason to talk any more in the "partitive" way. The "aspective" naturalist program has gone from strength to strength, while the "partitive" dualist program, with Sir John Eccles as its sole eminent champion of recent decades, has gone nowhere.

Murphy maintains that the difficulties associated with a theological program that bases itself on a naturalist position are often exaggerated. Much of the detail of her case is directed towards showing that the naturalist framework offers a plausible and fruitful alternative for describing human beings and that it can accommodate most of our traditional concerns. This requires a demonstration of credible naturalist equivalents for the aspects of human beings which dualists cite as evidence for special spiritual "parts." Her argument relies heavily on two related concepts, those

wanted a condemnation of cloning: "don't worry. None of us has a soul and we all get along perfectly well!" *Bodies and Souls, or Spirited Bodies?*, 1.

11. Dunn, *The Theology of the Apostle Paul*, 54. Cf. Murphy, *Bodies and Souls, or Spirited Bodies?*, 21.

12. Murphy, "Nonreductive Physicalism," 139–40.

of "top-down causation" and "emergent properties." Top-down causation is best seen in an example like that of the heating-system which turns itself off when the apartment is empty. Here various material parts support the articulation of a whole system which in turn controls the movement of the parts from which it arises. The notion of "emergence" covers a wide range of cases, usefully listed and discussed by William Hasker.[13] For Murphy, a significant emergent property is one which arises not from the parts of the material base, but from the whole system, first appearing as a property when the whole system is in place. Emergent properties are not reducible to the combination of properties of the parts. Sensitivity to the economics of heating an empty apartment cannot be deduced straightforwardly from the properties of the parts which make up the system, but emerges only when the whole system is in place. What we refer to as "consciousness" is regarded as a property of this sort.[14] Murphy thinks that with the help of the concepts of top-down causality and emergent properties, she can avoid what she describes as "reductive physicalism," the view that, as Paul Churchland puts it, the notion of "soul" is no more than a name for "a particularly exquisite articulation of the basic properties of matter and energy."[15] For reductive physicalism, there is, in the end, nothing more than the building blocks, along with their physical properties.

Murphy wants to resist this "no more than" approach. She describes her position as "non-reductive physicalism." The position sees humans and other animals as natural bodies which have developed interesting emergent properties which enable a fair measure of top-down causation. The processes of an organic body loop round on themselves, sometimes objectifying their own states and reacting to them. Humans do this to a higher degree than other animals. Murphy mentions an experiment where chimpanzees always choose the larger of two piles of candy, in spite of the fact that a researcher awards them the *other* pile of candy each time, and gives away the one they choose.[16] Even small children quickly come to a higher level of abstraction here, and choose the smaller pile, so as to be rewarded in turn with the larger pile. The chimpanzees lack the ability to turn the operation of choosing into an object of higher-level abstraction like this, and are frustrated again and again as the object of their choice is taken away from them. For Murphy, at a certain point in this ascent, we start talking about

13. Hasker, *The Emergent Self*, 171–203.
14. Murphy, *Bodies and Souls*, 77.
15. Churchland, *The Engine of Reason*, 211.
16. Murphy, *Bodies and Souls*, 88.

"freedom," of a sort which is admittedly not "libertarian," but which offers enough to satisfy many philosophers.

The End-Directedness of Life

The power of Murphy's position, like that of all naturalisms, comes from its use of a few simple principles, which can be easily grasped, and which have great explanatory force. We quickly intuit the kinds of answers the position will offer to most of the usual objections. Perhaps we sense that in its own terms it is impregnable. And yet, it gives an impression of overlooking one of the central things it is trying to explain, the most basic feature of life itself. While we sometimes have difficulty in knowing whether a particular thing should count as living or not, the simplest phenomenology of life as experienced seems to indicate a sharp distinction between living things and non-living things, implying that "living" does not just reduce to occupying a particular level in a continuity of material differences. This is reflected in the sense of alarm that often comes over us as we suddenly realize that something we had thought inanimate is in fact alive. The difference between the simplest living thing like an amoeba and an artificial thing like a heating-system seems somehow fundamental, so that it is of a different order from the difference between two sorts of artificial things, like a heating-system and a cooling-system. It is however difficult to argue for a qualitative difference here, which can withstand Murphy's proposal that the difference can be explained by quantitative factors.

A first piece of evidence for our intuitive sense of a qualitative difference comes from biology. The biologist Maureen L. Condic insists on the almost-instantaneous moment of change from the presence of seed materials and nutrients to the presence of a zygote, in that the materials are suddenly taken over, and become something that is self-directed, as though a new entity has suddenly arisen, rather than just a new moment in a continuous process.[17] Aristotle would see this as confirmation of a position he formulated long ago, that there is a qualitative difference between two kinds of change. In the first, which characterizes artificial things, a material base remains in place throughout the change, while it loses certain properties and acquires others. In the second, which characterizes living things, a new thing comes into existence, which was not there before.[18] With non-living things, parts move other parts around, while with living things, there is a mysterious unity, where something seems to come into

17. Condic, *When Does Life Begin?*, 3.

18. Aristotle, "On Generation and Corruption," 512.

existence as an integral whole. Aristotle uses this point as the basis of a sharp little argument against reductive physicalism. If the life principle were a just a moving material of some sort within the living body, then in principle we could imagine it leaving the body and returning, so that the body could die and come to life again.

> But, if this is possible, it would also be possible for a soul which has left the body to enter in again; and upon this would follow the possibility of resurrection for animals which are dead.[19]

The fact that this is not possible, indicates that we are dealing with a different sort of unity, which he refers to as soul-body unity, or "hylomorphism." His argument can be applied to the sort of non-reductive physicalism favored by Murphy. When the complex non-living systems which serve as her prime analogues for physical entities break down, they seem always in principle recoverable, in that we can repair the damaged parts and the system will work again. Living things are however subject to the strange transformation called "dying," from which they do not seem recoverable any more. For Aristotle, this is evidence that there is something in play which cannot be reduced to the interplay of physical parts. One can however imagine counterarguments from the non-reductive physicalist side. A particular combination of parts might lose the coordination which allowed it to develop top-down causality, in such a way that it cannot recover it again. This is what the phenomenon of dying comes down to. For all the power of a reply of this sort, the suggestion that such damage can be *irreparable* seems strange. We feel that in principle, something understood in this way is always repairable, and that the contrast with living things, which are not susceptible to such repair, needs explanation. The naturalist might of course take the bull by the horns and suggest that in the future, it might become possible to recover the lives of things which have died, if the conditions are right.

A second argument that the act of living is more than just a function of organization, comes from thought-experiments involving simulations. We seem always to be able to imagine the processes of a living thing occurring in a non-living simulation, with feedback loops from sensors playing the part assigned to animal vision and so on. We can imagine robots or zombies that mimic humans down to the last detail. The contrast between Murphy and some of her opponents can be neatly defined in relation to such examples. The opponents believe that the possibility of simulation shows that the concept of life involves more than mere top-down functioning, given that a simulation has all of the functioning without having any of the life.

19. Aristotle, *On the Soul*, 647.

Murphy can reply however that the appearance of a consequent simulation like a zombie, which by definition duplicates all of the outward activities of an ordinary human, is in fact the very kind of thing which qualifies for the description "living,"[20] given that such a thing is identical to humans in all respects that can be registered. It seems reasonable therefore to accept a continuity of "behavior" stretching from things that are not alive, like a heating system with a thermostat, to plants and animals and humans. Murphy wants us to recognize that once we reach a certain level of complexity, it is sensible to use the word "life."

These arguments focus on observed complexity, and assume that life can be defined in terms of such complexity. But while everyone accepts that living things have a high degree of complexity, it does not follow that "life" can be *defined* in terms of such complexity. I want to suggest that the missing piece, which turns mere complexity into "life," is the notion of "end-directedness." Complex mechanisms, like a heating system with a thermostat, might serve ends (of an apartment owner), but they do not *have* ends. By contrast, the simplest living thing *has* ends. It approaches some of its possible futures as better than others, in that they represent the completion at which it is aimed. This is to say that it has "ends" or "goods" or "goals." These notions seem to be primitive. While they have connections to other concepts (like "complexity," "responsiveness," or "reflexivity"), they are not reducible to these. Nor do they necessarily imply awareness or consciousness. They refer to a certain sort of relation, a tendency towards a completion, which humans experience directly in their own lives, and which they also attribute to other living things. The act of living seems to set up an entity in this way, standing with its interests over against the world, "wanting" some things, and wanting to avoid other things. Once we accept that life is like this, we can regard certain machines as simulating it, in that they perform the actions of the living things which have such interests. But they do not themselves share the interests.

The difference that this notion of end-directedness makes is seen in expressions where Murphy seems to attribute life-functions to organic parts. When talking about language, emotion and "decisionmaking," Murphy says that "(l)ocalization studies . . . provide especially strong motivation for saying that it is the brain that is responsible for these capacities. . . . In

20. This does not apply to Hollywood zombies, which show outwardly some of the effects of not having an inner life. Real zombies are outwardly indistinguishable from ordinary humans. The zombie argument is developed by Chalmers, *The Conscious Mind*, 94ff.

Owen Flanagan's terms, it is the brain that is the *res cogitans*—the thinking thing."[21] She often repeats this point:

> As neuroscientists associate more and more of the faculties once attributed to mind or soul with the functioning of specific regions or systems of the brain it becomes more and more appealing to say that it is in fact the brain that performs these functions.[22]
>
> In brief, this is the view that the human nervous system, operating in concert with the rest of the body in its environment, is the seat of consciousness (and also of human spiritual or religious capacities).[23]

While these statements are not without ambiguity, they clearly exhibit the difference between an Aristotelian approach to living things, and the approaches of contemporary naturalisms. For an Aristotelian, we cannot imagine the brain or the nervous system as having ends, or as engaging in end-directed activity, at least in the fundamental meaning of these terms. To imagine such a thing is to see the brain or nervous system as having a kind of life, aimed at sets of fulfillments which satisfy them, in much the same way that life around a pond satisfies a frog. But we cannot make sense of an organic part like a brain as having life-ends like this.

The difference between the two is shown in a humorous example in the television series *The Addams Family*, which shows a hand (called "Thing") which seems to have a life of its own, transporting itself around as though it were a species of small animal. This shows what it might be like for a hand to exercise existence in the way that a living whole does. Probably to complete the picture we need to think of it as nourishing and repairing itself in some way, so that it includes broadly reflexive activities. But it is significant that to think this, we cease to think of the hand as an organic part, and start to think of it as a straightforward animal, with a whole life of its own and a set of characteristic goods. The example stands at the boundary line between two different categories, that of a functioning part which might serve ends, but does not have ends, and that of a living whole which has ends of its own. The humor of the example comes from combining these two aspects, perhaps implying that in reality, it is not possible to do this.

Certainly a hand that has acquired a life of its own no longer resembles something like the brain or nervous system. We cannot imagine these as having *goods* that they pursue apart from their functioning as organic parts of a larger whole. (One of Aristotle's criteria for an end-directed substance is

21. Murphy, "Human Nature: Historical, Scientific, and Religious Issues," 1.

22. Ibid., 13.

23. Murphy, "Nonreductive Physicalism," 131.

that it not be *part* of something else.)[24] In attributing life-actions to the brain or the nervous system, Murphy is overlooking this distinction, and treating the brain as though it has a life that it wants to realize. But we find such a life unimaginable, because a brain, unlike an animal, has no ends. What would such ends look like—*a desire to get as much sugar as possible*? Similarly, we cannot imagine a computer as having life-ends, however sophisticated it may be. What would they be—to have a nice clean screen? The point is captured in a remark said to have been made by Noam Chomsky—one which I have never been able to source—that to attribute a living action like a conscious act to "the brain" is like awarding an Olympic weightlifting medal to a forklift.

For Aristotle, a living thing is something whose very existence consists in having and seeking ends. The point is encapsulated in the famous Latin formula *vivere est viventibus esse*, that when it is a question of living wholes, "their being is to live . . ."[25] Life is a kind of background activity which forever seeks further fulfillment, and is identical with the existence of the subject whose life it is, so that the existence of a living thing is always a pursuit of completion. It means that for Aristotle there is a fundamental difference between the processes of change which characterize a living thing, and those which characterize mere materials. Materials exercise causal influence on one another in a way which strikes us as "external." A fire increases as fuel is added, growing by accretion, in that new parts simply join on to it as the process continues. Aristotle notices that the process of a living thing's nourishing itself is not like this.[26] A living organism takes food into itself, but does not simply join new parts to its existing exterior. Rather it uses the food as material for an action of a different sort, which oddly completes the living organism, representing not only an end-point of a process, but also the *good* of the process, the completion at which it was aimed. This striving for completion constitutes the very existence of the organism that is in question. Once it ceases, it is not as if the organism simply loses a quality, even an emergent quality. Rather, it is no longer there at all. The body of a living thing is not a stable base from which the emergent quality we call "living" proceeds. Rather it is itself a *product* of the act of living, the strange end-directedness which brings living things into existence in the first place.

24. "For a primary substance is neither said of a subject nor in a subject." Aristotle, "Categories," 6.

25. Aristotle, "On the Soul," 661.

26. Ibid., 662.

The Priority of End-Directedness

I believe that Murphy overlooks this original end-directedness of living things. But she nonetheless needs the notion, if she is to get her physicalist alternative off the ground. She defines a living thing as "a bounded organic structure capable of taking nutrients from the environment for the purposes of self-repair, growth, and reproduction."[27] This is to see living things as particular examples of general abstract systems, of which some non-living things are also examples. A sophisticated heating-unit exemplifies such a system at a low level. We can imagine a heating-unit which registers when one of its pipes is cracked, and immediately activates a repair mechanism which moves to seal the crack, or which activates a fuel pump when it registers that its own supplies are running low. This exemplifies the same structure as living systems, in that it maintains its own stability in relation to the wider world, and manages an ordered transformation of inputs into outputs. A living thing includes of course features that are specific to a living system, having a greater degree of complexity, and possibly displaying unusual emergent properties like awareness. It is constituted mainly from carbon, at least in our world. But these features inevitably look secondary when placed alongside the common structural elements.

It is striking that Murphy's description sees the differences between non-living and living things as the same *sorts* of differences as those which exist between non-living things and other non-living things. A heating system with a thermostat differs from a living thing in more or less the same way as a heating system differs from the autopilot system on an airliner, namely in degree of complexity and in materials used. The three hold their most significant identity in common, in that they all exemplify patterns of self-maintaining wholes, and differ only in that they realize these in more or less complex ways, with different materials. In the end, the framework of enquiry therefore determines the conclusion. Living and non-living things are basically alike, and their only difference lies in their respective degrees of complication. There is no need to appeal outside such quantitative factors to additional "parts," to account for the difference between them.

While Murphy's position overlooks the direction towards a good which sets living organisms apart from what is not living, it also *assumes* this notion in its attempted reconstruction of living things on the model of functional systems. This becomes clear if we look closely at how the parts of a heating system come to be seen as a functional whole. Away from the viewpoint of human beings there are no heating-systems, but merely parts

27. Murphy, *Bodies and Souls*, 85.

alongside one another in continuity with their surrounding parts, materials in continuity, where everything touches on something else. The philosopher Descartes noticed this when he described matter as a single continuous substance, whose nature consists in extension alone.[28] These parts and their relations produce an infinite number of effects, none of which is privileged. For example, the parts of a heating system block other things from moving into their space. They interfere with the movement of air, bring weight to bear on floors and walls, and react chemically with what is around them. The outcome of keeping a stable room temperature does not stand out among the many outcomes that such a system produces.

Some might argue that the maintenance of a constant room temperature is a privileged outcome, in that only if we keep *this* outcome in mind can we account for *all* the parts of the heating system, whereas if we take the system as a way of blocking spaces, we account only for part of it (the mass which keeps the space blocked). This is in fact a circular argument, in that it assumes that we know the boundaries of the heating-system (i.e., what counts as "all" the parts) *before* we have ascertained its purpose. In fact, it is only because we already have an idea of a purpose that we know what to include or exclude from the list of parts. By varying our glance, we can alter what is relevant or irrelevant, in principle rearranging the world into whatever systems we like, by taking different focal points around which we make sense of the rest. The French Renaissance thinker Montaigne has a philosophical goose who thinks that geese are the apex of the creation, for which all the rest has been designed, and in relation to which the rest can be understood. In this scheme, humans are means by which geese are provided with food.[29]

It is only when we single out one of the outcomes (constant room temperature) as the overarching goal, with all the rest directed towards it, that the heating-system comes into focus as an integral whole, something which can function more or less efficiently, and which can on occasion break down. The system is conceived as though it is *trying* to achieve something, though we know that in fact this is not so, as it is only a *simulation* of a living thing. But to do this, we need to import the notion of end-directedness. Where do we get it from? It obviously comes from the ends and purposes of the designer or maker or owner of the heating-system. We have a primitive experience of what it is to be directed towards something in this way. This experience is more primitive than any systems-theory, and is presupposed if we are to get the notion of a system off the ground. The irony of Murphy's attempt to understand living things, including human beings, as

28. Descartes, "Principles of Philosophy," 255.

29. Michel de Montaigne, "An Apologie of Raymond Sebond," 240.

types of "systems," now becomes evident. To think a "system" as such, we need to smuggle in the notion of end-directedness, our instinctive grasp of what it means to see some futures as better and others as worse. Only if this thought is allowed, can the notion of a system come together as an intelligible concept. This suggests that living things have an important priority over artificial things, in that they need to be presupposed in order to explain the notion of a system. Murphy wants to reverse this order, and explain humans by seeing them as particular sorts of systems.

If the notion of a system presupposes the notion of aspiration, it cannot be used to explain the notion. The idea of a system takes shape against a background of assumed aspiration. The argument brings us starkly against the strange notion of end-directedness, raising questions about how we arrive at it, and what kind of primacy it has. It might encourage us (or perhaps discourage us) to know that the dispute we are considering is centuries old in Western history. Bacon long ago banished consideration of the tendency which living things have towards a good ("final causes") from scientific enquiry, not in the first place because there were no such causes, but because it did not suit our purposes to consider them. Their investigation was "barren," as he famously put it.[30] Those who stand with Plato and his view that the notion of good is the ultimate principle of explanation, being "the authentic source of truth and reason,"[31] realize that final causes, for all their mysteriousness, will not go away.

Present-day controversies between theology and science tend to focus on the mechanisms of living organisms, asking whether it is conceivable that such mechanisms should come into existence without the direction of an intelligent designer. This way of framing the question focuses on the ways in which life articulates itself, and tends to overlook the strangeness of the phenomenon of life itself. Organic life is a form of existence whose core is aspiration towards something not yet possessed. That anything should be related like this beyond its current present states is surprising, and suggests a missing dimension to our explanations, as though things are haunted by a completion which has somehow insinuated itself at their origins. To be alive is to be restless for such a completion. While falling short of a deductive proof of the matter, such a state of affairs fits well with a view that sees living creatures as created participations in a life that was there before them, and which they obscurely seek throughout their earthly journey. In other words, it fits a view that sees the world and human life as fundamentally secondary, in thrall to an original fund of perfection to which it refers as the "creator."

30. Bacon, "De Dignitate et Augmentis Scientiarum," 473.

31. Plato, *Republic*, 750.

Bibliography

Aristotle. "Categories" 3a8. Translated by J. L. Ackrill. In *The Complete Works of Aristotle*, Vol. 1, edited by Jonathan Barnes, 3–24. Princeton NJ: Princeton University Press, 1984.

———. "On Generation and Corruption" 314a1–7. Translated by H. H. Joachim. In *The Complete Works of Aristotle*, Vol 1, edited by Jonathan Barnes, 512–54. Princeton NJ: Princeton University Press, 1984.

———. "On the Soul" 406b4-5, 415a28-29. Translated by J. A. Smith. In *The Complete Works of Aristotle*, Vol. 1, edited by Jonathan Barnes, 641–92. Princeton NJ: Princeton University Press, 1984.

Bacon, Francis. "De Dignitate et Augmentis Scientiarum." Translated by James Spedding. In *The Philosophical Works of Francis Bacon,* book III, chapter 5, edited by John M. Robertson, 5, 413–638. London: Routledge and Sons, 1905.

Chalmers, David. J. *The Conscious Mind.* Oxford: Oxford University Press, 1996.

Churchland, Paul. *The Engine of Reason, the Seat of the Soul.* Cambridge: MIT, 1995.

Condic, Maureen L. *When Does Life Begin?* New York: The Westchester Institute for Ethics & The Human Person, 2008.

Descartes. "Principles of Philosophy." Translated by Elizabeth S. Haldane and G. R. T. Ross. In *The Philosophical Works of Descartes* Vol. 1, Part II, Principle 4, 203–302. Cambridge: Cambridge University Press, 1931.

Dunn, James D. G. *The Theology of the Apostle Paul.* Grand Rapids: Eerdmans, 1998.

Hasker, William. *The Emergent Self.* Ithaca, NY: Cornell University Press, 1999.

Montaigne, Michel. "An Apologie of Raymond Sebond." In *Essays,* Vol II chap. 12. Translated by John Florio, 125–326. London: Dent, 1910.

Murphy, Nancey. *Bodies and Souls, or Spirited Bodies?* Cambridge: Cambridge University Press, 2006.

———. "Human Nature: Historical, Scientific, and Religious Issues." In *Whatever Happened to the Soul?* edited by Warren S. Brown, Nancey Murphy, and H. Newton Malony, 1–29. Minneapolis: Fortress, 1998.

———. "Nonreductive Physicalism: Philosophical Issues." In *Whatever Happened to the Soul?* edited by Warren S. Brown, Nancey Murphy, and H. Newton Malony, 127–48. Minneapolis: Fortress, 1998.

Plato. *Phaedo* 98D, 97c. Translated by Hugh Tredennick. In the *The Collected Dialogues of Plato*, edited by Edith Hamilton and Huntington Cairns, 40–98. Princeton, NJ: Princeton University Press, 1963.

———. *Republic* 517c. In *The Collected Dialogues of Plato*, translated by Paul Shorey, edited by Edith Hamilton and Huntington Cairns, 575–844. Princeton, NJ: Princeton University Press, 1963.

Taylor, Richard. "The Case for Materialism." In *Philosophy: Contemporary Perspectives On Perennial Issues*, edited by E. D. Klemke, A. David Kline, and Robert Hollinger, 179–89. New York: St. Martin's, 1994.

Wittgenstein, Ludwig. *Philosophical Investigations* n.109. Translated by G. E. M. Anscombe. Oxford: Blackwell, 1974.

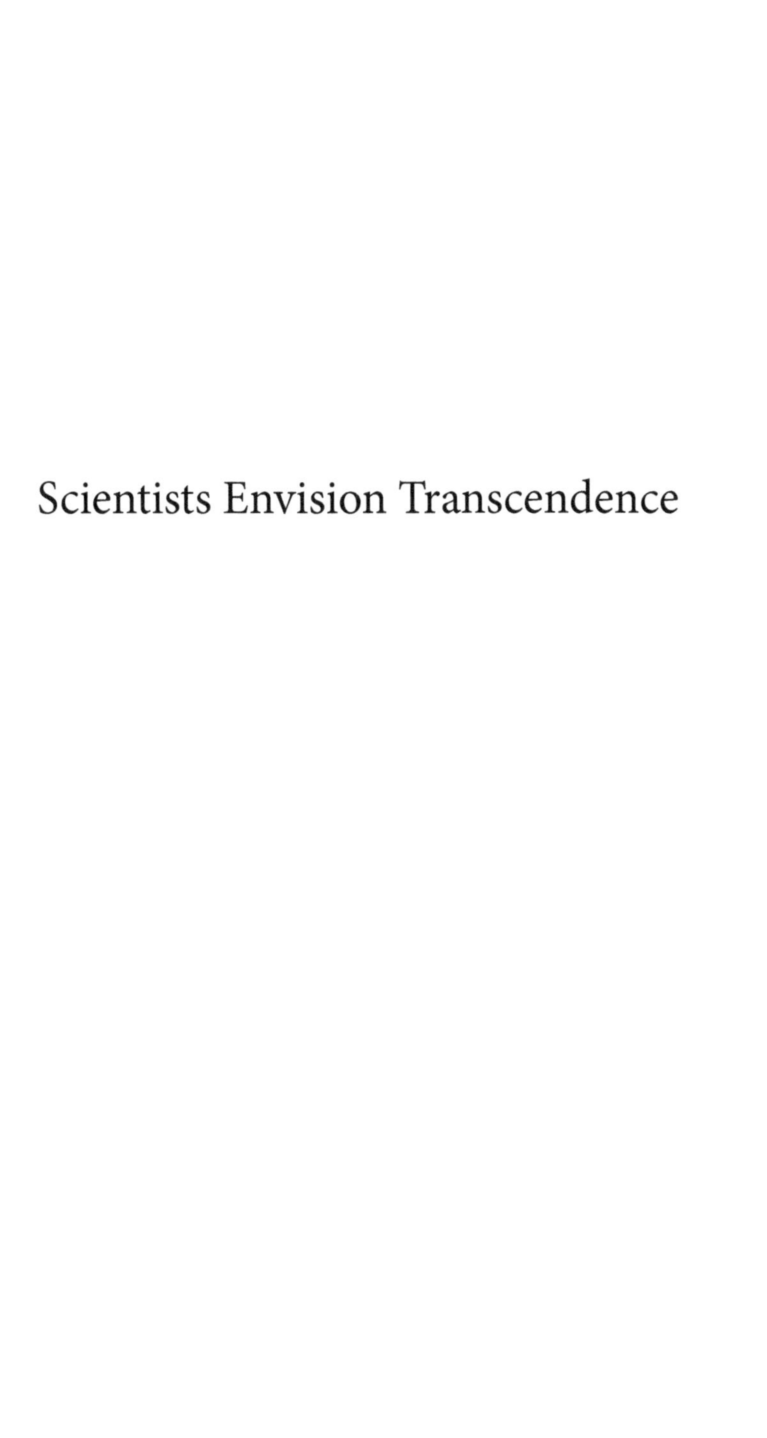

Scientists Envision Transcendence

6

Does Nature Suggest Transcendence?

Neil Broom

That the living world might, in some deep mysterious way, be expressive of a transcendent dimension is largely rejected by contemporary secular thinkers. Most will argue that modern science has demonstrated, at least in principle, that life in all its evolving complexity and sophistication is the inevitable product of entirely natural, unplanned, mindless processes. Biological materialism, or naturalism, is an all-embracing material explanation of how molecules evolved into complex living organisms including us humans. In this view all of life is accounted for in terms of the outworking of scientifically explicable chemical and physical processes guided entirely by rules and constraints resident within a wholly material universe. And so it asks—Why insist on a role for a Creator when science has shown there is nothing left for a Creator to do?[1]

The God versus no-God polarization is one of the big tensions troubling contemporary Western culture. The intensity of the debate is fuelled in part by the recent widespread publicity given to Christian religious fundamentalism and its frequent, and I believe, misplaced insistence that all scientific truth must be made subservient to a particular literal reading of the early chapters of Genesis. There is an added tension for many Christians genuinely engaged in science within the context of our secular scientific culture: there can be the threat of banishment to an academic gulag if one

1. Much of the material in this chapter is condensed from ideas developed in the author's two published books *How Blind is the Watchmaker* and *Life's X-Factor: The Missing Link in Materialism's Science of Living Things.*

dares to express religious and specifically theistic sympathies or raise doubts about the explanatory power of a wholly materialistic science.

In this paper I do not wish to explore the fundamental God versus no-God issue—that I shall leave to the theologians and philosophers. Rather, I want to linger briefly within the scientific "camp" and ask whether the particulars that science reveals—and science has done this task with remarkable rigor—do in fact point to a purposeful, transcendent dimension.

The Priority of Natural Selection

To begin our exploration it is important to note that naturalism's recipe for the unfolding of life is intimately bound up with the concept of Darwinian natural selection (NS). Although Darwin proposed his theory before the gene had been discovered, and we must not forget Alfred Russell Wallace's co-proposing of the same theory, our modern understanding of this concept is based on Darwin's unique insights into the interplay between biological variability, fitness with the local environment, and reproductive success.

Natural selection, now deeply informed by modern molecular biology, is really a description of biological transformation arising from the differential and adaptive survival of genes. Largely random alterations in an organism's genetic make-up result in variations in its phenotype. If these genetically sourced variations enable the organism to adapt more successfully to its environment it will reproduce faster, resulting in a lineage that is better able to survive than those variants less favorably endowed. This, in brief, is naturalism's primary explanation for life's evolutionary unfolding.

Again, we need to remind ourselves that naturalism is about a natural as opposed to a transcendent cause. It is committed to placing natural selection entirely within the material basket. For the materialist, the responsibility to deliver the richness of biological innovation rests squarely on the shoulders of natural selection. And it must bear this burden alone. There is no supporting cast. Single-handed, natural selection is charged with the monumental task of conquering the "Everest" of biological innovation. So, in Richard Dawkins' words:

> Natural selection, the blind, unconscious, automatic process which Darwin discovered, and which we now know is the explanation for the existence and apparent purposeful form of all life, has no purpose in mind. It has no mind and no mind's eye. It does not plan for the future. It has no vision, no foresight, no

> sight at all. If it can be said to play the role of watchmaker in nature, it is the blind watchmaker.[2]

Biologist John Avise presses home this almost sacral duty:

> Only natural selection comes close to omnipotence, but even here no intelligence, foresight, ultimate purpose or morality is involved. Natural selection is merely an amoral force, as inevitable and uncaring as gravity.[3]

A particularly eloquent piece of prose in the same materialist vein comes from the distinguished French biologist Jacques Monod:

> Even today a good many distinguished minds seem unable to accept or even to understand that from a source of noise, natural selection could quite unaided have drawn all the music of the biosphere. Indeed natural selection operates upon the products of chance and knows no other nourishment.[4]

How Natural Is Natural Selection?

But we need to ask—can natural selection be so easily dismissed as a wholly material, unconscious, purposeless process? I think it is fair to say that at one popular level the expression natural selection serves as a kind of mantra, an almost magical utterance that quickly allays any doubts a skeptic might entertain. It is uttered with power and authority when any kind of biological achievement has to be explained, and in the currency of a wholly material world. My argument is that the claim that natural selection explains the extraordinary (read: life processes) while drawing only on the ordinary (read: material processes), is not only bad science, it is also contradicted by the very narrative the materialist seems compelled to employ to present his or her story of life.

So let me first give you several recent examples from the popular science literature to illustrate just how reliant on the use of this mantra biological materialism has become. London University geneticist Steve Jones, in his book *Almost like a Whale,* has a chapter on natural selection and explains its working in the following way. He describes his experience of working as a fitter's mate in a Liverpool soap powder factory. A soapy liquid is blown out through a nozzle and the pressure drop creates a cloud of soap particles.

2. Dawkins, *The Blind Watchmaker,* 5.
3. Quoted in Larson and Witham, "Scientists and Religion in America."
4. Monod, *Chance and Necessity*, 114.

But the process originally utilized a simple nozzle that narrowed at one end. This design led to several quality control issues. Jones describes the problem of finding an improved nozzle design as simply too difficult for scientists to solve so the company resorted to evolution—"design without a designer." Here are Jones' words:

> The engineers used the idea that moulds life itself: descent with modification. Take a nozzle that works quite well and make copies, each changed at random. Test them for how well they make powder. Then, impose a struggle for existence by insisting that not all can survive. Many of the altered devices are no better (or worse) than the parental form. They are discarded, but the few able to do a superior job are allowed to reproduce and are copied—but again not perfectly. As generations pass there emerges, as if by magic, a new and efficient pipe of complex and unexpected shape.[5]

Now Steve Jones should, of all people, know better than to use such a misleading illustration. The trial and error or hit and miss type of process which he claims is analogous to natural selection is actually loaded with intentionality, or to be exact, intelligent scrutiny. Firstly, a better nozzle is being sought. So, a nozzle, said to have been modified at random, is tried and found to do a better or worse job than another. And who decides whether it is an improvement or not? A rather discerning "nozzle operator," one skilled in the art of recognizing whether the change is for better or for worse, one who is able to detect subtle degrees of improvement or deterioration.

Even the expression "trial and error" presupposes an expectation against which an altered performance can be judged. "Hit and miss" is all about a target that is being aimed for. The men on the Liverpool soap factory shop floor knew precisely what end result they wanted (a better performing nozzle) and this surely robs Steve Jones of his convenient metaphor for natural selection. The words "design without a designer" are little more than misleading sloganeering and what he presents to his readers is more a piece of materialistic fiction. Natural selection, even if simplistically illustrated with the soap powder analogy, is a truly intentional process.

Interestingly, Darwin had, some 150 years earlier, resorted to the same language of intentionality in order to convey to his readers the discerning power of natural selection:

> It may metaphorically be said that natural selection is daily and hourly scrutinising, throughout the world, the slightest variations;

5. Jones, *Almost like a Whale*, 91.

> rejecting those that are bad, preserving and adding up all that are good; silently and insensibly working, whenever and wherever opportunity offers, at the improvement of each organic being in relation to its organic and inorganic conditions of life.[6]

Darwin's picture of natural selection "scrutinising," "rejecting" the bad, "preserving" the good, carries the same idea of there being a profoundly important element of intentionality that operates in the living world—the very world he was attempting to explain in naturalistic terms.

But where does this quality of purpose or intention come from? Few would suggest that it could come from atoms or molecules themselves, unless of course we attribute to them qualities akin to mind or personality. Natural selection is certainly a biological reality but it is intimately linked with a dimension that would appear to be much more than material. Its persistence in the evolutionary literature *as a wholly material process* is, in my view, unfortunate. For while it serves rather well the particular ideological assertion that reality is ultimately unthinking matter, I do not think that it is consistent with the facts of science and especially biology.

The Achievement of Biological Complexity

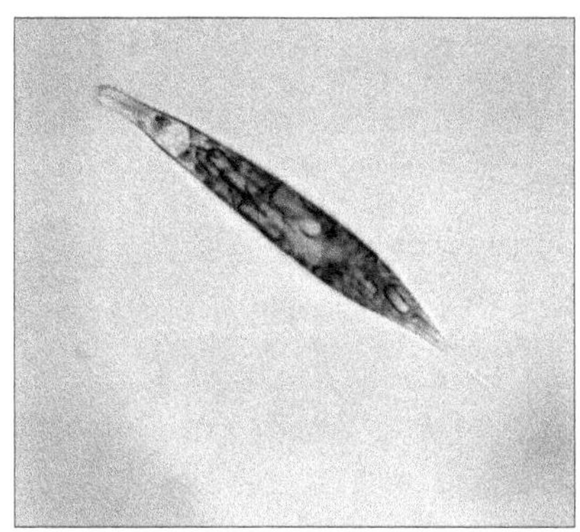

Fig. 1A: The tiny aquatic animal *Euglina*

A fundamental issue for biology is how organs of great complexity might have evolved. The answer is generally framed in terms of gradualism and the creative power of cumulative small changes. Scientifically there seems nothing wrong with such an approach. Certainly, in modern animals there are enormous differences in the degrees of sophistication of, for example, the organs of sight. The eye of the microscopic aquatic animal *Euglena* consists of a tiny light-sensitive spot.

6. Darwin, *The Origin of Species*, 84.

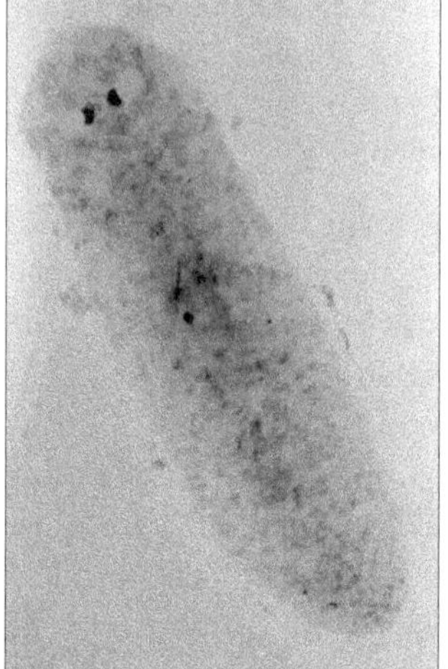
Fig. 1B: The flat worm *Planaria*

Further up the complexity ladder, the two eyes of the little Tubellarian flatworm *Planaria* are each formed from an arrangement of cup-shaped cells that are heavily pigmented.

The interior of each cup is filled with special nerve cells which feed sensory signals back to the brain. Then there is the compound eye found in the vast family of arthropods with its built-in ability to adjust optically to varying levels of lighting, and especially "tuned" for detecting rapid movements.

Finally, the vertebrate eye provides us with a truly staggering leap in optical sophistication.

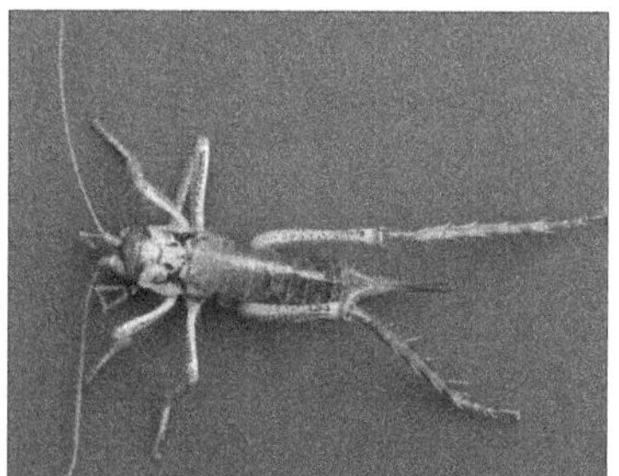
Fig. 1C: The New Zealand *Weta*

Fig. 1D: Compound eye of the *Weta*

The eye is, of course, just one of many impressive examples of a single physiological function that is supported by an enormous range of complex biological technologies. It is this that suggests to Richard Dawkins a gradual upgrading or evolving of a primitive eye into a more sophisticated eye, and on this point he may well be correct.

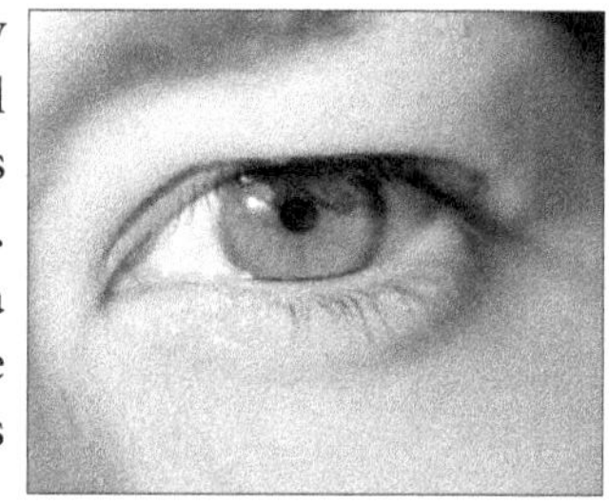
Fig. 1E: The vertebrate eye

Dawkins draws on a computer model devised by two Swedish biologists Dan Nilsson and Susanne Pelger and which "evolves" a virtual eye object from a flat layer of virtual cells sandwiched between virtual pigmented and transparent layers.[7]

7. Dawkins, *Climbing Mount Improbable,* chap. 5; Nilsson and Pelger, "A Pessimistic Estimate of the Time Required for an Eye to Evolve."

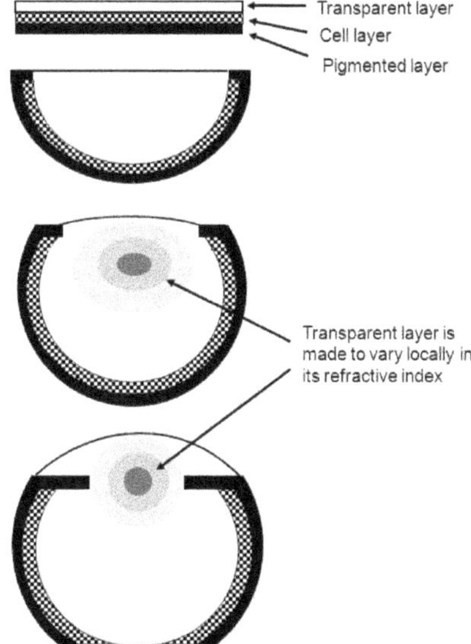

Fig. 2: Schematic showing major transformation steps in computer-generated eye object. Author's adaptation of the Nilsson-Pelger model.

The model works by producing at random small percentage changes in the degree of curvature of the sandwich, in the size of a light-restricting aperture, and in the local value of its refractive index (light-bending ability). The computer is programmed to perform a simple calculation of the focusing or resolving power of the sandwich each time a small random change (read virtual mutation) occurs in any of the three variables.

In a relatively small number of generations the computer model is shown transforming the flat sandwich layer through continuous minor improvements into a configuration representing a virtual, focused, lens-shaped object. Dawkins argues that this transformation is exactly analogous to climbing the mountain of biological complexity and in his own words:

> Going upwards means mutating, one small step at a time, and only accepting mutations that improve optical performance. So, where do we get to? Pleasingly, through a smooth upward pathway, starting from no proper eye at all, we reach a familiar fish eye, complete with lens.[8]

But one can immediately see that Dawkins' supposedly wholly material explanation is anything but material. He is required to impose a nonmaterial constraint on the behavior of the eye model—he inserts the crucial condition of "only accepting mutations that improve optical performance." Or, in terms of his mountain-climbing analogy, one must aim for the summit. Thus again, in order for his model to transform into a symbolic eye object, he is required to impose a profoundly purposeful constraint on the model's function.

Just for the record, neither the originators of the computer program, Dan Nilsson and Suzanne Pelger nor Richard Dawkins, appear to have

8. Dawkins, *Climbing Mount Improbable*, 151.

contributed much that is conceptually new in presenting their evolving eye model. Some 135 years earlier Charles Darwin proposed a near identical schema with his own "thought" experiment. Here is what he wrote:

> . . . we ought in imagination to take a thick layer of transparent tissue, with spaces filled with fluid, and with a nerve sensitive to light beneath, and then suppose every part of this layer to be continually changing slowly in density, so as to separate into layers of different densities and thicknesses, placed at different distances from each other, and with the surfaces of each layer slowly changing in form. Further we must suppose that there is a power, represented by natural selection or the survival of the fittest, always intently watching each slight alteration in the transparent layers; and carefully preserving each which, under varied circumstances, in any way or in any degree, tends to produce a distincter image. . . . [V]ariation will cause the slight alterations, generation will multiply them almost infinitely, and natural selection will pick out with unerring skill each improvement. Let this process go on for millions of years; and during each year on millions of individuals of many kinds; and may we not believe that a living optical instrument might thus be formed as superior to one of glass, as the works of the Creator are to those of Man?[9]

Note too how Darwin constructs for his readers a scenario that aims for a "distincter image", one that will "pick out with unerring skill each improvement". It is this principle of aiming for enhanced function that is absolutely crucial to the materialist's theory of life but one which defies any purely impersonal or material explanation.

Object Versus System

There is another layer of misrepresentation made by the biological materialist that needs to be exposed. And it concerns the confusing of material objects, however ordered they might be, with living systems. Richard Dawkins uses the example of such objects in an attempt to show his readers that evolution proceeds by virtue of the power of cumulative selection acting on small random changes. He describes his invention of a computer program which begins to draw from a simple predetermined form and which "evolves" an array of intriguing shapes that he calls biomorphs.

9. Darwin, *Origin of Species*, 170.

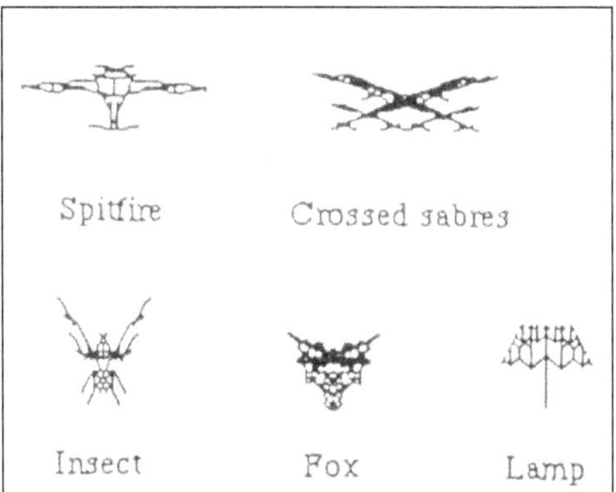

Fig. 3: Examples of Richard Dawkins' computer-generated biomorphs (reproduced with permission of Richard Dawkins)

These arise from small random changes occurring in the instructional "genes" contained in his program. Dawkins describes his own utter surprise and delight when he first ran his computer program:

> When I wrote the program, I never thought that it would evolve anything more than a variety of tree-like shapes. I had hoped for weeping willows, cedars of Lebanon, Lombardy poplars, seaweeds, perhaps deer antlers. Nothing in my biologist's intuition, nothing in my 20 years' experience of programming computers, and nothing in my wildest dreams, prepared me for what actually emerged on the screen. I can't remember exactly when in the sequence it first began to dawn on me that an evolved resemblance to something like an insect was possible. With a wild surmise, I began to breed, generation after generation, from whichever child looked most like an insect. My incredulity grew in parallel with the evolving resemblance. . . . Admittedly they have eight legs like a spider, instead of six like an insect, but even so! I still cannot conceal from you my feeling of exultation as I first watched these exquisite creatures emerging before my eyes.[10]

Dawkins' main point is that as the generations pass, the total amount of genetic difference between a particular "offspring" and its original "ancestor" can become extremely large. And while the offspring in any one generation are different from their parents in random directions, the choice of which progeny goes forward into the next generation is determined by a non-random selection process—the human eye.

10. Dawkins, *The Blind Watchmaker*, 59.

He does admit that the model is deficient in that it uses an artificial method to do the selecting, and goes on to suggest that a really clever programmer might be able to devise a form of natural selection that in some way modelled a mechanism of survival or death based on his so-called "biomorphs" interacting with a simulated hostile environment.

But there are glaring conceptual flaws in Dawkins' whole analogy. Firstly, he has committed a fatal error by mixing his metaphors. In effect he confuses systems that achieve with objects that simply *are*. What he produces is a series of computer-generated objects, in essence, digital doodles that certainly go through an interesting sequence of transformations resulting from the accumulation of small random alterations in the values of his shape-determining instructional "genes". But they are nothing more than *objects* and can never be used to explain, in even the simplest analogous sense, how any living system might have arisen.

Dawkins appears to be exploiting the fact that his computer model generates shapes that crudely resemble all manner of objects, both living and non-living, and he even calls them by a name designed, I suspect, to evoke in the reader's mind a living connotation—biomorphs. An unsuspecting reader might then imagine a plausible connection between these computer-generated pictures and the real thing. In reality, however, Dawkins' program produces pictorial representations of anything and everything, living and non-living—a great variety of recognizable shapes or "digital doodles", Lego-like biosymbolic fantasy objects, crude and simplistic symbols of reality, but little more.

His computer program is a fantasy-generating machine—of a digital kind! His biomorphs offer nothing in the way of explanation as to how any functioning system, living or non-living, might have come into existence. They provide no more satisfactory explanation than does a child's crayon drawing of an elephant or a mouse account for the existence of the real animal.

Dawkins' biomorph analogy contains yet other glaring misconception. Here is a human being deliberately programming a computer which itself has been built with an immense amount of human creativity. This computer is then *instructed* to generate an intriguing array of images by sequential, random changes (mutations) in the values of the program's various shaping "genes." In other words, Dawkins requires an intelligently structured, non-random, and highly sophisticated environment in which to produce his biomorphs. This is a far cry from what one would expect from a wholly impersonal set of material processes.

For Dawkins' model to carry any real conviction, even as a mechanism for "evolving" an endless variety of geometric forms, he must be able to produce his biomorphs beginning only with the impersonal, and enriched only by the chaotic action of brute chance. All *meaningful influences* must be excluded. There must be no intelligence available to design, build, and program the computer. There must be no mechanism whereby one "morphic" trend is preferred or selected over another, for that would then amount to cheating by invoking a non-material agency. He must be able to demonstrate that such grimly primitive and impersonal conditions can produce a "system" whose interacting parts combine to *achieve* in a truly creative sense. Merely producing an object, however symbolic of living "things" its shape might be, simply will not do.

Dawkins could, of course, draw a much more modest conclusion from his biomorph model. And it might go something like this. Given the necessary resources of human intelligence, computer hardware and software, the "random-walk" biomorph analogy demonstrates how random changes in the input instructions can be used to generate an endless variety of shapes that bear some purely superficial resemblance to the shape of both non-living and living things.

Fig. 4A: Metallic dendrites growing from the molten state

While Dawkins' biomorph model tells us virtually nothing about how living systems might have evolved, nor what they are, it does illustrate rather nicely the distinctive appearance of many material or non-living objects. For example, when liquids freeze solid, structures called dendrites will often be produced. The snowflake takes on an almost endless array of repeatedly branched dendritic shapes of considerable geometric beauty. When certain molten metallic alloys freeze from a high temperature "fir tree"-shaped dendrites of solid metal crystals form first in the melt.

Fig. 4B: Robert Hooke's drawing of dendrites growing in freezing urine

The famous seventeenth-century mathematician and natural philosopher, Robert Hooke, constructed the first compound microscope consisting of two lenses, rather than one. With the much greater magnification provided by this instrument,

Hooke proceeded to examine the minutia of his surroundings including the crystalline symmetry of frozen urine.

His book provides some of the most beautiful hand-drawn microscopic images from nature ever made.[11]

Few might relish the prospect of freezing and then examining their own waste-water. However, let me suggest a comparable experiment almost anyone with access to some basic chemicals can perform. Take small amounts of the two common chemicals sodium chloride (salt) and sodium acetate and dissolve them in a small amount of water. Leave the solution to slowly evaporate on a glass slide in a warm airing cupboard until all that remains is a thin spread of solid particles. Rather quickly the dried out salt crystals will reabsorb moisture from the atmosphere leaving microscopic little puddles. But within these puddles a myriad of morphic delights await to be viewed under a low-powered microscope.

Fig. 5A: Sounding whale

On one of my slides I found the tail of a sounding whale. There were short and long-tailed dinosaurs enjoying a moment of intimacy and an out-of-balance propeller.

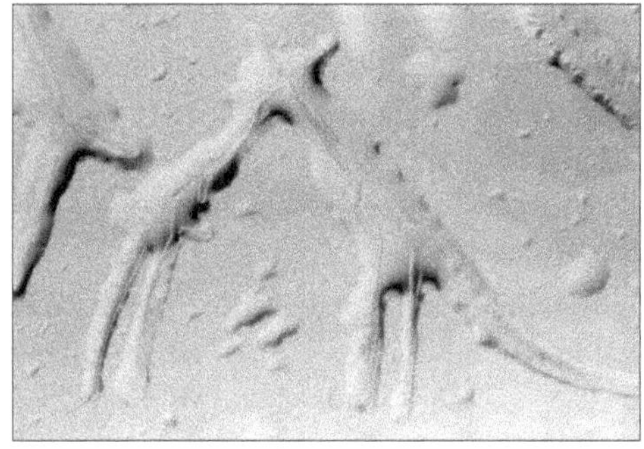

Fig. 5B: Dinosaurs sharing an intimate moment

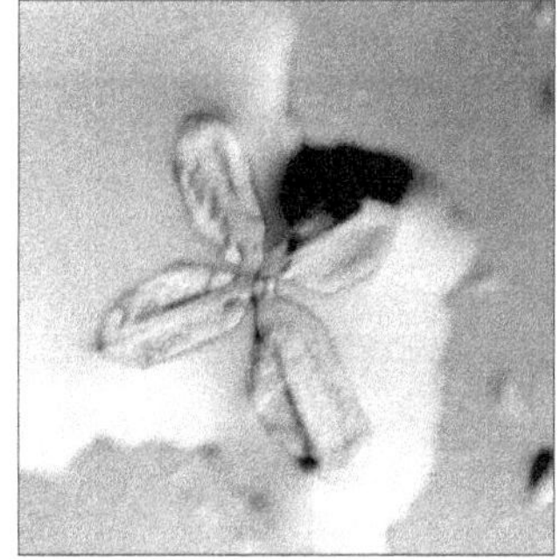

Fig. 5C: Out-of-balance propeller

These morphic wonders were all generated entirely by natural processes. As the water in my salt solution evaporated, the chemical species within began to aggregate, atom to atom, into crystalline arrays. This process, in accordance with the rules of chemical bonding, produced solid crystals growing in directions defined by their three cubic axes in space. Subtle and local variations in conditions within the evaporating solution meant that any given growth direction was in or out of favour at any one place and time—hence the never-ending variety of these crystalline shapes or morphs.

11. Hooke, *Micrographia.*

Importantly, no computer with a fancy instruction program was required to produce these crystalline delights though I think they compete rather favorably with those biomorphs generated by Richard Dawkins on his computer. But equally I would never want to suggest that these chemical morphs offer even the slightest hint of how living things might have come into existence. Crude symbolism certainly, but helpful insight into biological realities—I think not!

What my morphs do demonstrate is the servile role played by the unthinking laws of chemistry. They operate with untiring faithfulness, and always under higher influences. And in my case these influences were the unthinking fluctuations within the solution itself. The end product is a series of objects whose shapes conform entirely to the known rules of chemistry and possess some vague resemblance to the shapes of living things.

Returning briefly to Dawkins' biomorph model, what it does illustrate is a principle that goes against the very grain of his own materialistic philosophy. And it is this: in order to *achieve* (note my deliberate choice of this purposeful word) even a series of objects that are interconnected by a progression of small alterations in shape (i.e., intermediates), and where those alterations are triggered by small random changes in the shape-altering instructions, a creatively designed and constructed system is required. In brief, Dawkins needs a computer. This is certainly not analogous to the workings of raw, material forces alone; rather it is an example of a sophisticated system deliberately built to achieve a certain end—the production of objects he calls biomorphs.

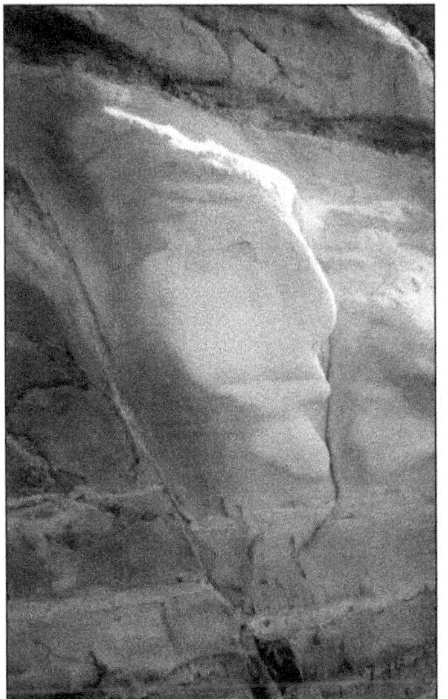

Fig. 6A: The crude form of a human face sculptured in rock by the unthinking forces of nature

The confusing of objects with purposeful systems is in many ways at the very heart of the debate between the materialist and the transcendentalist. However, there is no question that quite complex objects can arise entirely from the mindless action of the brute forces of nature.

The image in Figure 6 shows, with a little stretch of the imagination, a "human face" sculptured in a soft sandstone coastal cliff near my home. No artist had dreamed up and shaped this face. Over time the erosive action of wind, sand, sun, rain and tide had done its unthinking thing on the variable strata of soft sandstone and produced by chance an object which possessed some symbolic resemblance to a human face.

While sufficiently pleased with my find to record it on camera, I was unable to experience anything like the "feeling of exultation" that Dawkins admits to in seeing his biomorphs appear on his computer screen. And yet my sandstone face is in many respects much more of a material achievement than Richard Dawkins' computer generated images. His biomorphs depended on an intelligent computer programmer and operator. My sandstone sculpture was crafted by the raw forces of nature. What we both have in our possession are crude, naive symbols of reality and nothing more. But there is a single important difference. His biomorph was one of a continuum of objects produced because he employed a richly structured system to create them. My rocky face was completely and utterly original, it was a genuine collector's piece. There were no others even vaguely like it on the beach. There was no carefully thought-out scheme that had harnessed the material forces of nature in order to produce a sequence of sandstone shapes that led finally to my symbolic profile. This was mindless, undirected artistry at its best.

What we can see then is that objects, many of them of considerable symbolic interest, can be produced by the brute forces of an unthinking material world. In contrast, it would seem that purposeful systems will always be the result of carefully contrived arrangements that only some influence, akin to mind, can provide.

Life Transcends Order

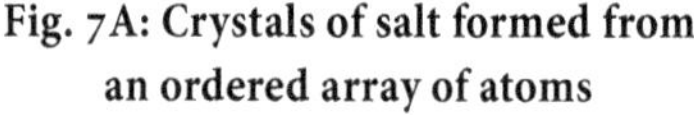

Fig. 7A: Crystals of salt formed from an ordered array of atoms

Fig. 7B: Pebbles on the beach sorted into a gradation of sizes by wave action

There is a related problem and it concerns the frequent assertion that because biological systems, like nonliving systems, exhibit order that they can be explained in wholly material terms. The evolutionary biologist Douglas Futuyma makes exactly this point arguing that the generation of order that we see for example in a crystal or in the sorting of beach pebbles into a gradation of sizes by wave action is clear evidence that order in nature is no evidence for design and, importantly, that this same class of impersonal/unthinking natural forces can equally explain the living organism. I quote from his book *Science on Trial:*

> Biological systems, like nonliving systems, are ordered—and like nonliving systems, they can be explained in terms of detailed physical mechanisms. Physiologists may be daunted at times in attempting to understand how a cell carries out the intricacies of metabolism; but as physiology has grown, it has shown these intricacies to be the consequence of fairly simple laws of chemistry, not of a mysterious "life force."[12]

Compare now the above statement of Futuyma with that of the systems scientist Leon Brillouin who takes a completely contrasting and, I believe, more candid, more honest view of the living organism and its behavior:

> The living organism heals its own wounds, cures its sicknesses, and may rebuild large portions of its structure when they have been destroyed by some accident. This is the most striking and unexpected behaviour. Think of your own car, the day you had a flat tire, and imagine having simply to wait and smoke a cigar while the hole patched itself and the tire pumped itself to the proper pressure, and you could go on. This sounds incredible. It is, however, the way nature works when you "chip off" while shaving in the morning. There is no inert matter possessing a similar property of repair.[13]

The contrast between these two positions is glaring: the crudely ordered strata of pebbles that we see on the beach are engulfed by the external forces imposed on them. They have no choice but to "go with the flow". The granules of salt that I sprinkle on my boiled egg at breakfast consist of sodium and chlorine ions that have aggregated with boring regularity into a particular crystalline order. Compress one of these salt crystals and you will get an utterly predictable response—it will crush! It cannot anticipate this assault on its shape or make up for any loss of cohesive strength. It cannot, of itself, embark on a program of self-repair or reproduction to ensure the continuity of the sodium chloride species in that particular form.

The grain of salt certainly possesses order, and it is the kind of order that materialists like Douglas Futuyma misleadingly imply can account for

12. Futuyma, *Science on Trial*, 115.

13. Brillouin, *Life, Thermodynamics, and Cybernetics*, 154.

the living organism. But the idea that the order observed in the non-living world provides a key to our understanding of how living organisms might have developed seems little more than a naive materialistic fantasy.

Purpose Denied, on Purpose Relied

Oxford chemist Peter Atkins is a prominent scientist who promotes with considerable vigor the idea of a mindless, purposeless set of material processes that have transformed "Molecules into Men". Here is a brief extract from his book *Creation Revisited* illustrating this grand materialistic unfolding of life:

> The whole course of evolution can be regarded as a geared and co-operative dissipation of energy. Every stage of evolution, including the steps that gave rise to complex molecules out of simpler ones, to people out of slime, and the processes involved when species are confronted with competition, proceeds by dissipation. Molecules did not aim at reproduction: they stumbled upon it. Accretion of complexity reached the point where one molecule was so structured that the sequence of reactions it could undergo, under the casual pressure of dispersal, led by chance to the formation of a replica. . . . At every stage of replication there was opportunity for modification because slightly different smaller molecules were in the vicinity and could be incorporated. Many of these daughters may have been unviable, or less successful at replication than their ancestors and sisters; but some were more successful, and flourished into elephants.[14]

Atkins sketches for his readers a series of ancient, aimless molecular happenings: a local pocket of molecules, driven by a tendency for everything in the universe to gravitate towards a more uniform or more spread-out and lower energy state, which are continually bumping into each other (in chemical terms, reacting). In their haphazard meanderings, these molecules "stumble" into some different configuration which just happens to possess some new qualities. For example, copies of this new arrangement might somehow be made more easily. Remember, in Atkins' molecular world, nothing is aimed at. There can be no actual purpose or intended outcome in this wholly material world.

This new tendency of the molecules to stumble upon a mechanism of copying or replication, also embodied failure—a failure to copy faithfully. A kind of molecular variety concert is launched on the primordial stage of the ancient, still lifeless, earth. Act after aimless act is performed, each a

14. Atkins, *Creation Revisited*, 31.

subtle twist on the previous as other molecules straying in the vicinity are conveniently co-opted. A "yes, we got through that act," or "no, that was a disaster" kind of primordial culling pressure (read—natural selection) acts on this molecular concert, resulting in more replication, more variety, more cancelled acts, more complexification and producing, eventually, elephants and humans!

Now the above is, I believe, a fair summary of how Peter Atkins' imagines life to have unfolded. But what is he really asking his readers to believe? Keeping in mind Atkins' reigning dictum that complex life came from simple molecular interactions via entirely inanimate processes, it stands to reason that if a living cell could have been created in the fullness of time by such starkly material happenings, the origin of *much less* complex non-living things should be even more easily explained by equally material processes.

So let me try and explain Atkins' primordial drama by way of an analogous scenario, one that is, indeed, incomparably simpler than any primitive life form, but comparably material and thus much more plausible given the conditions he espouses. My scenario might read something along the following lines:

Imagine some hot little spot on the surface of the ancient earth, maybe a crevice near an active volcano (technically termed a *fumarole*). Some iron oxide molecules just happen to meet up with some unlikely carbon atoms which, at the prevailing temperature, just happen to bring about the reduction of some of the iron oxide to its metallic state (equivalent to Atkins' "random, motiveless jostling" of his "crowd of atoms").[15] It just so happens that this iron, now further heated by the reduction reaction (equivalent perhaps to Atkins' "geared and cooperative dissipation of energy"),[16] begins to flow as a liquid and find its way, quite by chance, into a collection spot where it gradually cools. The form it assumes on solidifying is of course a nothing-in-particular shape.

But, the lottery of primordial events grinds relentlessly onwards and upwards. More molten iron is produced, shape is added to shape, a corner is knocked off here, a bit added there and soon that nothing-in-particular shape is modified into something that, quite by chance, begins to take on a more cylindrical form. Volcanic explosions generate scoria "bombs" and cause movement in the rocky environment which pummels and distorts our piece of iron. A distinct bend is produced, the form of a crude "crank" shape is hinted at. The relentless heaving, tumbling and grinding movements eventually produces, quite by chance, a smooth, polished bearing surface on the

15. Atkins, *Creation Revisited*, 23.

16. Ibid., 31.

"crank" object—equivalent to Atkins' "Complex molecules can acquire even greater complexity in stages instead of attempting a single grand passion. One molecule may be able to discard a few atoms to a congenial partner, pick up a few others elsewhere, and in due course chance upon a destination."[17]

Nearby, equally material processes lead to the formation of another metallic "thing" that just happens to attach itself to the above "crank" as a crude connecting rod. This, together with several other metallic shapes—all produced by the same mindless, unguided physical processes—results in the accidental formation of a crank connected to a piston inside a cylinder. A mix of gases, quite by chance, happens to seep into the cylinder above the piston and gets accidentally compressed when the "crank" is struck at the "right" angle by another scoria bomb (equivalent to Atkins' "reaction by multiple misadventure").[18] This gaseous mixture turns out to be combustible. A spark from the volcanic vent triggers an explosion and thus the primordial earth, utilizing only unthinking material processes, yields the very first firing stroke of the internal combustion engine.

Of course, this first "stroke" of luck did not connect with an appropriate second stroke of luck. However, because we have both mega-time and mega amounts of material and energy this same kind of process is repeated endlessly and, after a mega-number of in-between models, leads eventually to an improved pre-engine (equivalent to Atkins' "complexity may be the outcome of chains of simplicity").[19] This last model now incorporates a first and second exhaust stroke which had an obvious functional advantage in that it was closer in form to an engine that could function (yes, we have here a suggestion of *natural selection* but not without a strong hint of a purposeful goal!). Although mega-failures abound, the four-cycle internal combustion engine eventually appears on the primordial stage complete with inlet and exhaust valving, electronic ignition, water cooling, extractors, intercooler and turbo-charger!

Now our functioning fantasy engine is incomparably simpler than any minimally functioning biological cell. But we are forever assured by Atkins' own writing that entirely material processes acting on endless amounts of matter bathed in endless flows of dissipative energy, are able to deliver in megatime whatever level of complexity we care to find in the living world. Mere extrapolation of simple unthinking processes is supposedly sufficient to explain how life entered onto the primordial stage. And so for Atkins, "if there are atoms there will in due course be molecules; and if there are

17. Ibid., 29.

18. Ibid., 31.

19. Ibid., 7.

molecules on warm, wet platforms, there will in due course be elephants."[20] Using the same logic, one might equally assert that "if there is iron oxide and carbon on very hot platforms there will in due course be iron and steel, and in due course there will be internal combustion engines."

It soon becomes apparent that any attempt to discuss the issue of life's origin within a purposeless material framework very quickly turns messy, in fact decidedly ridiculous! However, materialists all too often attempt to skirt round the mess by inserting purposeful elements into their narratives describing the action of natural selection, albeit in a not so subtly disguised form. In this regard it should be sufficient to remind readers of two examples already referred to in this chapter—Steve Jones' soap powder factory analogy in which the workers are in *pursuit of an improved nozzle*; or the evolving eye model of Nilsson and Pelger (also exploited by Richard Dawkins) which requires that *increased spatial resolution be aimed* for.

Mindless Mechanicity Or Mindful Machinations

Evolutionary philosopher Daniel Dennett is similarly imbued with the need to covertly insert purpose but deny its need. His recurring theme is the "mindless mechanicity" of the evolutionary process.[21] He sees Darwin's concept of natural selection as the "universal acid" that dissolves away all but the "purposeless, mindless, pointless regularity of physics." And in Dennett's brutally unthinking, unfeeling universe this same physics leads eventually to "products that exhibit . . . purposive design."[22]

But Dennett all too frequently betrays his need for the extra-material. Take for example his description of natural selection as an algorithmic process, a "set of individually mindless steps succeeding each other without the help of any intelligent supervision."[23] To assist his reader to grasp the concept of an algorithmic process, and one that makes use of chance or randomness as occurs in Darwinian natural selection, Dennett uses the example of long division. He rightly argues that when wanting to divide a large number by another, one can simply choose a digit at random, try it and then check out the result. If the initial guess is too large or too small, simply adjust and retry. The point he correctly makes is that one eventually gets the process to work even if the first guess was stupidly far out—it just takes a bit longer to do the job.

20. Ibid., 5.

21. Dennett, *Darwin's Dangerous Idea.*

22. Ibid., 65.

23. Ibid., 59.

But can Dennett's long division example be described as just mindless mechanicity? Certainly not! Despite the guessing element, a solution is being *sought*. We actually want to solve an arithmetic problem using long division. It is powerfully goal-driven. Dennett claims you "don't need to have any wit or discernment" but this is patently untrue. The process has been *set up* in such a way that there is a constant testing of the rightness or wrongness of a particular guess against a correct outcome. In an entirely mindless, purposeless world surely nothing is being sought, nothing is being judged right or wrong, correct or incorrect. Things *just are* and this is precisely what Dennett's long division analogy fails to illustrate.

Tell-Tale Signs from Living and Non-Living Systems

Any commonsense comparison of the living and non-living world points powerfully to properties and characteristics of life that remain inexplicable in terms of the material laws and processes revealed by science. David Holbrook notes that the living organism *strives* to realize its full potential.[24] Michael Polanyi sees the organism as goal-centered; it might succeed or fail to achieve this goal and the science of pathology is rightly applied to account for such failure.[25] By contrast, when a candle flame "dies" one does not immediately consult a pathology text book. Whereas the candle flame can be adequately accounted for in terms of the material laws of chemistry, the living organism, although dependent on such laws, plays to a higher tune. It embodies purposeful orchestration of these material laws.

Philosopher Eric Tomlin likens the behavior of the living organism to a musical melody consisting of cycles of unified "movements" in which the first notes are as important as the last.[26] The organic themes are played out phase by phase and in anticipation of those that follow. The material laws can perhaps be viewed as the individual notes that are played but they do not, of themselves, define the musical theme. Rather they are exploited in the service of a higher purpose, one reflecting the creative genius of the composer.

Natural selection certainly relies on an oddly non-material principle, namely the prolife drive that all living organisms express, the tendency to want to flourish, what Darwin called the fecundity principle. This "flourishing" surely contradicts materialism's assertion that life is merely a special arrangement of matter. Each living organism, however simple or complex, possesses this truly remarkable quality—it wants to live and to this end it

24. Holbrook, *Evolution and the Humanities*.

25. Polanyi, *Meaning*, 161–81.

26. Tomlin, "The Concept of Life."

performs intensely purposeful, anticipatory tasks. It is "possessed" of a drive to go on surviving in the midst of what are often enormous external pressures bearing down on its organic well-being.

This ceaseless striving to live and keep on living, and to self-repair when damaged, is quite alien to any non-living system. A plant will build up reserves of food for those anticipated periods of leanness. A tree or a bone will actively remodel and self-strengthen certain parts of its structure in response to forces repeatedly imposed by the wind or heavy exercise. There is a constant turn-over of components in the living organism in response to damage and decay.

The fundamental quality that seems to stand out in the living organism, whether simple or sophisticated, is its *awareness* of both its "organic responsibility and destiny." It *knows* what it should be in a functional sense. And when this function is disrupted by trauma or disease the organism orchestrates a sequence of restorative acts aimed at enabling it to fulfil this destiny.

A comparison of the *performance* of a living organism with that of a complex material system such as, for example, a motor car engine is instructive. It highlights the fundamental difference between innate, creative, anticipatory behavior and imposed, programmed activity. The motor car engine is certainly made to perform, but only because a certain combination of external forces and constraints (devised by a human mind) extracts from it a particular activity—the generation of motive power. The engine is entirely at the mercy of these forces: remove them and it reverts to a "lifeless" metallic corpse. The engine is a *subject* without rights. It is subject to the choice of materials used in its component parts and to their exact shape and arrangement, to the quality of lubrication and cooling supplied, to the preciseness of the ignition timing etc. These are all external factors imposed on the engine by a creative mind.

By contrast, the living organism is a *monarch* within its own ecological niche. It is able to creatively challenge and adapt to a significant degree the forces that are imposed on it from the external world. Of course there are limits to any organism's adaptability. It can be so easily overwhelmed. But the mere fact that it has even limited adaptive potential sets it fundamentally apart from any non-living system or object.

An engine, left by the careless driver to overheat, soon results in its lubricating oil thinning dangerously. Unchecked, the resultant frictional heating soon ends in a total systems collapse—engine seizure. Now compare this with a lettuce plant. Every home gardener knows just how important it is to supply the plant with plenty of water. But if its thirst is not met, especially in hot weather, the lettuce will "bolt" or go-to-seed, thus attempting to ensure its continuity as a species. The lettuce responds to the harsh heat of high summer in a profoundly creative manner. Not so with the motor car engine. It can only wallow in the victim role.

It is frequently argued that because living systems behave in a mechanical manner they are therefore reducible to wholly material laws. For example, the American evolutionary biologist George Williams has this to say of the evolution and operation of biological mechanisms:

> When I use the term *protein-based machinery*, I implied that the workings of the human body can be understood in ways closely similar to our understanding of metal and plastic machinery. I assumed that we can, metaphorically at least, take the body apart and see what makes it tick. This understanding can make use of any and all known physical principles, but no modern physiologists would invoke anything immaterial[sic] or supernatural. . . . Biologists never conclude that physics and chemistry are not a sufficient basis for understanding how a biological mechanism works.[27]

A recurring assertion in Williams' book is the adequacy of mechanism (read wholly material processes) in explaining the operation of organisms. Here is a familiar illustration he uses in support of this assertion:

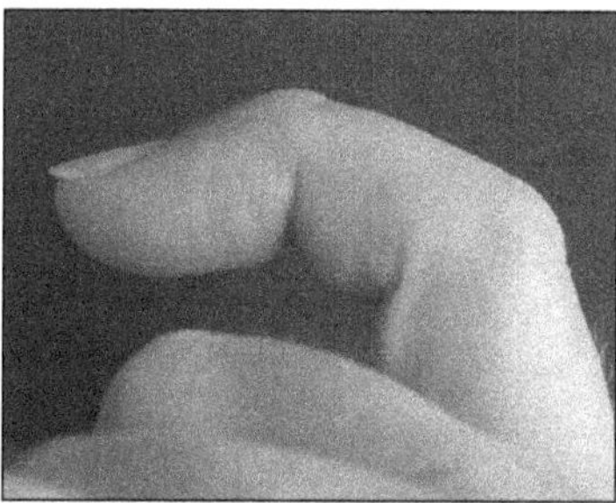

Fig. 8A: Curling and straightening out of a finger

> A finger does not curl up or straighten out because its wants to, but because it is forced to by the pulling of tendons. These tendons pull only because they are pulled by muscles. Why do the muscles pull? Their pulling is an active shortening of the muscles as a whole, and this shortening in the realm of the readily visible reflects a shortening process in the realm of the ultramicroscopic. Muscles are densely loaded with parallel protein fibers running from one end to the other. These fibers actively shorten, and provide the muscle with its forceful contraction. . . . Their normal relaxed state is stretched out. Their contraction

27. Williams, *Plan and Purpose in Nature*, 65.

> requires a supply of energy from a substance called adenosine triphosphate (*ATP*). The energy taken from the metabolism of this substance comes ultimately from the food we eat and the oxygen we breathe. Understanding all this requires an impressive array of technical knowledge of the molecular machinery of the cell, but this knowledge is entirely of physics and chemistry. No subtle immaterial [sic] processes are employed.[28]

Now it is certainly correct to say that biological systems are machines which rely on well-established physical and chemical principles. The heart is a muscle-driven, beautifully synchronized multi-valve pump delivering a flow of blood into the circulatory system in accordance with well-known laws of fluid mechanics. The articulating joint works as a hinge exploiting properties of stiffness and low friction. The eye is an auto-focusing camera harnessing well-established principles of optics. The inner workings of the cell operate as an incredibly sophisticated biochemical processing factory. Living systems are indeed mechanical. And George Williams' curling finger is equally mechanical in respect to each of the various levels he describes. But can he really claim that the processes involved are "entirely of physics and chemistry"?[29]

One way of critiquing Williams' claim is to apply his same line of reasoning to any human-engineered system. Consider again the workings of an internal combustion engine. We might ask "Why does the crankshaft rotate and deliver power to the transmission system"? Following almost exactly his line of argument, we can say that the crank receives a push from the piston via the connecting rod and rotates. This push is, in turn, produced by a high pressure explosion at the top of the piston, this explosion resulting from the ignition of an appropriate mix of compressed air and petrol. Finally, the explosion is triggered by a spark generated from an electrical circuit. Put simply, what we have in reverse order is a sequence of

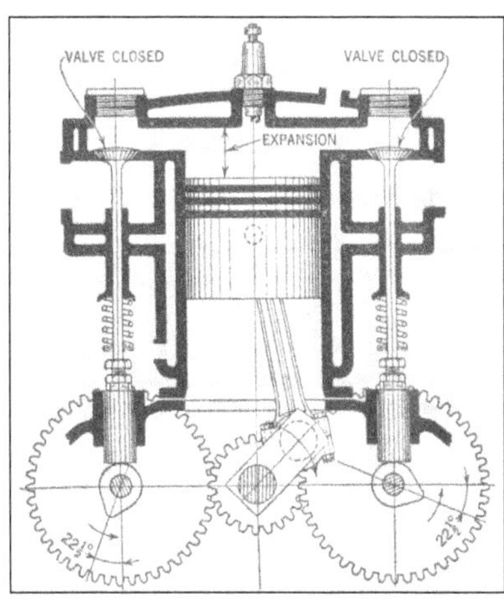

Fig. 8B: Schematic showing basic operation of the internal combustion engine (Taken from Audel's *New Automotive Guide*, New York: Audel & Co., 1938)

28. Ibid., 68.
29. Ibid., 67.

events—a rotation, a force, a pressure, a violent chemical reaction, a pulse of "lightning"—all processes that can be described in purely material or physico-chemical terms and that clearly parallel George Williams' curling finger.

We should note too that Williams emphasizes that his finger does not curl up "because it wants to." In the same way our petrol engine doesn't "roar into life" because it wants to. It starts running because an appropriately sequenced chain of physical events has been externally triggered.

Michael Polanyi's Critique of Machines

It might therefore seem at first glance that both our living finger and our inanimate engine can be explained in wholly material terms. But such a conclusion does not stand up to closer scrutiny, and to press home this point I would like to draw on the common sense insights of Michael Polanyi, one of the great integrative thinkers of the last century.

Conscious that the biological sciences have bought liberally into mechanism as an over-arching explanatory philosophy, Polanyi seeks to dispel the idea that because living systems are demonstrably mechanical in their various functions they can therefore be explained in purely physico-chemical or material categories. Whilst acknowledging the validity of the mechanical model in understanding biological systems, Polanyi insists that it points to something beyond and above purely material entities. Here is what he says:

> There is a great deal of truth in the mechanical explanation of life. The organs of the body work like machines, as they are subject to a hierarchy of mechanical principles. Biologists pursuing the aim of explaining living functions in terms of machines have achieved outstanding success. But this must not obscure the fact that these advances only add to the features of life which cannot be represented in terms of laws manifested in the realm of inanimate nature.[30]

Polanyi argues that just as the material properties and laws of nature are harnessed within the boundaries defined by the design of any man-made machine, so material laws operate within the boundaries defined by the organism's structure. But this living structure is no more determined by these laws than the material properties of steel determine the shape of a crankshaft in our engine. In the case of non-biological machines, Polanyi

30. Polanyi, *The Tacit Dimension*, 42.

states quite categorically where the material laws of nature lie in relation to the emergence of such machines:

> If all men were exterminated, this would not affect the laws of inanimate nature. But the production of machines would stop, and not until men arose again would machines be formed once more. Some animals can produce tools, but only men can construct machines; machines are human artifacts, made of inanimate material. . . . The structure of machines and the working of their structure are thus shaped by man, even while their material and the forces that operate them obey the laws of inanimate nature. In constructing a machine and supplying it with power, we harness the laws of nature at work in its material and in its driving force and make them serve our purpose.[31]

This harness is not unbreakable; the structure of the machine, and thus its working, can break down. But this will not affect the forces of inanimate nature on which the operation of the machine relied; it merely releases them from the restriction the machine imposed on them before it broke down.

When we pass on to living organisms, we are similarly faced with machinelike systems, whether these be whole organs such as the heart, an individual cell, or one of the many molecular machines contained within the cell such as the sodium-potassium membrane pump. Each of these living mechanical systems involves an enormously complex sequence of interactions among their component parts.

In the same way in which the material properties and inanimate laws of nature are harnessed within the boundaries defined by the design of our man-made machine, so the inanimate molecular and chemical laws operate within the boundaries defined by the organism's structure. But this living structure is no more determined by these laws than the material properties of steel determine the shape of a crankshaft in an internal combustion engine. Paul Weiss expresses rather succinctly the same concept: "There is no phenomenon in a living system that is not molecular, but there is none that is only molecular either.[32]

The reductionist assertions of biological materialists like George Williams rest on the presumption that because living systems are "mechanical" they are therefore explicable in terms of the impersonal laws of physics and chemistry. The hierarchical structure of both inanimate and living machines is surely incompatible with this view. The very moment one claims that life is mechanical and is therefore reducible to a complex set of inanimate

31. Polanyi, "Life's Irreducible Structure."

32. Weiss, *Within the Gates of Science and Beyond*, 270.

biochemical mechanisms, one tumbles into a logic trap. For to admit to "mechanism" in the living world is to admit, as Michael Polanyi so clearly shows, to the need for boundary conditions that cannot be accounted for by these inanimate processes. By their very "mechanical" nature, biological systems "demand" a higher level of explanation.

Conclusion

Biological materialism appears fixated on a one-line causal economy of wholly material influences. In acknowledging only the unfeeling laws of a mindless, purposeless material world, it offers an absurdly truncated theory of life that fails to account for the "aliveness" of the living world.

If unthinking material laws are unable to produce biological innovation, what is it that draws atoms and molecules together into systems that exude a sense of purpose and destiny? I would argue for a model of an evolving creation that doesn't shrink from placing the essential activity of God right at the very core of the organic process. In other words, right down the evolutionary line to primordial "ground zero" we are confronted with a dimension that relates to something akin to the activity of a transcendent Mind. It would seem from examining the facts revealed by science alone that nature does indeed suggest a transcendent dimension.

Bibliography

Atkins, Peter. *Creation Revisited.* New York: Freeman, 1992.

Brillouin, Leon. "Life, Thermodynamics, and Cybernetics." In *Modern Systems Research for the Behavioral Scientist,* edited by W. Buckley, 147–56. Chicago: Aldine, 1968.

Broom, Neil. *How Blind is the Watchmaker.* Downers Grove, IL: InterVarsity, 2001.

———. *Life's X-Factor: The Missing Link in Materialism's Science of Living Things.* Wellington, NZ: Steele Roberts, 2010.

Darwin, Charles. *The Origin of Species by Means of Natural Selection.* 6th ed. London: Dent, 1928.

Dawkins, Richard. *The Blind Watchmaker: Why the Evidence of Evolution Reveals a Universe Without Design.* London: Penguin, 1988.

———. *Climbing Mount Improbable.* Harmondsworth, UK:Viking, 1996.

Dennett, Daniel. *Darwin's Dangerous Idea.* London: Penguin. 1995.

Futuyma, Douglas. *Science on Trial: The Case for Evolution.* New York: Pantheon, 1982.

Holbrook, David. *Evolution and the Humanities.* New York: St. Martin's, 1987.

Hooke, Robert. *Micrographia.* London, 1665.

Jones, Steve. *Almost Like a Whale.* London: Transworld, 2000.

Larson, E. J., and L. Witham. "Scientists and Religion in America." *Scientific American* 281 (September 1999) 78–83.

Monod, Jacques. *Chance and Necessity.* London: Collins, *1972.*

Nilsson, Dan, and Susanne Pelger. "A Pessimistic Estimate of the Time Required for an Eye to Evolve." *Proceedings of the Royal Society of London* 256B (1994) 53–58.
Polanyi, Michael. "Life's Irreducible Structure." *Science* 160 (1968) 1308–12.
———. *Meaning*. Chicago: University of Chicago Press, 1975.
———. *The Tacit Dimension*. Garden City, NY: Doubleday, 1966.
Tomlin, E. W. F. "The Concept of Life." *Heythrop Journal* 18.3 (1977) 289–304.
Weiss, Paul. *Within the Gates of Science and Beyond*. New York: Hafner, 1971.
Williams, George. *Plan and Purpose in Nature*. London: Weidenfeld and Nicolson, 1996.

7

Thinking about God and Infinity

Can Mathematics Contribute?

WILF MALCOLM

I WILL FIRST SET out some preliminary intuitive ideas and language about the nature of infinity as we encounter it in ordinary circumstances, and in common thinking about God. One immediate context is our growing awareness of the seeming lack of any spatial boundaries to the universe in which we find ourselves. Space seems to be unlimited in its extension—it goes on to infinity. But, then, what is the nature of that infinity?[1]

Closely intertwined with our notions of spatial infinity are the notions of time and eternity. Interestingly, some current scientific thinking suggests a possible time boundary to our physical universe looking backwards—the "time" of the big bang—but leaves open the question as to whether there will be an end-time.

Mathematically, it is through the sequence of counting numbers; one, two, three, and so on forever and ever, that we encounter the notion of the infinite—an unending sequence of counting units. Indeed this unending sequence of units underlies the notions of infinity associated with contexts involving unending application of units of measurement, or of units of conceptual awareness. The infinities of the notions of time and space illustrate such an unending sequence of measuring units. Concepts such as self-awareness or self-consciousness and the nature of personal identity, involving units of comprehension, also involve notions of the infinite.

1. This paper was originally presented as an address to TANSA, Thursday 25 March 2010.

Certainly the unending sequence of counting numbers gives rise to a fundamental understanding of the nature of mathematical infinity. On the one hand it leads to ideas of infinite size or magnitude—a magnitude greater than any magnitude of finite measure. But on the other hand, through the related sequence: 1, 1/2, 1/3, 1/4, and so on forever and ever, we gain an idea of infinitely small magnitudes. As we shall see later in the article, it is the concept of the infinitely small that plays a significant part in the mathematics that supports the physical sciences through the differential and integral calculus. It is also important to note that we can make true statements about each and every counting number without actually separately identifying each number in our mind on its own. For instance, the statement that every second number is even is such an example.

A somewhat different intuitive concept of the finite to infinite relationship is the philosophically inclined conceptual desire to draw together a diversity of awareness and experience into a unity of understanding and concept. The finite is recognized in the individuality of the diverse components, with the infinite reflected in the desire for a unified understanding. Perhaps this desire underlies the wish of some scientists to construct a "theory of everything."

Certainly, too, it is the case that notions of the infinite become inextricably involved with our thinking about God. The Bible resonates with such terms. God is omnipotent—all powerful; omniscient—all knowing; omnipresent—within and outside of space and time. In more philosophical terms God can be regarded as the Being behind all being; the Meaning behind all meaning; the Sense behind all experience; the Creator and Sustainer behind the given world; the Word behind all aspects of our knowing. In such contexts the infinity of God is closely associated with the notion of having no limit or boundary in terms of our conceptual understanding. But does this remove the idea of God from our ability to understand or comprehend?

Basic Approach

In the above comments I think it is plain, that in thinking about God intuitive ideas of the infinite and the finite become involved. It is also plain that in thinking about our encounter with our immediate world we, too, become involved with notions of the finite and the infinite. The development of mathematics and its effective utilization of concepts about infinity in its critical contribution to scientific developments, is a major expression of this latter encounter.

And so the question would seem to arise naturally: "Can understanding of the way in which ideas of the infinite develop in mathematics help us in our understanding of the infinity of God?" Saint Augustine of the fourth to fifth centuries CE, and one of the great theologians of church history certainly thought so. In an article written by Adam Drozdek and entitled, "Beyond Infinity: Augustine and Cantor," he summarized three important aspects of Augustine's discussion of God and infinity. First, infinity is an inborn concept which enables any knowledge. *Second, infinity can be found in the purest form in mathematics, and thus mathematics is the best tool of acquiring knowledge about God.* Third, God is neither finite nor infinite and his greatness surpasses even the infinite.[2]

Later theologians such as Anselm and Aquinas, and others also, accepted and developed Augustine's thinking in this regard. As well, I have to confess, that until reading in preparation for this paper I had not known that Georg Cantor, German mathematician of the eighteenth and nineteenth centuries CE and one of the major contributors to the development of understanding of the mathematical infinite, considered that his work on the mathematics of infinity would have greater consequences for theology than for mathematics itself.

For the middle part of this article I will seek to give a gentle introduction to aspects of the ways in which mathematics has developed the concepts of the finite and the infinite. In so doing I will comment on the following stages:

1. Basic classical Greek/Aristotelian notions of the infinite and Zeno's paradoxes;
2. Limit concepts of infinity;
3. Notion of the derivative in the calculus; and
4. Cantor's set-theoretic concepts of the transfinite and its distinction from the absolute infinite.

Then, in conclusion, I will seek to indicate some tentative directions that I consider these mathematical notions might open up for further theological consideration.

2. Adam Drozdek, "Beyond Infinity," 127–40.

Basic Mathematical Ideas Involving Infinity

Greek/Aristotelian Notions and Zeno Paradoxes

For most classical Greeks, and Aristotle in particular, infinity was not an actual entity but unlimited potential. It was this notion of unlimited potential, illustrated in the unending sequence of counting numbers which Augustine inherited and incorporated as a continuing element in Christian theology. For many mathematicians, too, right up to the nineteenth century, this was the primary component of infinity—unlimited potential.

Again for many in classical Greek philosophy, the reality underlying all knowledge had a primary unity that was not subject to change or partition. The desire to support understanding of this primary unity may have been the motivation for the development by Zeno, in the fifth century BCE, of his famous paradoxes. Through them, perhaps, he sought to demonstrate that notions of change and motion as elements of the primary reality led to contradiction and false understanding. Let me indicate the nature of three of these paradoxes. The first is based on an apparent analysis of a person crossing a room from one side to another. First that person must cross to the half-way point, then to the half-way point of the remaining distance, then to the half-way point of the next remaining distance, and so on. But this process is an unending one, like the sequence of counting numbers. It goes on without end and the person will never reach the other side of the room—paradox indeed, when we consider our actual experience in crossing a room.

A second such paradox is the well-known story of the race between Achilles and the tortoise. At the start of the race the tortoise is given a start, say of a one hundred meters. When Achilles reaches the point where the tortoise first started, the tortoise has moved to a further point along the race track. But when Achilles reaches this further point the tortoise has again moved on. And so on, for an unending sequence of points. Thus Achilles will never catch up to the tortoise. Again a paradox when we consider actual experience.

A third Zeno paradox would seem to deny the possibility of actual observed motion in space. Take an arrow moving along a line in space. In any space of time its tip, say, will have moved from one point in the line to another distinct point. Therefore the tip of the arrow cannot be in motion at any point of time, because a single point of the line cannot be subdivided into two distinct points. Thus at each point along the line the arrow is at rest.

We shall look later at these kinds of paradoxes from the point of view of later developments in the concepts of mathematical thinking. We shall also consider the impact of paradoxical concepts on theological thinking, including a mathematical parallel to the doctrine of the Trinity.

Limit Concepts of Infinity

Limit concepts in handling encounters with notions of infinity have a long history in mathematical developments. Archimedes, the great Greek mathematician of the third century BCE, used forms of such concepts in calculating lengths of curved surfaces, such as the circumference of a circle. In the seventeenth century CE, Newton and Leibniz used such notions, somewhat intuitively, in their independent developments of the calculus. Let me seek to give you a brief insight into the nature of these limit concepts.

Consider the sequence of numbers given by the formula $1/n$, where n progresses through all the counting numbers. What is immediately apparent is that $1/n$ gets smaller and smaller as n gets bigger and bigger. In mathematical language we say: The sequence $1/n$ has limit zero as n tends to infinity. We write this as: $\lim_{n\to\infty}(1/n) = 0$ The great strength of this concept is the precise formal definition that supports it. To say that $\lim_{n\to\infty}(1/n) = 0$, means that whenever you choose a real number ϵ greater than zero, but no matter how small, you can then always find a counting number, M, such that whenever n is greater than M, then $1/n$ is closer to zero than ϵ. If you change the value of ϵ to a smaller, but still non-zero number, then you can find another counting number M, for which the statement will still be true. It is amazing that such a descriptive statement, involving only finite numbers, can make precise the limit concept.

This notion of a limit has a wide range of deep and extensive outcomes involving notions of infinity. One straight forward example is the notion of adding together an infinite sequence of numbers. For instance let $S_n = 1/2 + (1/2)^2 + (1/2)^3 + (1/2)^4 + \ldots + (1/2)^n$, where n is any counting number. By a little school algebra it can be shown that $S_n = 1-(1/2)^n$, and so $\lim_{n\to\infty}(S_n) = 1-0 = 1$. That is adding this infinite sequence of numbers gives us the finite number 1. A fascinating way in which one can add together an infinity of numbers.

Such a method gives a way of working through Zeno's paradox about crossing the room. If the room is taken as 1 unit wide, then the sequence Sn adds up the distances of first going half way, then going half of the remaining distance, then again half of the remaining distance, and so on for n times. Taking the limit as n tends to ∞ gives us the sum of all these steps taken an infinite number of times, and as we have seen this sum is 1. That is we have crossed the room!

Taking limits does not just involve counting numbers. It can involve real numbers as well. One well known example is $\lim_{x\to 0}(\sin x/x) = 1$. That is the limit of $\sin x/x$ as x gets smaller and smaller is 1. For those without knowledge of trigonometry and hence of sinx, this example can be illustrated by the following diagram.

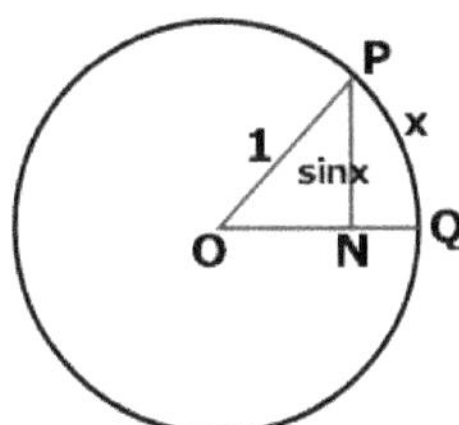

Fig. 1: The limit of sinx/x as x gets smaller and smaller is 1

The length of the circumference of the circle from P to Q is the value of x, and the length of the line PN is the value of sinx. As x tends to 0, that is as P tends to Q around the circle, then the ratio of the length of PN to the length of PQ tends to 1, notwithstanding the fact that when P coincides with Q the two lengths are separately zero. Even though the statements involve only finite numbers, the limit process itself involves an infinite notion. For all intervals of numbers close to 1 we can find an interval of numbers x close to zero such that the ratio sinx/x is always in the interval close to 1. This example leads us directly to the notion of a derivative as encountered in the mathematical calculus.

Notion of the Derivative in the Calculus

With Zeno's paradox in mind about the moving arrow being motionless I will develop the notion of derivative in the context of the concept of the velocity of a moving object. If a moving object P moves in a line from a point A to a point B and takes a time t units to do so, then we say the average velocity of P from A to B is given by the ratio AB/t, where AB is the distance from A to B. That is the average velocity over a distance from A to B is the distance from A to B divided by the time taken to travel that distance. So far then Zeno is on track. A measure of average velocity requires two distinct points. For if B is taken as the same point as A, then the velocity from A to B is 0/0, which is meaningless.

This then is where the genius of Leibniz and Newton comes into play, through reaching out to an intuitive concept of limit. In the diagram below the particle is at the point A with plane vertical coordinate x as distance and plane horizontal coordinate t as time.

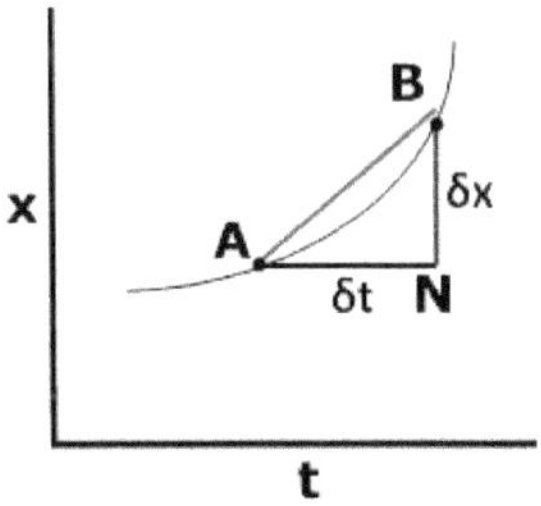

Fig. 2: An intuitive Concept of Limit

Take a small, non-zero, increase in time, which we will call δt. This means the particle will have moved to the point B, a distance δx from A, represented by the vertical line on the graph, BN. So the average velocity of the particle from A to B is given by the ratio of $\delta x/\delta t$. Then the velocity of the particle at A is defined as the limit of this ratio as δt tends to 0. Thus Zeno's moving arrow paradox is overcome by the limit concept which enables velocity to be defined at a single point. This limit is also known as the first derivative of x as a function of t.

Thus it is that this limit process, incorporating a mathematical notion of the infinite, provided the basis for major and significant developments in the physical sciences. It is the case that both Newton and Leibnitz, while developing the calculus on an intuitive basis of the limit processes, did not have a clear concept of the limit notion as developed by men such as Weierstrass more than a century later. It was this lack of clarity that gave opportunity to Bishop Berkeley to develop his criticism of the emerging scientific method thought by some to be threatening theological understanding. It is also the case that the limit process, while clearly involving infinite processes, yet does so more in the context of infinity as a potential, rather than as an existing entity.

Cantor's Set Theoretic Concepts of the Infinite

It was in the second part of the eighteenth century CE that the German mathematician Georg Cantor developed a precise mathematical concept of the transfinite. Note that I have called it the *trans*finite, that is across the finite, because not withstanding these transfinite concepts, Cantor still believed there was an absolute infinity transcending all the transfinite levels he identified. It is interesting to note, too, that Cantor received much criticism, indeed persecution, from some mathematical colleagues who opposed his ideas, including his onetime mathematical mentor Leopold Kronecker. It is not only religious authorities that oppose radical thinking!

Cantor's concepts of finite and infinite are based on the very simple notion of one-to-one correspondence between two sets or collections of entities and, thereby, being able to say that two such collections have the same numerical magnitude if they can be put into one-to-one correspondence with each other. Thus it is that the set of fingers on my left hand has the same numerical magnitude as the set of fingers on my right hand. The process of counting each set to five demonstrates the one-to-one correspondence!

More formally, we say that θ is a one-to-one correspondence between sets A and B if for each a in A there is a unique b in B such that $\theta(a)=b$; and for each d in B there is a unique c in A such that $\theta(c)=d$.

But it is when this notion of numerical magnitude based on one-to-one correspondences is applied to the non-finite that we find surprises. For instance the set of counting numbers can be put into one-to-one correspondence with the set of even counting numbers, a proper subset of itself. The diagram as set out illustrates the correspondence.

↓	0	1	2	3	4	5	6	7	...	n	...
		2	4	6	8	10	12	14	..	2n	...

Thus the set of counting numbers has the same numerical magnitude as a proper subset of itself, that is to say the even counting numbers. This is something that could never happen with a set of finite magnitude. Indeed it is this occurrence that leads to a straightforward definition of an infinite set as against a finite one. A set is said to have infinite magnitude if there is a one-to-one correspondence between itself and a proper subset of itself, a proper subset being one that has some members of the parent set not in it. This gives rise to interesting paradoxes.

Galileo, some two hundred years before Cantor, pondered on these paradoxes as to how you could take away even an infinite number of members of a given set, or add to it additional members, and yet not reduce or increase its numerical magnitude. David Hilbert, a leading mathematician of the late nineteenth and early twentieth centuries CE, illustrated this through the story of what came to be known as Hilbert's Hotel.[3] The hotel had an infinite number of rooms, one corresponding to each counting number. One night all the rooms were occupied when another person turned up seeking accommodation. Sorry, said the man on the desk, all the rooms are taken. We cannot fit you in. Fortunately the manager overheard the conversation. Don't be silly, he said to the desk man, just ask each of the present guests to shift to the room numbered one greater than their present one, (that is 1 to 2, 2 to 3, and so on right through all the rooms), and this will leave room numbered 1 for our new guest. But it even got worse for the poor desk man. A little later an infinite bus load of people turned up, one for each counting number, and sought accommodation. This time the desk man sought the help of the manager before turning this huge mob of people away. Not a problem said the manager. Ask each of the present guests to move to the room which has twice the code number of their existing room. Thus the existing guests were shifted to occupy all the even numbered rooms, leaving all the odd numbered rooms to be occupied by the new bus load!

Another surprising outcome to Cantor's basic ideas of the numerical infinite was the realization that there was ever increasing levels of infinite numerical magnitude. To establish this he used the notion of taking a given set and then looking at the set of all subsets of the given set. For instance, if the given set was A ={a,b,} then the set of all subsets of this set could be written down as P(A)= {∅, {a},{b},{a,b}}, where ∅ is the empty subset. We can

3. See http://en.wikipedia.org/wiki/Hilbert's_paradox_of_the_Grand_Hotel, accessed Sept 17, 2012.

see immediately in this case that the size of the set of all subsets is greater than the size of the given set.

But what if we took the given set to be the set of all counting numbers, call it N. Then let P(N) be the set of all subsets of N. It is immediate that P(N) cannot have numerical magnitude less than that of N, as every member of N gives rise to a subset consisting of just that member. But just because P(N) has other subsets of N, subsets of N containing two or more of its elements, does not mean, as we have seen earlier, that P(N) may not have the same numerical magnitude as N. Cantor's brilliant argument can be sketched as follows.

If P(N) has the same numerical magnitude as N then there must be a one-to-one correspondence, let's call it θ, between N and P(N). That is, if n is a member of N then θ(n) is the corresponding subset of N, that is the corresponding member of P(N). But now we can show that there is a member of P(N) that does not correspond to a member of N, contradicting the claim that θ is one-to-one.

To find a member of P(N) that is not connected by θ to a member of N, we take B = {n: n is not a member of θ(n) }. That is B is the subset of N made up of those counting numbers n, such that n is not a member of the subset corresponding to n under θ. Suppose that B corresponds to the counting number m under θ. That is θ (m)=B. Now ask if m belongs to B. If you say yes, it belongs, then it has to have the property defining B which gives that m is not a member of B. But if you say no, then it has the property for inclusion in B. Either way you get a logical contradiction (not a paradox!) and so B is not connected to any counting number m by θ. That is, there is no one-to-one correspondence from N to P(N). And so P(N) is a level of infinity above the infinite magnitude of N, the counting numbers. But this can go on without stopping. For now take the set Q as the set of all subsets of P(N), that is P(P(N)). The same argument will show that the numerical magnitude of Q is another level of infinity beyond that of P(N), and so on.

By a similar argument Cantor was able to show that the infinite magnitude of the set of all real positive numbers is at a higher level to the infinite magnitude of the set of all counting numbers. One of the still open questions of mathematics is whether there is a level of infinite magnitude between that of the counting numbers and that of the positive real numbers. The claim that there isn't an intermediate level is known as the continuum hypothesis.

No doubt some may wonder about the reliability of this argument of Cantor, given its similarity to the style of the classical argument of Bertrand Russell developed at the beginning of last century and which led to the crisis in the set theoretic foundations for mathematics. But I can assure you Cantor's argument as described above is consistent within the accepted axiomatic framework for set theory today.

Thus it is that Cantor has opened up for mathematics a sophisticated theory of infinite numerical magnitudes. Such development has certainly demonstrated the capacity of human thought to deal rationally with many aspects of the infinite and the finite, and their relationship to each other, that are encountered in our intuitive experience of the world in which we find ourselves. It is worth noting, too, that it was as recent as the 1960s that the Jewish German and American mathematician Abraham Robinson published ground-breaking work on non-standard analysis in which infinite and infinitesimal numbers can be used as an alternative approach to the limit processes we discussed earlier, as a basis to developing the mathematical calculus.

All this mathematics is all very well. Mathematics is irrevocably connected to a variety of concepts of infinity and the infinitesimal. The more challenging question still remains to be addressed. Can these ideas of mathematical infinity help us in our thinking and understanding of the nature and person of God? It is this question to which we now turn.

God and Infinity

Epistemological, Not Ontological

It is important to first note that any carryover from mathematical concepts of infinity to theological ones will be of an epistemological character, not ontological. That is, there are possible links between how we might go about thinking about God and ways of thinking about mathematical infinity, but these are not claims that God's being reflects the nature of mathematical infinity.

At least since the times of the classical Greeks and certainly within the history of Christian theology as demonstrated in the works of Augustine, Anselm, and especially, Aquinas there has been a desire to establish rational proofs of God's existence. Such proofs inevitably depend upon an understanding of God's infinite nature or being, together with analysis of sequences of concepts such as cause and effect, or intention and outcome, or such like. Analysis of such sequences leads to claims of ultimate first or last members of such sequences and God's existence as the ultimate first cause or ultimate final purpose or outcome. But awareness of such a numerical sequence as: . . . 1/2n, 1/n . . . ¼, ½, 1, 2, 4, . . . n, 2n . ., where each member of the sequence is got from the previous one by multiplying by 2, and there is not a first or last member to the sequence, leads me to question the rational nature of such proofs. For the present let me say that I do not believe that rational formulation of the nature of God will lead to independent proofs of "his" or "her" existence. As with mathematics, the rational formulation, necessary as it is to our understanding, is dependent on our intuitive engagement with reality. It is not an independent and a priori expression of that reality.

Paradoxes, Not Logical Contradictions

Earlier we looked at the paradoxes of Zeno, possibly developed with a view to demonstrating that the primary unity of reality could not be broken up by rational analysis. But we then saw how a more developed notion of the mathematical infinite gave us ways of working through the apparent contradictions presented by the paradoxes. Paradoxes should not be taken as logical contradictions. They seem to arise in our initial rationalization of some field of intuitive experience giving rise to seeming contradiction in understanding of that experience. But such apparent contradiction then becomes a challenge to clarify and extend that initial awareness so that our understanding becomes more consistently formulated.

A seeming mathematical paradox that has analogies in theological thinking, and indeed with the doctrine of the Trinity, is the possible expression of the infinite within finite boundaries. The following diagram illustrates such a possibility.

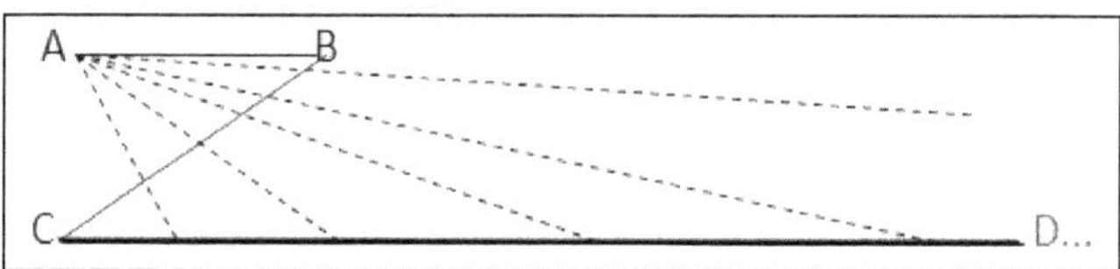

Fig. 3: Analogies with the Trinity: the expression of the infinite within finite boundaries

In this diagram we see illustrated how the infinite magnitude of the horizontal line CD, beginning at C and continuing to the right for ever can be fully expressed within the finite open segment CB (that is all the points on the segment CB, but not including B) through the one-to one correspondence of points established through the collection of dotted lines through the point A. As points on the bounded line CB get closer and closer to the point B, so the lines connecting these points to A get closer and closer to the line through A and B, parallel to CD, and the corresponding points on CD get further and further out to the right without limit. Those with a knowledge of projective geometry would identify the point B with a point at infinity on CD.

Such expressions of the infinite within finite boundaries gives us, I believe, possible analogies in thinking about God and Jesus, the eternal Word become flesh. Paul writes in Colossians: "For in Christ all the fullness of the Deity lives in bodily form" (Col 2:9). Does the relationship of the unbounded horizontal line CD with the bounded open interval CB, expressed through the collection of lines connecting each point of the open interval CB with each point of the unbounded horizontal line CD, parallel the relationship between Father, Son, and Holy Spirit of the doctrine of the Trinity? Perhaps, too, the identification of the point B with the point at infinity on the line CD can be linked to "the Word became flesh"!

In this regard, too, Cantor's identification of different levels of infinity opens up our theological thinking to possible different forms of the expression of the divine. This has consequences for thinking about the nature of the Trinity and perhaps understanding some of the traditional differences in thinking about the person of Jesus, such as represented in the thinking of Athanasius and the thinking of Arius, in the background to the Nicene creed.

Immanence and Transcendence

One of the chief analogies between thinking about mathematical infinity and theological thinking about God is the interdependence between the concepts of finite and infinite in mathematical thinking and the concepts of God's immanence and transcendence.

In the initial intuitive notions of the infinite we think of unlimited time and space, reality without bounds or limitations, that which is beyond our knowledge and awareness. But as human understanding has developed, the realization of the infinite within experienced reality has become a critical factor. This is illustrated in the development of the mathematical calculus, and its ability to make precise concepts of motion and change.

And so it is with our theological thinking. It is the immanence of God, present in all aspects of reality that I believe is the critical factor in ongoing theological thinking, understanding, and experience. Understanding the nature of that immanence and its relationship to God's transcendence is a challenge, but a challenge which has the potential to deepen and extend human understanding and experience. The fact that through science we can develop an understanding of our world without explicit appeal to the concept of God does not deny God's immanence within it. Rather, it is the recognition of such immanence that enables us to find a responsible and enriching pathway of life within it.

A Basic Concept for Thinking about God

There is no doubt that it was the precise notion of a limit that played a major role in the mature development of the mathematical calculus and its major role in the physical sciences. Also it was the development of the idea of numerical magnitude based on the concepts of one-to-one correspondence that enabled Cantor to develop his theories of the mathematical transfinite, and provide a conceptual framework for the understanding of notions of infinite magnitude. Based on such examples one has to ask: Does theology have available to it such basic concepts which could lead to a fuller and clearer understanding of the being and nature of God?

No doubt you will have your own choice of such possible basic concepts. For me I am increasingly drawn to what I shall call the concept of an I–You relationship, or, if you prefer, an I–Thou relationship. The first component of this concept is of course self-identity, or consciousness of self. I am who I am! But the second essential component is of you, another self with whom I can enter into relationship. Such a relationship belongs to you as much as it belongs to me, and is the outcome of you being you and I being me, leading to a shared awareness each of the other. The whole reality of life is based on the diversity and character of such relationships. Right from birth such relationships shape and form every aspect of our living and understanding. Current philosophical thinking would seem to give a lot of attention to the first component, but not to the second.

It is in the context of the reality of human relationships that we become aware of the immanent presence of the transcendent I AM, the Spirit of God, and the actual and potential relationship we have with that personal being, whose identity is both reflected in our own identity, but also other than it. Perhaps we should address God directly, like Moses. "Who are you God?" To which God responds: "I am, that I am!" Perhaps if Moses had been René Descartes, (*Cogito ergo sum*—I think, therefore I am) he might then have replied, "But I am. How can you be me?" The nature of this relationship is crucial to the message of Jesus. In his prayer for his disciples and those who would believe through their message, he prayed: "that all of them may be one, Father, just as you are in me and I am in you. May they also be in us so that the world may believe that you have sent me" (John 17:21).

The amazing claim that God is Love can only be understood in the awareness of the basic reality of personal relationship, both human and divine. Yes, the paradoxes will present themselves, but seeking to deepen our understanding of the nature of personal relationship can provide, I believe, a way to deeper and clearer understanding of God and humanity, and the world of experience we share.

Bibliography

Drozdek, Adam. "Beyond Infinity: Augustine and Cantor." *Laval theologique et philosophique* 51.1 (1995) 127–40.

Wikipedia. *Hilbert's Paradox*. Online: http://en.wikipedia.org/wiki/Hilbert's_paradox_of_the_Grand_Hotel.

8

Scientific Origins of God

JEFFERY L. TALLON

"THE SCIENTIFIC ORIGINS OF God" was title of a session led by Emeritus Professor Lloyd Geering[1] in a Café-Scientifique-style meeting in May 2007 at "Te Papa"—the Museum of New Zealand. The meeting was sponsored by the Royal Society of New Zealand (RSNZ) and GNS Science.[2] Some will question whether theology is a suitable topic for RSNZ sponsored meetings. Science is concerned with data and hypotheses which are testable. So where does one draw the line? I would suggest that theological propositions which are purely ideological probably have no place in a scientific context. But Lloyd Geering's thesis was testable and I propose to challenge it.

His provocative title needs a little explanation. The word "science" is derived from *scientia,* meaning knowledge. Though modern science is empirically based, primitive science was just a *body of knowledge*—a curious mix of observation, folklore, legend, and religion. Having established his definitions Geering then suggested that the biblical[3] idea of a monotheistic universe-creating God, as in Genesis chapter 1, emerged from *primitive Babylonian science* during the Jewish exile in Babylon (587–20 BC) following the sack of

1. Lloyd Geering is Emeritus Professor of Religious Studies at Victoria University in Wellington. While teaching at Knox Theological College in Dunedin in 1967 he faced heresy charges for denying the resurrection of Jesus. The charges were subsequently rejected by the Presbyterian Assembly.

2. *GNS Science* is *Geological and Nuclear Sciences*—a New Zealand Government owned Crown Research Institute.

3. I wish to use the word "biblical," as it refers to the "Old Testament," in an inclusive sense to also mean the Hebrew Scriptures (the *Tanakh*) as well as the first thirty-nine books of the Bible. I use all three terms interchangeably.

Jerusalem and the large-scale deportation of Jews to Babylon. Over the course of many centuries the Judaic, Christian, and Islamic faiths emerged from this common source. Then beginning in the twelfth century AD *modern empirical science* began to emerge from within Christendom. In Geering's view, empirical science has now displaced not only the creation story of Genesis 1 but the Creator as well. There is a slick closure in this proposition. Primitive science spawned the idea of a single creator God which, in its maturity, gave birth to empirical science, which in due course interred both its grandparent and latterly, its parent. He presumes that God is not an external reality but a human construct: "man," we might say, was not created in the image of God, rather God was created in the imagination of "man."

A discussion opener is certainly more effective if provocative. And given the brief time to expound it there was little scope for fleshing out the basic ideas, let alone giving them some clothes. But it seems to me that the very skeleton of this idea is flawed and will never walk, however much flesh or clothing might be added.

Modern empirical science has certainly produced a grand meta-narrative of cosmic, biological, and human origins. It is an astounding saga stretching across 13.8 billion years, back to the first instant of the "big bang." And remarkably, the entire observable universe has contributed to the atoms and electrons of which our bodies are made.[4] Our knowledge of deep space and deep time is increasingly precise. Our modern creation narrative is vastly superior to the biblical creation narrative in terms of explanatory and predictive capacity. But we have to ask first, whether that was ever the purpose of the biblical creation story, and second, whether its eclipse in scientific terms necessarily also implies the demise of the Creator.

In response to Geering's propositions I make three rebuttal points. They are first, the polytheistic milieu of Babylonian science hardly seems a credible birthplace for monotheism; second, Hebrew monotheism is a consistent (and dateable) theme throughout their Scriptures stretching back to the very earliest accounts, long before the Babylonian exile; and third, modern empirical science cannot be claimed to have set aside the notion of a divine Creator.

4. Davies and Koch, "All the Observed Universe Has Contributed to Life."

Babylon and the Exile

Historical Background

The ancient confederation of Israelite tribes established a fledgling monarchy in the eleventh century BC, which flourished under David and Solomon. For a time they extended its borders well beyond Palestine. On Solomon's death in 931 BC dispute between his sons Reheboam and Jereboam led to a division into two kingdoms—Israel in the north and Judah in the south—and, with a few exceptions, the two states steadily declined in power and integrity thereafter. After centuries of debilitating warfare with adjoining nations Samaria, the capital of Israel, was eventually captured in 721 BC by the Assyrian King Sargon II after a three year siege by his father Shalmaneser V.[5] Large numbers of the northern tribes were deported to Assyria.

In the South, by siding variously with Egypt, Assyria or Babylon, Judah managed to hold out a little longer. But by the end of the seventh century BC it was a weak kingdom situated in a crucial trade and military corridor between these great empires—and Babylon was now the dominant power. Jerusalem broke treaty with Babylon and not surprisingly found the full might of empire launched against it by Nebuchadnezzar II. The last independent King of Jerusalem, Jehoiachin, surrendered the city and was deported to Babylon along with many nobles and artisans. This was 15 February (2 Adar) 597 BC and is described in detail both in the Bible[6] and in a cuneiform tablet known as The Babylonian Chronicle. This tablet was first translated in 1956 and it corresponds in precise detail with the biblical record.[7]

Moreover, that is not the end of Jehoiachin. The Bible recounts that

> in the 37th year of the exile of Jehoiachin King of Judah, in the 12th month, on the 25th day of the month, Evil-Merodach (562–60 BC) King of Babylon, in the year that he began to reign, graciously freed Jehoiachin King of Judah from prison; and he spoke kindly to him, and gave him a seat above the seats of the Kings who were with him in Babylon. So Jehoiachin put off his prison garments. And every day of his life he dined regularly at

5. 2 Kgs 17:1–6 Biblical references herein are taken from the New International Version (NIV) unless otherwise specified.

6. 2 Kgs 23:36—24:20; 2 Chr 36:5–10; Jer 52:1–30.

7. The cuneiform text states this was in the seventh year of Nebuchadnezzar while the Bible has it in his eighth year. However, the Babylonians counted the first year as the accession year, then commenced counting. So the two texts concur even in this detail.

> the king's table; and a regular allowance was given him by the king, every day a portion, as long as he lived.[8]

My astronomical calculations show this date to be 23 March 561 BC. The date precisely matches the reign of Evil-Merodach (Babylonian Amel-Marduk). More significantly, two and a half millennia later a cuneiform tablet was found in the ruins of Babylon. It was a rations list from this period. Among the recipients is listed Jehoiachin, King of Judah. This elevates our confidence that the biblical record of this period is reliable history. We pick up this point again later.

According to the biblical record Nebuchadnezzar installed Zedekiah as a vassal king and returned to Babylon. Subsequent civic and religious life in Jerusalem seems to have been chaotic and for a period of eight years the prophet Jeremiah remonstrated with the King, nobles, and priests for their religious waywardness and their ongoing politically suicidal provocation of Babylon. Finally Zedekiah refuses to pay tribute and on 17th December 589[9] BC Jerusalem finds itself under siege again. This time the entire region of Judah and all its fortified towns are targeted for destruction. On 26 July 587 BC the city falls, the temple is destroyed, the entire region is ravaged and the leading citizens as well as general public are deported to Babylon.[10] There they remain through the reigns of Nebuchadnezzar (605–562), Amel-Marduk (biblical Evil-Merodach 562–60 BC), Neriglissar (560–556 BC), and Nabonidus (556–39 BC), who later in his reign was co-regent with Belshazzar (553–39 BC). We may call this period Exile I and it is the period that the book of Daniel describes.

At this point Babylon falls to the Medo-Persian Empire under Cyrus. In his first year of reign in Babylon (536 BC) Cyrus decrees that the Jews may return to Palestine. Many leave, returning to Jerusalem to pick up the remnants of economic, social, and religious life after between fifty and seventy years in exile. The return is described in the book of Ezra. They start to rebuild the Temple. But, for various reasons, many also stay behind and remain in Babylonia through a succession of Persian rulers who may have been monotheistic Zoroastrian, though this is by no means certain as we shall see. We may call this later period Exile II and it spans the Kings Cyrus II (d. 530 BC), Cambyses II (530–523 BC), Darius I (522–486/5 BC), Xerxes

8. Jer 52:31–34 (English Standard Version).

9. The Gregorian dates which I quote here are my own calculations from the biblical lunar/solar dates using the astronomical software "Starry Night"—www.starrynight.com, accessed October 15, 2012.

10. For a detailed history of these, and subsequent, events see Lipschits and Blenkinsopp, *Judah and the Judeans*.

I (probably biblical Ahasuerus in the book of Esther, 486–65 BC), and Artaxerxes I (465–24 BC) of the book of Nehemiah. It is in the reign of this last Persian King that the second wave of returning exiles make their way back to Palestine (444 BC) actively encouraged by the King. They rebuild the city walls and re-establish their religious practices. Because in Babylon this was possibly a period of monotheistic faith, at least amongst the ruling class,[11] we have to consider Exile II as being possibly pertinent to Geering's thesis.

Babylonian Polytheism

The Babylonians, like most ancient peoples, conceived a veritable pantheon of gods. Each possessed a symbol and a number, and boasted a lineage of forebears and offspring. Amongst many more, there were Lahmu, Lahamu, Apsu, Anu, Tiamat, Kingu, Enlil, Nabu, Ea, Enurta, Anshar, Shamash, Kishar, and of course Marduk, the patron god of Babylon (often referred to as Bel), and Ishtar, the goddess of love. The moon god Sin, otherwise known as Nanna or Nannu was the son of Enlil, consorted with Ningal and fathered other gods Ishtar, Shamash and Erish Kigal. The priestess of Sin (Nannu) at the time of the biblical Daniel during the Jewish exile was Bêl-Shalti-Nannar. She resided at Ur the ancient Chaldean city which Abraham left one and a half millennia earlier and which was excavated in 1922 by a British Museum expedition under Sir Leonard Wooley.[12] She was the sister of Belshazzar. He is mentioned in the book of Daniel, in the context of the "writing on the wall," as the last King of Babylon before it fell to Cyrus. This Belshazzar was unknown to the ancient historians Berosus, Ptolemy, and Herodotus and was generally believed to be a fiction until the discovery of the *Nabonidus Chronicle*[13] in 1879. There he is confirmed as the co-regent of Babylon at its fall. His name reflects the common practice of appending the names of gods; and his sister has two. In fact the Mother of Nabonidus is also recorded as being a Priestess of Nannu.[14] These late discoveries, confirming both Belshazzar and his sister, not only illustrate the historical robustness of the biblical record but show the importance of multiple gods in Babylonian life throughout Exile I, the very time discussed by Geering.

11. Boyce, *A History of Zoroastrianism*, 28f.

12. Woolley, "Ur of the Chaldees" 185f.

13. The *Nabonidus Chronicle*, presumed to have come from the ruins of Babylon and acquired in 1879 by the British Museum, is a clay cuneiform tablet covering the period from 556 BC to about 539 BC, commencing with the accession of Nabonidus and describes the conquest of Babylon by Cyrus the Great.

14. See note 12.

Why he should suggest this was the nursery of Hebraic monotheistic faith remains a mystery.

A recently reported discovery illustrates my point further. A small Babylonian cuneiform clay tablet[15] in the British Museum was identified by Michael Jursa as referring to the Nebo-Sarsekim of Jeremiah 39:3 and 39:13. There he is described as Nebuchadnezzar's "chief officer" and he was present at the capture of Jerusalem in 587 BC. The clay tablet is a bill of receipt for payment of 0.75kg of gold to a temple by a Nabu-sharrussu-ukin, who is described as the "chief eunuch." He is presumably one and the same as the biblical Nebo-Sarsekim as his status is identical in both records. Nebo[16] or Nabu was the god of writing and wisdom. He was the son of Marduk and the tutelary deity of Borsippa. Once a year on New Year's day (1 Nisan) he was carried to Babylon so he could "converse" with his father Marduk. The full text of the tablet reads:

> (Regarding) 1.5 minas of gold, the property of Nabu-sharrussu-ukin, the chief eunuch, which he sent via Arad-Banitu the eunuch to [the temple] Esangila: Arad-Banitu has delivered [it] to Esangila. In the presence of Bel-usat, son of Alpaya, the royal bodyguard, [and of] Nadin, son of Marduk-zer-ibni. Month XI, day 18, year 10 [of] Nebuchadnezzar, king of Babylon.

Fig. 1: The "Nebo-Sarsekim tablet"

From astronomical simulations I calculate the day to be 29 January 594 BC,[17] five or six years before the final siege of Jerusalem, and less than three years after the first siege of Jerusalem. It is possible that the gold he offered at the Temple of Marduk was taken from the Temple of Jerusalem in this first siege. My point, however, is that in this short transactional record multiple Babylonian gods are mentioned—Marduk, Bel, Nabu, and Ukin. Like the sister of Balshazzar, Nabu-sharrussu-ukin also is dubbed with a double deity. Esangila (or Esagila) was the huge temple of Marduk in Babylon. Curiously, the Nebo-Sarsekim tablet was found, not in Babylon, but in Sippur where the tutelary deity was Shamash—the sun god. This further example of all-pervasive Babylonian polytheism, again, comes from the very time to which Geering refers. It is

15. A cuneiform tablet found in the ruins of Sippar and acquired by the British Museum in 1920, it was first translated in 2007 by Michael Jursa from the University of Vienna.

16. For other Biblical references to Nebo see Jer 48:1 and Isa 46:1.

17. I find that New Year (1 Nisan) was 23 March 595 BC.

not unreasonable to suppose that Nebo-Sarsekim might have heard Daniel coin, in the King's court, our now everyday expressions "feet of clay" and "writing on the wall"—terms, I would suggest, that might be applied to Geering's thesis that the Jews acquired their monotheism in Babylon.

Babylonian Polytheistic Science

Fig. 2: Cuneiform clay tablet BM 41462 describing Halley's comet and five different Babylonian gods

Still more surprising is Geering's suggestion that it was Babylonian *science* in particular that fostered monotheism. We can of course examine Babylonian science most closely. More than half a million clay cuneiform tablets have been excavated from Mesopotamia covering all aspects of life, administration, transactions, and discourse. A large number cover astronomical observations, and many have been published in the Babylonian Astronomical Diaries.[18] Consider the tablet designated BM41462 covering astronomical observations in 164/3 BC. Lines 15, 16, and 17 on the obverse side read as follows "month VIII, the 18th, Mercury's last appearance in the east in Scorpius. The comet previously seen in the east in the path of Anu in the area of Pleiades & Taurus, to the west . . . passed along in the path of Ea. That month, the 5th, 6th, and 7th sacrifices were made to Bel, Beltija, and Istar." This is quite a famous tablet because the comet referred to is Halley's, and the date is 8 November 164 BC. Modern simulations on my computer confirm the precise description and path. Again, the point here is that the gods Anu and Ea are mentioned and sacrifices to three more gods Bel, Beltija and Istar are recorded (the days being 26, 27, and 28 October 164 BC).

What of the Exile II period where it is supposed that the Achaemenid Persian kings exercising rule over Babylon were Zoroastrian? Even here, entries in the Astronomical diaries commence with the greeting "At the command of Bel and Beltija may it be well."[19] During this period for astronomical/astrological purposes the Persian Gods of Ahura Mazda and

18. Sachs and Hunger, *Astronomical Diaries and Related Texts from Babylonia.*

19. Ibid; see also Beaulieu, "Textes administratifs," 53–87, 79.

Mithra seem to have been incorporated into Marduk and Shamas (the sun god) respectively,[20] while Tiri or Tirya, the Persian god of the planet Mercury was subsumed into the Babylonian god Nabu.[21] Another principal Persian god Anahita was folded into the cult of Aphrodite modelled on the Assyrian Istar and the Babylonian Nannu.[22] The fact is that Babylonian science itself was enduringly polytheistic and to claim that this was the nursery of monotheism is both surprising and contrary to the evidence.

Hebrew Monotheism

Let us now consider Geering's proposition that the monotheistic concept of God as creator of the heavens and earth was a late addition to Jewish belief arising from the Babylonian exile somewhere between 587 and 520 BC, or perhaps later in the period 520 to 444 BC. The suggestion is that prior to this the Jewish God was Yahweh (or Jehovah) who was understood merely as a *local* god peculiar to the Hebrews and their limited geographic surroundings. This, however, is not borne out by the Hebrew Scriptures, as we shall see by considering just a few examples that push further back into antiquity. It is sufficient for our purposes merely to demonstrate conclusively that at any time prior to the exile the Hebrews embraced a monotheistic faith. However, in the interests of completeness, we will consider several such examples.

Jeremiah and the Last Kings of Judah

The books of 2 Kings, 2 Chronicles and Jeremiah report in some detail the closing phases of the southern Hebrew kingdom of Judah. The last three kings Jehoiakim (609–597 BC), Jehoiachin (597 BC), and Zedekiah (597–87 BC) were each confronted by Nebuchadnezzar (605–562 BC) in successive campaigns in Palestine. In view of the detailed correspondence with the available Babylonian records (e.g., the above-noted Babylonian Chronicle, Nebo-Sarsekim tablet, and the Jehoiachin rations tablet) I take it that this particular part of the biblical record is accurate historical data and proceed under that assumption. "In the 10th year of Zedekiah, which was the 18th year of Nebuchadnezzar"[23] (i.e., on both counts 589/588 BC, one year be-

20. Boyce, *A History of Zoroastrianism*, 28f.

21. Gnoli, "La stella Sirio"; Boyce, *A History of Zoroastrianism*, 31f.

22. Gnoli, "Babylonia ii."

23. Jer 32:1.

fore Exile I and fifty years before Exile II), Jeremiah the prophet makes the following statement "Ah, Lord God! It is you who has made the Heavens and the Earth by your great power and by your outstretched arm!"[24] This is an unequivocal monotheistic affirmation of Jehovah as Creator of the Universe, an affirmation that historically preceded both exilic periods.

In the following two chapters of Jeremiah occurs some of the most commanding monotheistic assertions in the entire biblical record. The author repeats the dating—590/589 BC during the final siege of Jerusalem. The passage concludes with the following statement from Jeremiah "Thus says the Lord: If I have not established my covenant with day and night and the fixed laws of the universe, only then will I reject the descendants of Israel and David my servant."[25] This is no local god, the tribal deity of a few self-absorbed Hebrew clans. The prophet speaks on behalf of One who stands astride vast corridors of time and speaks into existence the very laws of the Universe. If some doubt still remains as to whether this is historically faithful, the following chapter (34) repeats the date—589/588 BC during the final siege of Jerusalem. Then follows an episode that confirms the date, albeit indirectly. King Zedekiah had made a proclamation that all Hebrew slaves should be set free.[26] He and the nobles then subsequently renege and Jeremiah in no uncertain terms reproves them for this. According to Mosaic Law every seven years all Hebrew slaves were to be liberated in the so-called Sabbatical Year. The question then arises as to whether the immediately previous year was Sabbatical.

Working from Josephus and other records we can pin down the ancient sequence of Mosaic Sabbatical Years. Here are some examples:

1. The Babylonian Talmud states that the Temple (Herod's) was destroyed in the second half of a Sabbatical year.[27] This therefore extended from Autumn 69 AD to Autumn 70 AD.
2. Josephus states that Herod's army besieged Jerusalem in a Sabbatical Year.[28] This would therefore run from Autumn 37 BC to Autumn 36 BC.
3. 1 Maccabees 6:20 states that in the year 150 (of the Seleucid era) Lysias stormed the citadel in Jerusalem. Later (1 Macc 6:49) we are told that they then evacuated the city because there were no provisions in the

24. Jer 32:17.
25. Jer 33:25–26.
26. Jer 34:8ff.
27. Babylonian Talmud: Mishna Arakin 11b, 12b, see also Shab 33a.
28. Josephus, *Antiquities of the Jews*, XIV 16:2.

storehouses on account of it being the Sabbatical year. We know from the Babylonian Saros Tablet (of eclipses) and from many other sources that the Seleucid Era begins in the Spring of 311 BC. Thus the Sabbatical Year of 150 ran from Autumn 163 BC to the Autumn of 162 BC. Remembering that there was no 0 AD or 0 BC it is easy then to extend the seven-fold series back (or forward) in time and indeed 590/589 BC was a Sabbatical Year in which slaves were to be liberated. The historical context seems to be uniformly robust.

Hezekiah (726–697 BC)

As noted, in 931 BC the nation of Israel had split into a southern kingdom, *Judah*, with *Jerusalem* as its capital and a northern kingdom, *Israel*, with *Samaria* (eventually) as its capital. From 726 to 697 BC Hezekiah was king of Judah and he initiated a number of religious and public reforms. He rebuilt many cities, fortified others and, under threat of Assyrian siege, was responsible for the construction of a remarkable water tunnel into Jerusalem rediscovered only as recently as 1880. In an earlier siege, and under threat of imminent defeat, he and his people were taunted by the Assyrian throng massing at the city walls. Hezekiah, fearful but pious, went into the temple to pray, saying, "O Lord (Jehovah), God of Israel . . . thou art the God, thou alone, of all the kingdoms of the Earth; thou has made Heaven and Earth."

Again, this statement clearly compromises Geering's hypothesis if the date can be confirmed. Now 2 Kings 18–20 tells us that the siege began in Hezekiah's fourteenth year, that is *circa* 712/711 BC, and this was the Ashdod campaign of Sennacherib described in Assyrian records.[29] We can doubly confirm this from some subtle textual points. During the siege Hezekiah is assured by the prophet Isaiah that all will be well: "And this shall be a sign for you: this year you shall eat what grows of itself and in the 2nd year what springs of the same; then in the 3rd year sow, and reap, and plant vineyards and eat their fruit."[30] This is generally interpreted as meaning "the siege will last two years; you won't be able to sow crops this

29. There was another Sennacherib campaign and siege of Jerusalem in 701 BC described in the Taylor prism found in the ruins of Nineveh in 1830 by Colonel R. Taylor, British Consul General at Bagdad. It is possible that 2 Kgs 18–20 *conflates* both campaigns (or alternatively the Taylor prism *confuses* them). The parallel record in 2 Chr 32 shows that there was a significant time span between these two in which Hezekiah closed up springs, bored the water tunnel, built up the city wall and a second outer wall, he raised defensive towers and "made weapons and shields in abundance."

30. 2 Kgs 19:29.

year nor the next but in the following year the siege will be lifted and you will get on with life as before." There are obvious problems with this—how, for instance, would they gather in from the fields during a siege? It seems much more likely to be a reference to the year of Jubilee. Mosaic Sabbatical law decreed that, every seven years, fields should be left fallow and the following year one could reap only what grew of its own accord. Every seventh Sabbatical year (i.e., the forty-ninth year) was to be followed by a Jubilee year in which debts were to be cancelled, slaves released, lands returned to original owners, and fields were to be left fallow for the second year running. The language used is almost identical to the language of the law of Jubilees.[31] So the statement would mean "don't worry, the siege will be lifted and you will get on with your usual religious and pastoral routines, including the upcoming Sabbatical and Jubilee celebrations."

Now tradition has it that Antiochus Epiphanes captured Jerusalem in a Jubilee year. This was 170/169 BC[32] so simple arithmetic shows that 709 BC was a Sabbatical year and 708 BC was a Jubilee year and this is consistent with the siege commencing in 711 BC. We can thus date Hezekiah's statement to *circa* 711 BC, more than one hundred years prior to the exile.

Further support comes from an unexpected angle. At about the same time Hezekiah became gravely ill but the prophet Isaiah informs him that another fifteen years will be added to his life. As a sign that this would be so Isaiah stated that "the sun would go back ten steps on the dial of Ahaz." Now the Hebrew here is very obscure but it suggests a forward and backward movement of the shadow. It may therefore be relevant that on the 14th March 711 BC at 10:32 AM there was a solar eclipse of about 80 percent magnitude—just the type that would cause a small forward and backward movement of the shadow on a dial. This again points to the year of 711 BC. Finally, add the fifteen additional years promised by Isaiah and one obtains 697/6 BC, the very year of Hezekiah's death. The detail throughout suggests an accurate historical record rather than some fiction written two hundred years later in the Babylonian exile period as the minimalists would suggest. And most significantly, in the Hebrew text Sennacherib's father's name, Sargon, has the correct transliteration from the contemporary Assyrian, *SRGN* and not the later Babylonian form *ShRKN*.

31. Lev 25:1–17.

32. Josephus, *Antiquities of the Jews XII*, V3. Antiochus took Jerusalem in the 143rd Seleucid year (170/69 BC).

Earlier Times

Stepping back more than one hundred years earlier we come to Ahab, a king of *Israel* (875–53 BC). He was a contemporary of Elijah and he occupies as many as six chapters of the book of Kings.[33] The date of his last year may be ascertained from the biblical king lists but is precisely confirmed by the monolith *Kurkh stela*, of the Assyrian king Shalmaneser III (858–24 BC), found in Turkey in 1861. It describes Shalmaneser's victory over a coalition of twelve kings at the Battle of Qarqar. *Ahab the Israelite* is mentioned, as is also King Hadad Ezer of Syria who is the biblical BenHadad. This occurred in the summer of 853 BC.

Unravelling the detailed king lists and their chronology in the Hebrew Scriptures is complicated by the fact that the two kingdoms used different methods for describing the duration of a reign, and at times, one reverted to the other method. At length, significant errors could build up. The *Kurkh stela* in combination with the *Black Obelisk* of Shalmaneser III of Assyria, found in 1846 in the ruins of Caleh near Nimrud, together serve to pin down the last year of King Ahab and the first year of Jehu (841 BC) king of Judah. The two dates 841 and 853 BC are consistent with the Hebrew Scriptures and from thence the dates of the entire king list back to King David (*circa* 1010—970 BC) are established. Before that, times become increasingly uncertain. For example there is a possible early date (*circa* 1446 BC) and a late date (*circa* 1250 BC) for the exodus, though we favor the former which can be established on astronomical grounds.

Space will not allow a detailed analysis of the earlier period. Instead I tabulate below a set of examples, working back in time that show the continuity of the idea of a monotheistic creator God. This continuity extends back to the earliest records in the Hebrew Scriptures and is evidently incompatible with the thesis that this is a late exilic idea borrowed from Babylonian science. Dates are presented in the table along with the reference and the textual statement. (Of course these dates refer to the events described and not necessarily the dates of the books themselves which have clearly been subsequently redacted to some extent. However, a persuasive case can be made for contemporary source material.)[34]

33. 1 Kgs 16:29—22:40.

34. See for example Kitchen, *On the Reliability of the Old Testament.*

Reference	Text	Date
2 Kgs 19:15	Hezekiah prayed to the Lord: "O Lord, God of Israel, enthroned between the cherubim, you alone are God over all the kingdoms of the earth. You have made heaven and earth."	710 BC
1 Kgs 18:17–40	The confrontation between Elijah and King Ahab on Mount Carmel, at heart, concerns monotheism: "The Lord, He is God."	874–53 BC
1 Kgs 8:12, 27, 60	Solomon, at the dedication of the Temple: "The Lord has set the sun in the heavens" "But will God really dwell on earth? The heavens, even the highest heaven, cannot contain you. How much less this temple I have built!" "so that all the peoples of the earth may know that the Lord is God and that there is no other."	22 Oct 860 BC
2 Sam 7:22	David: "How great you are, Sovereign Lord! There is none like you, and there is no God but you"—after Nathan the prophet had blessed him.	1004/3 BC
Ps 8:3	David: "When I consider your heavens, the work of your fingers, the moon and the stars, which you have set in place, what is man that you are mindful of him?"	1010–971 BC
1 Sam 2:8	Hannah: "For the foundations of the earth are the Lord's; upon them He has set the world"—her prayer at the birth of Samuel.	c. 1070 BC
Exod 20:11	Moses: "For in six days the Lord made the heavens and the earth, the sea, and all that is in them"—part of the 4th Commandment.	c. 1446/5 BC
Ps 90:2	Moses: "Before the mountains were born or you brought forth the earth and the world, from everlasting to everlasting you are God"—psalm attributed to Moses.	c. 15th BC
Gen 14:22	Abraham: "I have raised my hand to the Lord, God Most High, Creator of heaven and earth, and have taken an oath that I will accept nothing belonging to you"—to the King of Salem.	c. 20th BC
Gen 9:6	"God made man in his own image"—the story of Noah which also implies God is creator of the earth and master of its destiny.	
Gen 5:1	"When God created man, He made him in the likeness of God."	
Gen 2:4	"In the day that the LORD God made the earth and the heavens."	
Gen 1:1	"In the beginning God created the heavens and the earth."	

Thus, contrary to Geering's hypothesis, I conclude that there is a unity of contention throughout the Old Testament—that there is one God who is Creator of all. As shown, a number of these monotheistic assertions can be independently dated as originating long prior to the exile period. There are, of course, minimalists who claim that the entire Hebrew Scriptures were a largely fictional construction from the period of the Babylonian exile. Though space does not permit a comprehensive treatment there is much direct and indirect evidence to indicate that the scriptural records were largely contemporary in their initial composition. As noted, there were editors/redactors who, over the centuries, perhaps merged older documents, inserted comments and to some degree "modernized" place names, for example. But generally names used reflected the contemporary etymological style and structure. So, for example, the transliteration of Sargon, mentioned above, or the many other Egyptian, Philistine, Canaanite, or Phoenician names that crop up in the text in their contemporary form as revealed from archeological studies. When King Solomon forms a treaty with Hiram, King of Tyre, he enlists Phoenician artisans to build his temple. The names in the narrative used for the months of the year are Phoenician[35] (Ziv, Bul, and Ethanim). This is a clue that the passage is authentic for these names appear nowhere else in the Hebrew Scriptures (and are certainly not the Babylonian names later adopted by the Jews). Tellingly also, in many cases there is no attempt to "modernize" the record. Consider for example the very frequent Old Testament use of the phrase "to this day." Clearly Josh 15:63, which states that Judah could not dislodge the Jebusites from Jerusalem "to this day," was written before 2 Sam 5:6 ff which describes David taking Jerusalem and defeating the Jebusites.

The faithful merging of older documents from previous centuries is well illustrated by the Babylonian Astronomical Diaries[36] which record stellar, solar, and planetary events over more than five hundred years. These were first recorded on a day-by-day basis using media of wood or vellum then later transcribed onto more durable cuneiform clay tablets and independently checked off as accurate copies. These records were then subsequently (sometimes hundreds of years later) compiled into different categories—eclipses, saros periods, Venusian occultations, and the like. In the Hebrew Scriptures the occurrence of accurate contemporary data in individual books covering long periods suggests compilation and redaction with just such integrity.

35. 1 Kgs 6–8.

36. See note 18.

Empirical Science and the demise of God?

Geering's final point is that if the notion of a single creator God emerged from primitive Babylonian science then the advent of modern empirical science (with its superior creation narrative) finally destroys that notion. God was once born of science and is now slain by science. But of his three hypotheses this is perhaps the weakest. What is the evidence that modern empiricism eradicates theism? The claim is often made that science provides explanations for origins and so has removed the conceptual need for an Originator. Science, over time, has nudged God out of thunder, aurorae, plague, drought, earthquakes, success in war, and mental illness. God is no longer responsible for "acts of God." But this presumes that the only motive for religious belief is to fill the gaps in our knowledge. This is a very narrow view of religion. In fact, the orthodox faith position is that God sustains all things within the universe: all matter and all physical law—both known and unknown.

So we[37] need to beware of the "God of the gaps" mindset. Nonetheless, modern science has exposed a puzzle of unprecedented proportions. The two scientific revolutions of the past fifty years, cosmology and molecular biology, have revealed just how incredibly unlikely the world about us is. The universe with its physical laws, fundamental constants, and boundary conditions is astoundingly finely balanced—it is "just right" to a degree never previously contemplated. If these conditions were ever so slightly different, atoms, molecules, organics, minerals, planets, solar systems, or galaxies would not exist. Much has been written about this.[38] Similarly, the biological world with its universal macromolecular complexity increasingly challenges explanation as to its origins. Once established in sufficient diversity and complexity, the biosphere can rely on evolution to sustain and develop it. But how these profoundly complex molecules bootstrapped themselves into existence (and so quickly) remains a serious challenge to science. Our existence is contingent upon a cascade of exceedingly low probabilities in the domains of cosmology, physics, and biochemistry.

Put another way, we have discovered just how unlikely it is that we are here by mere chance. We may be, but the odds are slim. The underlying scientific dilemma has provoked international conferences in mainstream mathematics, physics, and biology.[39] I do not state these facts to prove that we *are* created but merely to show that Geering's claim that we are not cre-

37. "We" meaning all—believers, scientists, and atheists alike.

38. See for example Barrow and Tipler, *The Anthropic Cosmological Principle*; or Davies *The Goldilocks Enigma.*

39. See for example Medawar, *Mathematical Challenges to the Neo-Darwinian Interpretation of Evolution.*

ated is by no means proven. To the contrary the wildly improbable universe about us has a distinct appearance of *createdness*. These facts eventually proved persuasive to the one-time, very public atheist Professor Anthony Flew.[40] Moreover, in the context of his friend Bertrand Russell's famous remark that God hasn't produced sufficient evidence of his existence,[41] Flew suggested that Russell "would have regarded these developments as evidence"[40] had he lived to learn of them.

As one who engages both with the world of science and of Christian belief I adopt the following three-fold hypothesis: First, God exists as an external purposive reality, by whose will and creative power the universe was brought into existence as a *coherent* system. Though one asserts this through faith, that faith is underpinned by much objective data. Second, in order to discover how God created one must turn to the methods of empirical science. Third, because the universe is coherent one can *in principle*, with enough experimentation, string together the broad-brush story of origins, back across time and space, to God's last creative act without subsequently invoking supernatural intervention. That is, I believe in the efficacy of the scientific method which is reliant on coherence. This does not push God away beyond the singularity of the Big Bang because, as I claim, He sustains all substance and all physical law by his ongoing, sovereign decree.

Geering presented nothing to controvert such a position. The Creator is not negated by the fact that modern science has elucidated some of the Creator's method. Nor have we diminished in the least his proposed power and transcendence by virtue of the fact that we have understood a little more of his universe. God, if he exists, is Creator of both the known and the yet to be known.

Summary

The proposition that Hebrew monotheism originated in Babylonian science, then later met its demise in modern empirical science is a shaky one indeed. I have suggested, rather, that Babylonian science was enduringly polytheistic, *orthodox* Hebrew faith (despite its vicissitudes) was enduringly monotheistic[42] and theism is perhaps increasingly scientific.

40. Flew and Habermas, *Philosophia Christi*.

41. Russell, *Bertrand Russell Speaks His Mind*, 19–20.

42. However Israel often departed from its orthodoxy and participated in the worship of local idols: Ba'al, Molech, Ashe'rah, and Chemosh.

Postscript: The Theistic Origins of Science

Having, I hope, raised a serious challenge to the hypothesized "scientific origins of God" I would want to reverse the proposition to affirm *the theistic origins of science*—and in so doing close on some common ground with Geering. I do agree that modern empirical science emerged from the Christian theological milieu, and probably uniquely so. There were crucial religious and cultural impediments in the Babylonian, Greek, Chinese, and Arabic worlds that prevented the emergence of anything like modern empirical science.[43] Much has been written on this[44] and I will not repeat the arguments. On the other hand, Christianity with its central theology of creation, posited a rational Creator whose creation was not only good but of such splendor as to bring constant praise and glory to his name. The study of God's creation was a practice of worshipful duty. And if the Creator was rational, so was his creation. If the Creator was not capricious neither was his creation. If the Creator could be sought, discovered and known, then so could his handiwork. Johannes Kepler wrote "The chief aim of all investigations of the external world should be to discover the rational order and harmony which has been imposed on it by God and which he revealed to us in the language of mathematics."[45] Over the doors of the Cavendish Laboratory, Cambridge University[46] are written the words of Psalm 111:2 "The works of the LORD *are* great, studied by all who take pleasure therein."

To close, I want to suggest that our twin instincts for science and religion spring from a common fount. God created this universe as a coherent material system, subject fully and consistently to physical law: "I have established my covenant with day and night and the *fixed laws* of heaven and earth,"[47] declares God through the prophet Jeremiah. We human beings are fully part of that material world. Yet God is not distant, residing aloof in unapproachable Platonic perfection. God is immanent for he continuously

43. By "modern science" I mean a methodological programme that involves both theory and experiment. Theoretical hypotheses are needed to integrate observations and empiricism is needed to test the predictions and prohibitions arising from the theory.

44. See for instance, Stark, *For the Glory of God,* chap 2.

45. Kepler, *New Astronomy*, n.p.

46. This highlights another critical factor in the uniquely Christian rise of empirical science: the international collegiality of the Christian universities established in the eleventh and twelfth centuries. Scientific advancement is not fundamentally predicated on the breakthroughs of a few elite individuals but is a collective movement of peer understanding.

47. Jer 33:25–26.

sustains the substance and laws of the universe about us.[48] Yet he does not intrude. He will not declare his reality by spectacular and supernatural intervention. (The reason for this is almost certainly linked to the gift of free will and lies at the heart of the three temptations of Jesus). Instead, he has endowed this race of humans with the wit to seek for explanations of the world about us and thus ultimately to seek and find him. The spiritual search and the scientific search are thus linked by the same faculties bestowed by our Creator—inquisitiveness, rational intellect, a sense of awe and a craving for synthesis. He is the waiting Guest. He knocks at the door. He speaks in whispers.[49] (The secrets of Nature also wait—knocking, whispering.) Our search for understanding leads us eventually to hear that Divine whisper. Paul, speaking to the philosophers in Athens, sums this up:

> The God who made the world and everything in it, being Lord of heaven and earth . . . made from one blood every nation of men to live on all the face of the earth, having determined allotted periods and boundaries of their habitation. God's purpose for all of humankind is that they should seek after God, to feel their way towards him and find him—though he is not far from any one of us. For in him we live and move and have our being.[50]

Bibliography

Babylonian Talmud, Arakin 11b, 12b, Shab 33a. Online: http://halakhah.com.

Barrow, John and Frank Tipler. *The Anthropic Cosmological Principle.* Oxford: Oxford University Press, 1988.

Beaulieu, Paul-Alain. "Textes administratifs inédits d'époque hellénistique provenant des archives du Bīt Rēš." *Revue d'Assyriologie* 83 (1989) 53–87.

Boyce, M. *A History of Zoroastrianism* II. Leiden: Brill, 1982.

Davies R. E., and R. H. Koch. "All the Observed Universe Has Contributed to Life." *Phil. Translated by Royal Society London* B334 (1991) 391–403.

Davies, Paul W. *The Goldilocks Enigma: Why Is the Universe Just Right for Life?* London: Penguin, 2007.

Flew, A., and G. R. Habermas. "My Pilgrimage from Atheism to Theism." *Philosophia Christi* (Winter 2005). Online: http://www.biola.edu/antonyflew/flew-interview.pdf .

48. Heb 1:3; Col 1:17.

49. "These are but the outer fringe of His power; how faint the *whisper* we hear of Him," Job 26:14 (NIV, reproduced on a plaque near Arthur's Pass National Park, New Zealand. A different version of the same verse is over the entrance to the Christchurch Museum)

50. Acts 17:24–28.

Gnoli, G. "Babylonia ii. Babylonian Influences on Iran." In *Encyclopaedia Iranica*, edited by Ehsan Yarshater. Online: http://www.iranica.com/articles/babylonia-ii.

———. "La stella Sirio e l'influenza dell'astrologia caldea nell'Iran antico." *Studie Materiali di Storia delle Religioni* 34 (1963) 237–45.

Josephus. Flavius. *Antiquities of the Jews*. Translated by William Whiston. London: Nelson and Sons, 1886.

Kepler, Johannes. "New Astronomy, Based upon Causes, or Celestial Physics, Treated by Means of Commentaries on the Motions of the Star Mars, from the Observations of Tycho Brahe, Gent." 1609. Translated by William H. Donahue. Cambridge: Cambridge University Press, 1992.

Kitchen, K. A. *On the Reliability of the Old Testament*. Grand Rapids: Eerdmans, 2003.

Lipschits, Oded, and Joseph Blenkinsopp, editors. *Judah and the Judeans in the Neo-Babylonian Period*. Winona Lake, IN: Eisenbrauns, 2003.

Medawar, Peter, editor. *Mathematical Challenges to the Neo-Darwinian Interpretation of Evolution*. Symposium Monograph No. 5. Philadelphia: Wistar Institute, 1966.

Russell, B. *Bertrand Russell Speaks His Mind*. Edited by Woodrow Wyatt. New York: Bard, 1960.

Sachs, A., and H. Hunger. *Astronomical Diaries and Related Texts from Babylonia Volumes 1–6*. Vienna: Verlag der Österreichischen akademie der Wissenschaften, 1988–1996.

Stark, Rodney. *For the Glory of God*. Princeton: Princeton University Press, 2003.

Woolley, C. Leonard. "Ur of the Chaldees: A Record of Seven Years' of Excavation." London: Faber and Faber, 1935.

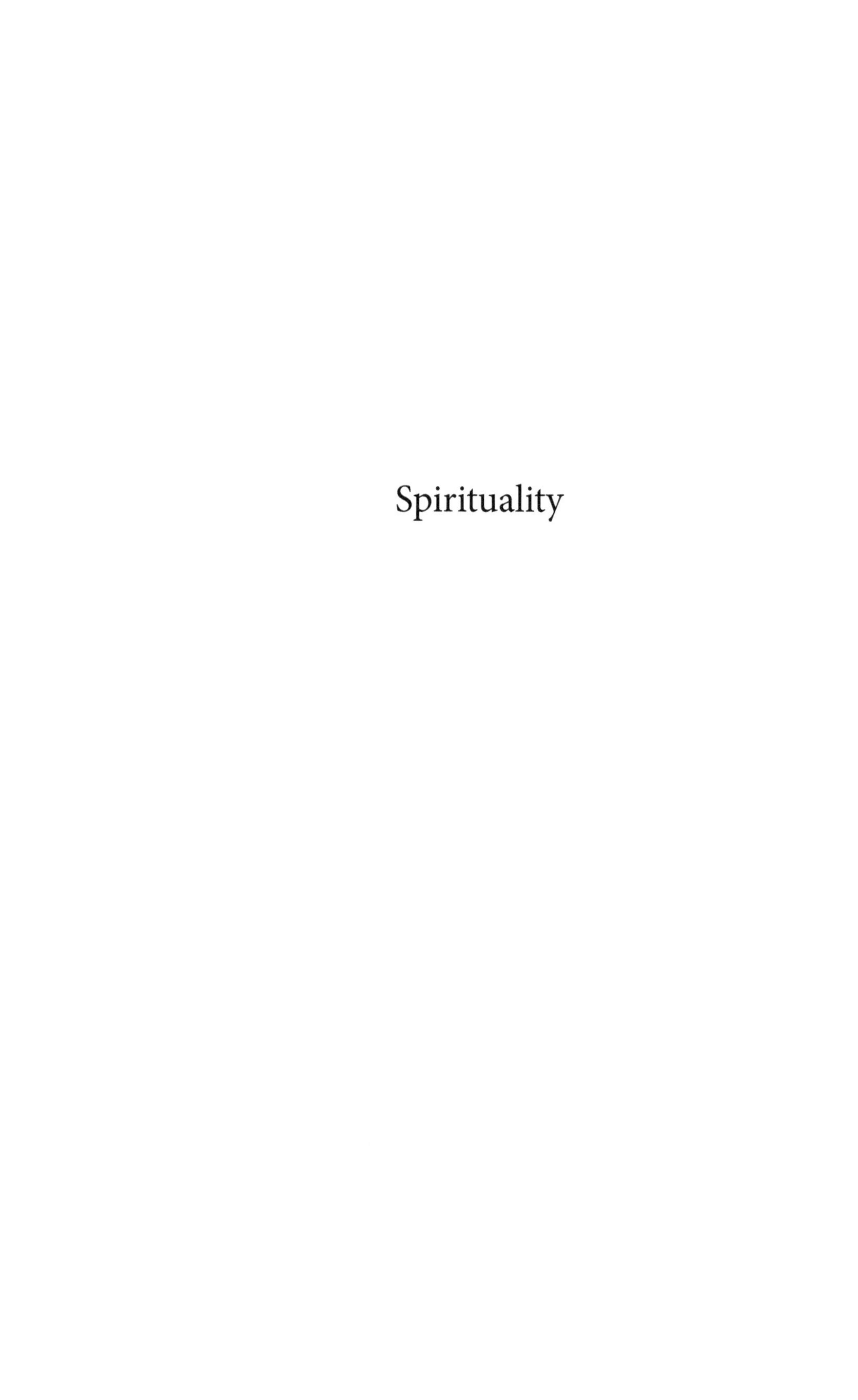

Spirituality

9

Christian Spirituality

Informed by, and Informing Science

Graham O'Brien

Introduction

Within Western civilization, secularization refers to the historic process of social differentiation resulting in the separating of the secular sphere from religious institutions and norms.[1] At an ontological level, secularism as an ideology views humanity as fully autonomous and as the ultimate measure of existence based on experience. With its origins in the seventeenth-century philosophy of René Descartes (1596–1650), secularism understands the natural world as a separate realm of knowledge from the spiritual; the natural world is open for exploration through scientific means where truth is objective scientific facts. Religious insight in contrast is subjective and religion is critiqued as a "primitive, pre-rational worldview."[2] Therefore, science became the greatest form of human rationality ruling the public sphere, so that in today's context Western culture can be considered scientistic,[3] in which culture without science would be unthinkable, even in a postmodern context. Secular belief devoid of any religious understanding is now seen as providing the fundamental view of reality, purpose and morality, a view captured within science by atheistic naturalism whereby

1. Casanova, "Beyond European and American Exceptionalisms," 17.
2. Ibid., 24.
3. Sanders, "Missiology, Epistemology, and Intratraditional Dialogue," 56.

the natural world is all that exists. Combining secularism as an ideology with science produces the dogmatism of *scientism*, where truth is only obtainable through science, in which scientific knowledge provides the "most profound and accurate knowledge" and provides "the paradigm for true knowledge."[4] As a result, science displaces Christianity in providing meaningful explanations of existence within Western culture, and the existence of God is easily rejected.

The notion of "spirituality" however, identifies a paradox in terms of human self-knowledge where humanity is both a product of nature and spirit. As a result, humanity has the unique ability *via* the human spirit to stand outside the creaturely self and the world, in what is termed "self-transcendence."[5] Spirituality is therefore a fundamental property of being human as evidenced by its being one of the "earliest special propensities or dispositions"[6] of modern humans detectable in the archaeological record. Religious awareness and behavior therefore is central to human uniqueness and must be considered a typical human behavior. Although not an exclusively Christian idea, spirituality can be understood in broad terms as "the development of the human capacity for self-transcendence in relation to the Absolute,"[7] or as the "conscious involvement in the project of life integration through self-transcendence toward the ultimate value one perceives."[8] The central question in the spiritual quest is the search for meaning centred on practical lived human experience. Human experience includes the natural world, which for many is an inspiration for praise of the Creator God and leads to a growing understanding of our interconnectedness with nature.[9] Rather than the modern idea of nature being a self-subsistent, self-enclosed system, a spirituality of nature can be embraced by understanding nature as a living entity of power and beauty. Humanity can then approach nature as wondrously given so that we encounter nature as a whole and recognize nature's beauty and integrity.[10]

There is common ground on which to base an interaction between spirituality and the scientific worldview, since both look for the depth-structure of

4. Turner, *Frames of Mind*, 241–42. Also see Haught, *Deeper Than Darwin*, 32, 48. Scientism can also be called "naturalism," "scientific materialism," or "scientific naturalism." See Broom, "Atheistic Science," 97; Haught, "Science and Scientism," 364–65.

5. Niebuhr, *The Nature and Destiny of Man*, 3–4, 14.

6. Van Huyssteen, *Alone in the Universe?* 204, 13.

7. Sheldrake, "What is Spirituality?" 39.

8. Schneiders, "Christian Spirituality," 1.

9. Lesniak, "Contemporary Spirituality," 11–12. The Psalms in particular utilize nature as a source of praise. For example, see Pss 8; 19; 36:5–10; 42:1; 84; 104; 139:13–16.

10. Foltz, "Nature's Other Side," 330–42.

reality including the search for meaning and truth, and both share the belief that the world is "characterised by regularity and intelligibility."[11] As a result, science and spirituality can together search the deeper layers of reality, motivated by the passion for truth and so make sense of the world in which we live. I am suggesting that this interaction is especially important in two areas—*knowledge* and the *sacred*—in which an emergent view of science provides space for spirituality within the public arena. Through a mutual interaction of knowledge and the sacred, religion can gain a deeper sense of wonder for creation through science, and science avoids becoming purposeless and even destructive by taking on "significance and direction from a religious affirmation concerning meaning and value of human existence."[12]

In order to understand how our views about spirituality and science can be mutually beneficial in the areas of knowledge and sacredness, I am going to use the science-religion typology developed by Willem Drees that identifies nine areas of interaction based on three challenges to religion posed by science (New knowledge; New views of knowledge; Appreciation of the world), and three characteristics of religion (Cognitive—attempts to grasp the true, ultimate nature of reality; Experience—religious interpretation of experience; Tradition—by which people live and shape their lives).[13]

The usefulness of this typology is that it broadens the areas of discussion away from the traditional categories of conflict, independence/separation, dialogue/partial integration, and integration[14] that are produced from the interaction of new scientific knowledge and the cognitive aspects of religion, and identifies both the experiential and traditional aspects of religion as significant. Therefore, dialogue with science moves from a discussion purely about knowledge *per se* and includes categories such as "appreciation of the world," "experience," and "tradition," all of which have a close connection with the understanding of spirituality. Within this context, I will focus on the relationship between religion and science identified in:

- The relationship between new views of knowledge from science and the cognitive character of religion: identifying the philosophy of science and opportunities for theology;

11. McGrath, *Nature*, vol. 1, 218. Also see Russell, "Spirituality and Science," 55.

12. John Green as quoted in Conway Morris, *Life's Solution*, 325. Also see Russell, "Spirituality and Science," 56.

13. Drees, *Religion, Science and Naturalism*, 39–49. Drees bases the elements of religion on the work of George Lindbeck.

14. These four categories or variations thereof, are used by a number of writers in science and theology. For a good summary of various positions see Polkinghorne, *Science and Trinity*, 1–32. Also see Barbour, *When Science Meets Religion*.

- Appreciation of the world provided by science and the cognitive character of religion: identifying a new covenant between humans and the universe;
- Appreciation of the world provided by science and religious tradition: a basis for hope.

These three areas avoid the reductionist view of religion/spirituality as purely evolutionary or psychological processes that would affirm a more atheistic position about the existence of God. Rather, the emphasis here is on identifying the places of mutual interaction and integration between Christian spirituality and science.

Although I accept the usefulness of Drees' typology, his overall metaphysics however falls short of truly identifying the spiritual. Drees adopts a form of ontological naturalism that he suggests does not have to be atheistic but can reflect the created integrity of the natural order. The divine is the primal cause, and so he distinguishes his ontological naturalism in terms of integrity provided by and dependent upon a transcendent creator, in contrast to the self-sufficient naturalism of atheism. As a naturalist however, Drees views the natural world as all there is to know, a world without any separable supernatural realm. In this context, religion is a natural evolutionary outcome of bio-cultural evolution and equated with a form of natural wisdom, so that evolution has resulted in a being with imagination and the ability of self-transcendence which ultimately leads to the formulation of notions of the divine.[15]

Although I can accept that humanity's ability to relate to God requires a level of brain function determined by evolution and that human existence is an embodied existence, the naturalist stance rejects any understanding of divine revelation and also rejects the idea of God's role in the process. While the typology of Drees is useful, I would suggest that Drees' view of God is best described as deistic, where God is identified as the transcendent creator but is removed from having an ongoing presence. In contrast, Christian spirituality affirms God's continuing and active role in the natural world, especially through the power of the Holy Spirit, so that our lived experience includes a daily experience with the living God present to us.

15. Drees, *Religion, Science and Naturalism*, 10–12, 18. Drees, "Postmodernism and the Dialogue between Religion and Science," 526, 529, 534, 537–39. CTNS, "Drees, Willem B. 'Evolutionary Naturalism and Religion.'"

Knowledge: Christian Spirituality Informed by Science

A central feature of the typology produced by Drees is an expanded view about human knowledge. Of particular importance is the autonomous view of nature resulting from the scientific revolution of the seventeenth century that produced a "separation of knowledge of the world and knowledge of the spirit."[16] As a consequence, divine revelation became a separate realm of knowledge dependent on the God of truth, and the natural world was opened for exploration through scientific methods.[17] The search for truth also changed from religious insight (subjective) to scientific fact (objective), resulting in the understanding of theology as describing symbolic inward truth rather than "divinely revealed concrete truth."[18] Significantly, this change also resulted in the loss of Christian doctrine as a vital presupposition for science. In particular nature was desacralized[19] and the Christian doctrine of human reason as a God-given gift was relinquished.[20]

Modern scientific knowledge has now taken on the mantle of true knowledge. It espouses a realist position that studies a reality independent of humans and independent of human attempts to find out about reality. As a result, science enlarges and changes our view of the known world, building on previously acquired knowledge and extending knowledge into new domains as well as extending our understanding in pre-existing domains. However, it is important to acknowledge that scientific realism is not unqualified and should be considered as a provisional human construct. Scientific knowledge is limited or incomplete knowledge that cannot give a full picture of reality, and as a result scientific enquiry produces "limit questions"[21] which are beyond science to answer. These limit

16. Schneider, "Setting the Context," 17.

17. Ibid., 33–44.

18. Deane-Drummond, *Biology and Theology Today,* 28–29. Science is now recognized to include the role of the scientist as subject, so that science is also recognized to include subjective truth which some see as evidence of the sacred, the embodied spirit and mind.

19. Turner, *The Roots of Science,* 54, 59–60, 76–83, 159–74. There is also a connection with the Islamic tradition within which the works of Plato and Aristotle were preserved and developed. See Schneider, "Setting the Context," 25–31; Turner, *The Roots of Science*: 112–18. However, Turner identifies an internal opposition within Islam based on the absolute nature of Allah's free will, the lack of a distinction between Creator and creation, and the retaining of a geocentric Platonic system. Therefore, a "modern science" failed to develop. Not all historians however accept this position.

20. Roger Trigg, "A Christian Basis for Science," 15; Trigg, *Rationality & Science,* 232–33.

21. Drees, *Religion, Science and Naturalism,* 17–18, 50. One example of limited knowledge is the understanding of "dark matter and dark energy". See

questions call for philosophical and religious/spiritual reflection so that reality can be seen more broadly.

There also needs to be a distinction made between science as a method of explanation, and the adoption of science within the general movement of the Enlightenment. Failure to understand this distinction, results in the commonly perceived conflict between religion and science. The combining of scientific methodology with the general impulse of Enlightenment thought has led to science becoming, "not only a method of studying the laws of nature or a canon of methodological agreements but a general movement of rationality against dogmatism and religious teaching"[22] resulting in scientism as a philosophical framework for scientific knowledge.

Two areas of critique against scientism can be identified that broaden our understanding of scientific knowledge. First, Roger Trigg focuses on the assumptions of empiricism, the belief that human experience is the only source of knowledge, and logical positivism that leads to the belief that science can verify everything. For Trigg, science is not the only means of studying reality. One can accept reality independent of our conception, but reject the belief that scientific investigation is the sole method for identifying reality. Furthermore, both empiricism and logical positivism fail to acknowledge the requirement for metaphysics, without which, there is no basis for understanding the order observed in nature that forms the basis for science itself, because ultimately reality did not have to be as it is.[23] As a result, complementarity identifies that multiple versions of the truth, including spiritual versions, are necessary to make sense of the world, because as the uncertainty principle in quantum physics suggests, we can never know all aspects of reality because our perspective of the world changes.[24]

Second, two other assumptions within scientism are the principle of "materialism," where matter is the "fundamental reality of the universe," and "reductionism" where all phenomena will eventually be explained by the actions of the material components.[25] Reductionism however occurs

---

Deane-Drummond, *Wonder and Wisdom*, 21–22, 36.

22. Walach and Reich, "Reconnecting Science and Spirituality," 426. Science is defined as "a way to understand the natural makeup of the world by means of rational methods of inquiry" or a "canon of methods for how to best gain experience and derive knowledge about our world from that experience." See pages 425 and 430 respectively.

23. Trigg, *Rationality & Science*: 70, 193–94, 210, 224–27, 235, 239. Trigg, "A Christian Basis for Science," 5–7. In particular, Trigg refers to the contingency of nature and the need for reflection on the conditions that make science possible. Also see McGrath, *A Fine-Tuned Universe.*

24. Lesniak, "Contemporary Spirituality," 11.

25. Barbour, *When Science Meets Religion*: 11.

in two forms, methodological and ontological. Scientific methodology as described by Drees utilizes methodological reductionism where higher levels of complexity are analyzed in terms of lower levels of complexity. This process is a "theologically benign[but] a scientifically fruitful technique."[26] However the danger is that insufficient attention is given to the organization of the constituent parts. Ontological (metaphysical) reductionism in contrast, is a philosophical position in which complex systems are described by their constituent parts and by doing so "everything worth saying about them has been said."[27] One problem with this position is that it assumes the modernist stance of seeing the universe as self-subsistent, and independent of anything outside of itself. Nature then becomes as philosopher Foltz says, "a faceless surface" that reflects human possibilities, "the product of our own hands."[28] Another consequence of ontological reductionism is determinism, whereby human life and actions are an inevitable consequence of biochemical properties.[29] However, as Trigg says, determinism and rationality are incompatible because determinism denies the possibility of a free ranging rationality and therefore the possibility of reason capable of both transcendence and truth.[30]

Emergence: Engaging Christian Spirituality and Scientific Knowledge

The above discussion emphasizes the difference between scientific methodology and philosophy, thereby challenging any scientific ontology that denies the possibility of God's existence. For Christian spirituality to engage with science however, it needs to account for new knowledge generated by science, in which integration provides the best approach especially where the new knowledge provided by science can be included in the truth of religion. Furthermore, a deeper understanding of what "knowledge" means has a significant role in justifying a legitimate place for spiritual perspectives alongside science.

26. Broom, *How Blind is the Watchmaker?* 82–84. Quote taken from Poole, "Nothing But a Pack of Neurons?" 17.

27. Poole, "Nothing But a Pack of Neurons?" 18. Also see Chan, "Homo Geneticus or Imago Dei?" 193–96.

28. Foltz, "Nature's Other Side," 330–33, 39–40.

29. Chia, "Biological Essentialism and the Person," 173–74.

30. Trigg, *Rationality & Science*, 83. As has been suggested, these metaphysical positions go beyond the boundaries of science, since "science is method, not a metaphysics." See Haught, *Deeper Than Darwin*, 112.

Both integration and understanding knowledge are critical in the engagement of spirituality with the new dynamic vision of the universe called *Emergence.* Emergence Theory, differing from the previous scientistic worldview, seeks to integrate cosmology and evolution and proposes that the universe is characterized by inherent unity, diversity and complexity. Philip Clayton, a leading figure in this field, identifies four basic claims of emergence:[31]

1. Reductionism is a false philosophy for science.
2. Empirical reality exists in multiple levels, and that over time new emergent levels emerge.
3. Emergent wholes are more than the sum of their parts and require new types of explanation adequate to the new level.
4. Emergent wholes produce new types of causal interactions.

The emerging universe is characterized by an evolving system of systems in the form of a nested hierarchy where parts exist within wholes, which are themselves parts within more complex wholes. Within an emerging world, new realities or properties come into existence over time by self-organization, resulting in an increase in complexity so that the "system-as-a-whole" influences the behavior of the parts at the higher levels of complexity through "top-down"[32] causality. The universe therefore is an open and unpredictable process because the emerging properties although constituted by their lower level components are not reducible to the sum of their parts. Furthermore, the universe is characterized by "emerging relations,"[33] an interrelation between the components and an interrelation between the entity and the environment. For the scientific disciplines, the view of an emerging universe characterized by increasing complexity alters the way the various disciplines understand knowledge. Paul Davis, a leading philosopher of science, points to the misconception that the laws of physics provide the fundamental level of order, and instead points to the creativity of emerging complexity at the macro-level, and not just simplicity and order at the micro-level.[34] The hierarchy of complexity then leads to a coordinated approach to scientific knowledge at the various levels of complexity, where the concepts and explanations for the higher-level wholes are not reducible to those used for their constituent parts resulting in a

31. Clayton, "The Emergence of Spirit," 293–94.

32. Peacocke, *Evolution, the Disguised Friend of Faith*, 70–71, 77. The converse relationship is bottom-up causality where the constituent parts define the behavior of the whole.

33. Edwards, *Breath of Life*, 131. John Polkinghorne calls this the "web-like character of interconnected integrity." See Polkinghorne, *Science and Trinity*, 74.

34. Davis, "Teleology without Teleology," 105.

non-reductionist epistemology. Rather than scientific knowledge taking precedence over, or replacing religious knowledge, today many scholars propose a "holistic epistemic network"[35] to describe a variety of disciplines studying increasingly complex systems, including the disciplines of science, theology and spirituality. Each epistemic level utilizes an analogous methodology of theory construction and testing, and although the knowledge from the lower levels places epistemic constraints on the upper levels, the upper levels still produce "new and irreducible properties and processes."[36] The effect is an interrelation of knowledge and a recognition of truth *via* the different disciplines, so that science and religion can be seen as mutually interdependent with the central issue being the relationship between the truth of science and the truth of religion. As a result, the new knowledge from science can inform spirituality by providing new visions of nature, and spirituality provides reflection on notions of meaning and the limit questions produced by science.

Emergence and the Human Person

Emergence theory is proving especially fruitful for relating science and a theistic worldview, especially when considering the naturalness of spirituality within human personhood. Biologically, the highest level of emergence is human personhood, where the mind (mental properties) emerges from the most complex biological structure known—the human body-and-brain. Humanity is therefore continuous with evolutionary history, being made of the same matter and energy, while also being discontinuous as a qualitatively different being. In a recent study of human uniqueness, van Huyssteen provides a greater appreciation of the role of spirituality/religious imagination within human evolution through what he calls *transversality*, a non-hierarchical, multi-perspective approach to human knowledge that understands "the voices of science, theology, religions, and art as different but equally legitimate ways of looking at the world."[37] Therefore, theology shares in the standards of interdisciplinary discourse as an equal partner with science as they both converge on commonly identified problems. The central presupposition to this approach is a holistic view that identifies hu-

35. Russell, "Natural Sciences," 330–31.

36. Ibid., 330–31. As Alister McGrath notes however, the relationship between religion and science is made more complex because of the differing relationship between religion and the various branches of science. See McGrath, *Science and Religion*, 28.

37. Van Huyssteen, *Alone in the Universe?* 23, 30–31, 219, 270. Quote taken from page 23. Transversality utilizes the disciplines of theology, evolutionary epistemology, paleoanthropology, neuroscience, and evolutionary psychology. An in-depth discussion of transversality is given on pages 10–42.

mans as embodied persons, whom, as such, are the locus of rationality—in contrast to a rationality based on abstract ideas.

In accepting the physical evolution of *Homo sapiens* as one unique node of biological inevitability,[38] van Huyssteen points to the unique human ability of transcending the biological origins resulting in the uniquely human activities that compose human culture such as art, science, and religion. The result is, as van Huyssteen says, that the "human person has emerged biologically as a centre of self-awareness, religious awareness, and moral responsibility."[39] Therefore, *Homo sapiens* can be considered a new entity, a qualitatively distinct being compared to the rest of creation, an understanding intrinsically linked to the linguistic capacity of humanity. Van Huyssteen argues that it is language that is thought to have led to the unique human imagination through "cognitive fluidity," where the various domains of the human brain freely interacted resulting in imagination and the symbolic revolution seen in cave art from 60,000–30,000 years ago.[40]

Most significantly, in using a multi-disciplinary approach, van Huyssteen has identified the naturalness, meaningfulness, and rationality of religious imagination and religion in human experience, where embodied humanity transcends its biological origin in the search for fulfilment and meaning. Religion therefore is one of the earliest special properties of modern humans detectable in the archaeological record.[41] This position is supported by Clayton, who suggests that the search for meaning is a ubiquitous human activity, and the religious response is intrinsic to human existence in the world.[42]

Emergence, Spirituality, and Theology

In the context of an emergent view of knowledge, the naturalness of religious imagination challenges the viewpoint of scientism that sees religion, religious imagination, and spirituality as an isolated faculty of the human mind that developed later. The unique human characteristics of consciousness, languages, symbolic mind and behavior directly relate to religious awareness and religious behavior. Therefore, it is possible to talk of a predisposition to religious belief as "one of the most complex and powerful forces

38. Conway Morris, *Life's Solution*, 303, 10, 12; Haught, *Deeper Than Darwin*, 155.

39. Van Huyssteen, *Alone in the Universe?* 10, 55–59, 70, 99, 147. Quote is taken from page 147.

40. Ibid., 190–91 and 194–236. "Cognitive fluidity" is a concept originally developed by Steven Mithen and used by van Huyssteen.

41. Ibid., 94, 108, 140, 175–76, 192, 203–5, 225–26, 268, 312.

42. Clayton, "The Emergence of Spirit," 297–98.

in the human mind, one of the universals of human behaviour."[43] Clayton goes even further by suggesting that emergence supports theism, whereby the religious object is more than a bundle of emerging properties. As an "upwardly open" system, the world at its most complex manifests aspects of divine influence, revealing the possibility of a self-revealing divine agent. As a result, "God" is not less of an agent in the world than humans, but is everything that humanity is, yet infinitely more.[44]

As suggested by Drees' typology and the above discussion, new views of knowledge as suggested by emergence also lead to opportunities for theology. Emergence has resulted in a renewed emphasis on the immanence of God as Creator, the living God who is continually active "in, with, and under" the creative natural processes.[45] The theological understanding of human personhood has also been deepened, with personhood now defined in terms of psychosomatic unity including physical, mental, and spiritual capacities.

The Sacred: Christian Spirituality Informing Science

In relating science to spirituality we enter the realm of the sacred, where the interiority of nature as an organic, living spiritual entity is recognized,[46] and where as Drees suggests, science provides a new and greater appreciation of the world that can then be reflected upon theologically. As a result, humanity can gain a deeper understanding of the world without making nature a product of human construction. In this context, the ability of spirituality to inform science through an understanding of the sacredness of creation can be discerned in four ways: wonder, depth, mystery, and hope.

1. Scientific enquiry has increased our sense of wonder at the universe leading to "new and wider concepts of reality."[47] However, as previously suggested, scientific enquiry as a limited form of knowledge produces limit questions at the boundary of knowledge, when nature as a reality transcends our inquiry and allows for other avenues of explanation. Limit questions represent the mystery of the universe which then leads to a sense of wonder and gratitude about reality. It is this mystical sense of awe and wonder in nature that often occurs in childhood and

43. Van Huyssteen, *Alone in the Universe?* 240.

44. Clayton, "The Emergence of Spirit," 302–3.

45. Peacocke, "Articulating God's Presence in and to the World Unveiled by the Sciences," 143–44, 152. See also O'Brien, "The Story of our Creation," 146–64; O'Brien, "Perfecting Not Perfect," 407–19.

46. Foltz, "Nature's Other Side," 334–36.

47. Gilkey, "Nature, Reality, and the Sacred," 295, 298.

provides the inspiration for becoming a scientist, an inspiration that gets lost in the "process of emotional distancing"[48] that reductionism effects. The natural extension of limit questions leads to metaphysics, which includes theological reflection resulting in wonder and gratitude (to God) for creation and our existence. As Deane-Drummond suggests, purely scientific wonder fails to appreciate the religious roots of wonderment which links transcendent and natural wonder.[49]

2. The sacredness of the natural world also relates to the depth of knowledge, including the notion of truth. As Haught suggests, since both religion and science share in the search for truth, an understanding of depth invites both religious and scientific readings of human knowledge.[50] In relation to spirituality, evolution provides a case in point, where the deeper patterns of evolution (emergence, complexity, convergence) identify the world as underpinned by deeper commonalities, which Conway Morris describes as a "genuine creation."[51] Haught goes on to suggest that the universe may then be thought of in-depth as a story filled with "promise," where the promise of life and evolution were present at the beginning of the universe. His resulting metaphysics of promise identifies "a promising God who opens up the world to the future is the ultimate explanation of evolution," so that the fundamental meaning of the evolving universe is found in the carrying of a promise. Evolution therefore is both "adaptation and anticipation," as God awaits the world in this unfinished universe.[52]

    The notion of depth is also reflected in the order exhibited in nature, a central presupposition for the natural sciences and also implying the contingent nature of existence and order that points to a non-contingent ground or cause. Theologically, orderliness is understood to result from God's character (rationality) in the act of creation and as McGrath suggests, it could have been another way.[53] There is, however, a paradox where the order identified with the laws of nature, which operate in analogous ways in the different dimensions of nature, also

48. Fox and Sheldrake, *Natural Grace*, 180–82. Also see Deane-Drummond, *Wonder and Wisdom*, 38–55.

49. Deane-Drummond, *Wonder and Wisdom*, 55. The first two chapters provide a good discussion on wonder in the natural world. Chapter 7 looks at the biblical, philosophical, and spiritual view of wonder.

50. Haught, "Science, Religion, and the Sacred Depths of Nature," 338–39.

51. Conway Morris, *Life's Solution*, 20, 290, 303.

52. Haught, *Deeper Than Darwin*, 53, 63, 128, 142–44.

53. McGrath, *Nature*, 1: 220–33.

includes spontaneity and openness. Therefore as Langdon Gilkey identifies, order plus change/novelty produces order.[54] An understanding of order is also linked to an understanding of value, where the ultimate traits of things provide a deep ground of permanence and value which has always been identified as sacred.

3. The search for depth/truth/knowledge shared by religion and science leads to a view of "nature-as-mystery"[55] in which our understanding of power and order includes traces of the sacred. The sacred aspects of reality (unity, meaning and value) are indicated in the intuitions necessary for science (power, life, order, and unity). The sacred nature of which have been lost in our secularized world so that compared to archaic religions who viewed nature as the "source and ground of our being,"[56] nature has been placed at a level below humanity. For Gilkey, in particular, the view of nature as "power" produces unity at the most fundamental level of being and value. As a stream of both energy and matter, power connects the past and present, and projects itself into an open future. Power functions in a dynamic process, converting itself into energy and then into matter, leading to the forms in our reality including humanity, functioning differently at different levels, resulting in the property of "vitality" at the level of life.[57] As such, matter becomes "more than matter,"[58] an emergent property dependent on the unity of the organism including the notions of meaning, purpose, and the fulfilment of goals. One example is the arrival of sentience in humanity as a being sharing the terrestrial creation, which points to the mysterious as matter transcends its biological properties. For humanity then, power also includes knowledge and therefore the demand for constraint, discipline, and sacrifice in the utilization of power.

4. Finally, as Drees suggests, an appreciation of the world provided by science can relate to the traditional character of religion that provides a basis for hope. Hope is a central feature of Christianity, identified in the resurrection of Jesus Christ, an event with universal and eschatological significance. Christian hope contrasts with the scientific

54. Gilkey, "Nature as the Image of God: Reflections on the Signs of the Sacred," 492–500.

55. Gilkey, "Nature, Reality, and the Sacred," 287, 296. Also see Yerkes, "Toward a New Understanding of Nature, Reality, and the Sacred," 438–39.

56. Gilkey, "Nature, Reality, and the Sacred," 297. Gilkey, "Nature as the Image of God," 490–91.

57. Gilkey, "Nature as the Image of God," 491–94.

58. Gilkey, "Nature, Reality, and the Sacred," 295.

predictions of a cosmological future without hope, where the universe will end either in fire or by freezing which as Peters suggests, highlights the dissonance between theological and cosmological eschatology.[59] Furthermore, as Deane-Drummond identifies, a sense of wonder at the vastness of the universe is just as likely to produce fear as it is comfort and gratitude.[60] Therefore, religious wonder joined with hope is distinguished from natural wonder without hope.

Conclusion

Christian spirituality can both inform and be informed by science providing a wondrous picture of nature's complexity, and by reflecting on limit questions produced by science and the notion of meaning itself. The typology developed by Willem Drees identifies significant areas of interaction within which Christian spirituality and science can engage. Significantly, this typology has allowed a discussion of knowledge in which scientific and spiritual perspectives can both be validated and integrated, in contrast to the view of scientism/atheism where religious knowledge is rejected. In particular, the emergent view of science identifies spirituality as a central feature of what it means to be human, and provides a broader definition of knowledge where both spirituality and science can engage.

A central feature of the interrelationship between Christian spirituality and science is the recovery of the sacred within the created order, a position that provides a balance to the naturalistic ontology of scientism. By emphasizing the sacred dimensions of nature, the notions of wonder, depth, mystery, and hope provide the ground where spirituality and science can engage and enhance each other. As a result of this discussion, I would suggest that religion/spirituality must be included in the public discourse relating to matters of science. This is especially true in the area of ethics, where scientific knowledge and the application of that knowledge lead to limit questions regarding meaning, values, and purpose that require metaphysical reflection.

Bibliography

Barbour, Ian G. *When Science Meets Religion: Enemies, Strangers or Partners?* San Francisco: HarperSanFrancisco, 2000.

59. Peters, *Science, Theology and Ethics*, 6–7.
60. Deane-Drummond, *Wonder and Wisdom*, 31.

Spirituality

Broom, Neil. "Atheistic Science: A Broth of Contradictions." In *Science and Christianity: Festschrift in Honour of Harold Turner and John Morton*, edited by L. R. B. Mann, 87–103. Auckland: University of Auckland Centre for Continuing Education, 2001.

———. *How Blind Is the Watchmaker? Theism or Atheism: Should Science Decide.* Avebury Series in Philosophy. Aldershot, UK: Ashgate, 1998.

Casanova, Jose. "Beyond European and American Exceptionalisms: Towards a Global Perspective." In *Predicting Religion: Christian, Secular and Alternative Futures*, edited by Grace Davie, Paul Heelas, and Linda Woodhead, 17–29. Aldershot, UK: Ashgate, 2002.

Chan, Mark L. Y. "Homo Geneticus or Imago Dei? Beyond Genetic Reductionism." In *Beyond Determinism and Reductionism: Genetic Science and the Person*, edited by Mark L. Y. Chan and Roland Chia, 190–214. Adelaide: ATF, 2003.

Chia, Roland. "Biological Essentialism and the Person." In *Beyond Determinism and Reductionism: Genetic Science and the Person*, edited by Mark L. Y. Chan and Roland Chia, 171–89. Adelaide: ATF, 2003.

Clayton, Philip. "The Emergence of Spirit: From Complexity to Anthropology to Theology." *Theology and Science* 4.3 (2006) 291–307.

Conway Morris, Simon. *Life's Solution: Inevitable Humans in a Lonely Universe.* Cambridge: Cambridge University Press, 2003.

CTNS. "Drees, Willem B. 'Evolutionary Naturalism and Religion.'" Online: http://www.counterbalance.net/ctns-vo/drees1-body.html.

Davis, Paul. "Teleology without Teleology: Purpose through Emergent Complexity." In *In Whom We Live and Move and Have Our Being: Panentheistic Reflections on God's Presence in a Scientific World*, edited by Philip Clayton and Arthur Peacocke, 95–108. Grand Rapids: Eerdmans, 2004.

Deane-Drummond, Celia E. *Biology and Theology Today: Exploring the Boundaries.* London: SCM, 2001.

———. *Wonder and Wisdom: Conversations in Science, Spirituality, and Theology.* Philadelphia: Templeton Foundation, 2006.

Drees, Willem B. "Postmodernism and the Dialogue between Religion and Science." *Zygon* 32.4 (1997) 525–41.

———. *Religion, Science and Naturalism.* Cambridge: Cambridge University Press, 1996.

Edwards, Denis. *Breath of Life: A Theology of the Creator Spirit.* Maryknoll, NY: Orbis, 2004.

Foltz, Bruce V. "Nature's Other Side: The Demise of Nature and the Phenomenology of Givenness." In *Rethinking Nature: Essays in Environmental Philosophy*, edited by Bruce V Foltz and Robert Frodeman, 330–42. Bloomington, IN: Indiana University Press, 2004.

Fox, Matthew, and Rupert Sheldrake. *Natural Grace: Dialogues on Creation, Darkness, and the Soul in Spirituality and Science.* New York: Doubleday, 1996.

Gilkey, Langdon. "Nature as the Image of God: Reflections on the Signs of the Sacred." *Zygon* 29.4 (1994) 489–505.

———. "Nature, Reality, and the Sacred: A Meditation in Science and Religion." *Zygon* 24.3 (1989) 283–98.

Haught, John F. *Deeper Than Darwin: The Prospect for Religion in the Age of Evolution.* Oxford: Westview, 2003.

———. "Science and Scientism: The Importance of a Distinction." *Zygon* 40.2 (2005) 363–68.
———. "Science, Religion, and the Sacred Depths of Nature." *Quaterly Review* 21.4 (2001) 333–48.
Lesniak, Valerie. "Contemporary Spirituality." In *The New Westminster Dictionary of Christian Spirituality*, edited by Philip Sheldrake, 7–12. Louisville: Westminster John Knox, 2005.
McGrath, Alister E. *A Fine-Tuned Universe: The Quest for God in Science and Theology.* Louisville: Westminster John Knox, 2009.
———. *Nature.* 3 vols. *Vol. 1. A Scientific Theology.* Edinburgh: T. & T. Clark, 2001.
———. *Science and Religion: An Introduction.* Oxford: Blackwell, 1998.
Niebuhr, Reinhold. *The Nature and Destiny of Man: Human Nature.* Edited by Robin W. Lovin, Douglas F Ottati, and William Schweiker. 2 vols. Library of Theological Ethics 1. Louisville: Westminster John Knox, 1996.
O'Brien, Graham J. "Perfecting Not Perfect: Christology and Pneumatology within an Imperfect yet Purposeful Creation." *Theology and Science* 7.4 (2009) 407–19.
———. "The Story of Our Creation." *Colloquium* 41.2 (2009) 146–64.
Peacocke, Arthur. "Articulating God's Presence in and to the World Unveiled by the Sciences." In *In Whom We Live and Move and Have Our Being: Panentheistic Reflections on God's Presence in a Scientific World*, edited by Philip Clayton and Arthur Peacocke, 137–54. Grand Rapids: Eerdmans, 2004.
———. *Evolution, the Disguised Friend of Faith.* London: Templeton Foundation, 2004.
Peters, Ted. *Science, Theology and Ethics.* Ashgate Science and Religion Series. Aldershot, UK: Ashgate, 2002.
Polkinghorne, John. *Science and Trinity: The Christian Encounter with Reality.* New Haven: Yale University Press, 2004.
Poole, Michael. "Nothing but a Pack of Neurons?" *Dialogue Australasia* 12 (2004) 15–18.
Russell, Robert John. "Natural Sciences." In *The Blackwell Companion to Christian Spirituality*, edited by Arthur Holder, 325–44. Oxford: Blackwell, 2005.
———. "Spirituality and Science." In *The New Westminster Dictionary of Christian Spirituality*, edited by Philip Sheldrake, 55–61. Louisville: Westminster John Knox, 2005.
Sanders, Andy F. "Missiology, Epistemology, and Intratraditional Dialogue." In *To Stake a Claim: Mission and the Western Crisis of Knowledge*, edited by J. Andrew Kirk and Kevin J. Vanhoozer, 55–77. Maryknoll, NY: Orbis, 1999.
Schneider, Laurel C. "Setting the Context: A Brief History of Science by a Sympathetic Theologian." In *Adam, Eve, and the Genome: The Human Genome Project and Theology*, edited by Susan Brooks Thistlethwaite, 17–51. Minneapolis: Fortress, 2003.
Schneiders, Sandra M. "Christian Spirituality: Definition, Methods and Types." In *The New Westminster Dictionary of Christian Spirituality*, edited by Philip Sheldrake, 1–6. Louisville: Westminster John Knox, 2005.
Sheldrake, Philip. "What Is Spirituality?" In *Exploring Christian Spirituality: An Ecumenical Reader*, edited by Kenneth J Collins, 21–42. Grand Rapids: Baker, 2000.
Trigg, Roger. "A Christian Basis for Science." *Science and Christian Belief* 15.1 (2003) 3–15.

———. *Rationality & Science: Can Science Explain Everything?* Oxford: Blackwell, 1993.

Turner, Harold W. *Frames of Mind: A Public Philosophy for Religion and Cultures.* Auckland: The DeepSight Trust, 2001.

———. *The Roots of Science: An Investigative Journey through the World's Religions.* Auckland: The DeepSight Trust, 1998.

Van Huyssteen, J. Wentzel. *Alone in the Universe? Human Uniqueness in Science and Theology*. Grand Rapids: Eerdmans, 2006.

Walach, Harald, and K. Helmut Reich. "Reconnecting Science and Spirituality: Toward Overcoming a Taboo." *Zygon* 40.2 (2005) 423–41.

Yerkes, James. "Toward a New Understanding of Nature, Reality, and the Sacred: A Syllabus." *Zygon* 33.3 (1998) 431–42.

10

Knowing with Heart and Mind

IRENE ALEXANDER

Our Language Deceives Us

THOSE OF US WHO are native English speakers are at a disadvantage when it comes to talking about knowing God. Any frequent churchgoer will assure you that they know God, when in reality they know *about* God, and can tell you the "facts," the doctrines of their faith. Many other languages have at least two words for knowing—knowing facts, and knowing people. In Swedish, for example, the word for knowing people is closer to the word for sensing or feeling. Implicit in their language is a recognition of relational knowing, whereas those of us in the West who speak English can be deceived into thinking we know someone when really we know some*thing*. We have privileged so-called objective, cognitive knowing and thought this was the better way, the way of the educated.

Three Ways of Knowing

The model I explore in this chapter is a triadic one—weaving together academic knowing, relational knowing, and inner knowing. Each of these ways of knowing has immature forms, undeveloped ways of knowing that are narrow and unexplored. Imagine an inverted pyramid with three faces leading upward from a smaller, narrower beginning to a broad horizontal surface, an open and expansive way of knowing. Each face is one way of knowing: academic knowing is one face, with its rigorous discipline of scientific method, which, when acknowledging its presuppositions and tacit knowledge can lead to a place of commitment and continual development. Relational or connected knowing is another face, with its relational understanding and the development of empathy and awareness of self and other. The third face is inner knowing, comprising increasing self-awareness and intuitive knowing that is part of spiritual and emotional maturity. Inner knowing is the willingness to engage with one's inner experience, what some may call the soul, and the challenges of the unconscious, of projections, and blind spots. While implicit in the other two ways of knowing—especially at the mature levels, this face focuses on the transformation of the self as knower. An exploration of each of these ways of knowing clarifies the differences, and demonstrates how, when she or he interweaves them, the person can stand in a spacious place of wisdom.

While our society may purport to value wisdom, in fact our educational institutions, our places of "higher learning," seldom use the term, focusing rather on knowledge. What do we mean by being wise, as opposed to being knowledgeable? How would we describe spiritual maturity? What are the wisdom ways of knowing? How would we recognize one of the wise ones?

Wisdom

Imagine yourself a theology lecturer, and you hear of a man visiting the city, turning people's ideas about God and the Scriptures upside down. From what you can gather he doesn't have any theological training, and yet the reports about what he says make more sense than anything you have heard in years. You decide to try and meet him in private and sound him out. When you meet him, you find him very compelling, quietly spoken, yet utterly authoritative. He tells you that you need to change your way of knowing, that there is a deeper way of knowing that is essential for any theological or spiritual perception. He says, "Are you a teacher in Israel and yet you do not understand this?" This is the experience of Nicodemus confronted by Jesus.

Our universities have cultivated a particular way of knowing, a knowing that relies on reason and evidence, gathering data, and weighing possibilities. It is a very productive way of knowing, disciplined and thorough. It is everything we think of when we speak of academia. I believe Nicodemus, so challenged by Jesus to reassess his way of being, was well schooled in the academic way of knowing, no doubt he could argue and interpret and deduce and dispute with the best of them. But he was attracted to the deeper knowing that Jesus spoke of—and lived. A knowing that was of the spirit, that followed where the Spirit led, that transformed the knower.

In this chapter I am proposing that we too can become wise ones, transformed by the Spirit in an ongoing relationship, knowing God relationally, with an ability to interweave ways of knowing, yet always with a tentativeness, a knowing of our own limitations and our need of God, and God's greater wisdom. Wisdom then is the wide base on which we stand, when each of the ways of knowing are developed and broadened. Academic knowing is a part of this broad base, but needs maturity and humility in order to be interwoven with other ways of knowing.

Academic Knowing—One Path to Mature Knowing

Wise academic knowing is the result of a maturing process of which only the beginning is at university. The early stages of academic knowing are typified by "right or wrong" dualism, as if all truth can be known absolutely. The process of epistemic development—the learning of ways of academic knowing, is described particularly by William Perry. His scheme of epistemic development was formed from interviews with undergraduate students at Harvard University as they completed each year's study. From the interviews Perry described successive epistemic positions from which the students interpreted their world. Perry's developmental scheme shows the shifts from black and white dualism to a thoughtful and contextual relativism.

The first position, although only described in retrospect by the students, Perry termed Dualism, because of the basic duality perceived as we-right-good versus other-wrong-bad. For students in this position, right answers for everything are believed to exist, and authorities know these answers and are responsible to teach them.

While many adults live their life through believing they (or at least "the experts") know the Truth, university students, especially in the humanities, are not given the luxury for long of believing that they can simply "learn more," to find out what is "Right." They meet a diversity of ideas in fellow students, texts and academic faculty. One of their first challenges is to negotiate the quagmires and quicksand of theories and possibilities and opposing ideas—rather than the solid ground of Truth they may have been expecting. Many an unwary student has lost her faith, or retreated from the scene of battle, not knowing how to find Truth gradually, as an unfolding revelation, an ongoing dialectic.

As these students are challenged with a diversity of ideas from their peers and their instructors, as experts are recognized as not knowing all the answers, uncertainty becomes unavoidable, leading to the next major position. This is termed Multiplicity, expressed as an egocentric personalism, in which, if there is uncertainty, one person's opinion is just as right as anyone else's.

Perry then described a transitional period in which students reassessed their understanding and evaluation of knowledge and authority, learning to examine their own thinking, and recognizing theories as models rather than "truth." Their next stage of development, unless they "retreated" (regressed to Dualism), or "escaped" (avoiding the responsibility inherent in the next stage), was Contextual Relativism, in which the students perceived all knowledge and values as contextual and relativistic.

"Theories become not "truth," but metaphors or "models," approximating the order of observed data or experience . . . even after extensive analysis there will remain areas of great concern in which reasonable people will reasonably disagree. It is in this sense that relativism is inescapable and forms the epistemological context of all further developments."[1]

Most students remained in this position for some time, exploring alternative perspectives and learning to compare the assumptions and processes of different ways of thinking. It is at this stage that the students discovered that they have moved from a "received belief" to a "creative faith." They found within themselves, as it were, the origin of meaning. Some students experience this process as destructive of faith—they may interpret this relativizing of knowledge to mean that no one can know if God exists. Unless they recognize other ways of knowing—the personal and connected—they may lose faith, thinking that if something cannot be "proven," it cannot be "known."

The final stages of Perry's scheme, focused on personal commitment, in which the learners recognized the need to let go of some alternatives, and to narrow their course of action. They began to make choices in terms of academic work, values, career, and relationships as well as their knowledge and understanding. This involved action, reassessment, and establishing priorities in the midst of complexity. The final position in this scheme, Commitment, was one of ongoing, unfolding action in which the knower is both committed (a "faith" position), and tentative, in a continuing dialectical process. This final stage inevitably includes aspects of personal and connected knowing.

In this scheme of epistemic development Perry describes not only a process of maturation, but also an endpoint, an ideal—a recognition of what mature academic development looks like. At the most mature level, as Perry proposes it, are knowers who recognize the limitations of academic

1. Perry, "Cognitive and Ethical Growth," 88.

knowing. Philosophers of epistemology explore the same question, recognizing these limitations and calling us to other ways of knowing. One of these limitations is the conceptualization that knowing is separate from the knower, as if neutral, objective, detached observers can know facts and truth as an "entity" separate from themselves. This way of thinking is more typical of the students at the earlier dualistic levels. It is not that academic knowing is in itself immature, unspiritual, wrong or to be disparaged. Rather, the issue is that it is not sufficient in itself, especially in its less mature forms. We in the West, and in academia, have tried to make it sufficient.

Polanyi and Gadamer

Michael Polanyi and Hans-Georg Gadamer, both philosophers with an interest in epistemology and spirituality, tell us objective, academic knowing is not enough. It is important, but not sufficient. Held to alone, it merely "puffs up" to use St. Paul's phrase (1 Cor 8:1), it inflates us, it does not lead us to life. So how are we to know? What is a spiritual epistemology, a mature epistemic process and position? And how is that a part of wisdom?

It is the thesis of this chapter that what both Polanyi and Gadamer describe is a mature epistemology, or, to use a more interdisciplinary term, a position of mature epistemic development, a position which represents both wisdom and various ways of knowing. While Polanyi himself was a philosopher of science and Gadamer a philosopher with a particular interest in hermeneutics, both men sought to apply their ideas to the human sciences and to religion, and to explore a more general and more personal way of knowing. Polanyi specifically stated "I want to establish an alternative ideal of knowledge, quite generally."[2]

As a psychologist with an interest in development across the lifespan, I find Polanyi's descriptions of "an alternative ideal of knowledge" fitting well with the higher levels of epistemic development described by researchers such as Perry and other feminist researchers (see below), whose focus was psychology and education. Wisdom then, is not objective, disconnected knowing—it is a knowing which is lived out in relationship and life experience. Whereas in previous decades objective detached knowing was thought to be the pinnacle of knowing, Gadamer and Polanyi argued passionately for Relational knowing as a better model.

Gadamer, in his discussion of hermeneutic experience, and the reality that the learning/knowing process is a "conversation," a dialectic process, says: "To reach an understanding in a dialogue is not merely a matter of

2. Polanyi, *Personal Knowledge*, vii.

putting oneself forward and successfully asserting one's own point of view, but being transformed into a communion in which we do not remain what we were."[3] Gadamer is recognizing that mature knowing is not an adversarial stance where the person is separate from the known or the other person (or text), but rather the knower is transformed through the relationship of which knowing is a part.

Polanyi, similarly, sought to disprove the idea of the detachment of the knower, seeking rather to put the knower at the centre of the knowing process. He believed detachment "exercises a destructive influence in biology, psychology and sociology, and falsifies our whole outlook far beyond the domain of science."[4] One of the important characteristics of this alternative ideal was the connection of the knower with the known, and with the community of knowers.

Academic knowing separated knower and known, perceiving this objectification as an aspect of critical inquiry. The method of critical inquiry is an important part of university training involving careful observation, critical reasoning, impersonal objective analysis, and awareness of context. Feminist researchers[5] labeled these analytical, impersonal procedures we aim to teach university students as "separate knowing" because the knower learns to be "separate" from her knowledge. She learns to weigh evidence, recognize opinion as no more than opinion, to logically compare ideas and to recognize what is personal projection and bias—and thus to hold knowledge as separate from herself as an important part of procedural knowing.

Relational Knowing

Mary Belenky and her colleagues described another way of procedural knowing. A knowing which still incorporates analysis, and awareness of personal biases and an objective stance, but which is not separate. "Connected knowing" is so named because it is relational and it retains the connection between the knower and her knowing.[6] This necessary communal and relational context makes relational knowing possible, and acknowledges the place of tradition and authority as part of relational knowing.

Connected knowing, then, is just as complex, just as "procedural," as the rigorous process of separate knowing, but it is based on empathy and a willingness to suspend judgment. There is a story about the recognition of

3. Gadamer, *Truth and Method*, 379.
4. Polanyi, *Personal Knowledge*, vii.
5. Belenky et al. *Women's Ways of Knowing*, 102.
6. Ibid.

connected knowing in a University tutorial. The tutor was teaching students to critique literature and found the all-female class slow in responding to the critical process. He decided to present a very poor critique in order to provoke a response. There was silence until finally one woman asked "What experiences have you had in your life that make you think like this?" She was automatically using a style of connected knowing—trying to put herself in the shoes of the other—to understand what life was like from inside his skin.

Connected knowing involves learning to hear another person from the inside of their world. Not that we learn to put aside our own feelings and reactions. Rather we learn to use our own feelings and reactions to resonate with the other person. We learn to notice our own reactions and responses and to work out—as much as we can—what is "ours" and what "belongs to the other." Using our own reactions we begin to know what life is like for the other, where their pain is and where life is for them. Carl Rogers, the founder of person-centered therapy explains this empathetic way of knowing: "To sense the clients' anger, fear or confusion, as if it were your own fear, anger or confusion but without getting bound up in it, is the condition we are endeavoring to describe."[7] Marcia Magolda also described gender related ways of knowing as interpersonal (collecting others' ideas), and impersonal (including being challenged by others and therefore being forced to think logically).[8] Peter Elbow, in a similar identification of these differences, wrote about the believing game (connected) and the doubting game (separate).[9]

The findings of these researchers alert us to this other way of knowing—not a less mature or less objective way of knowing—but certainly a contrasting one. Connected knowing is not less objective in the sense that it is also rigorous, analytical, self-aware, and conscious of bias. However, it is "less objective" in the sense that it does not make either the knowledge—or the other person—"object." Knowing is connected with the knower, it is an empathetic process, and it is connected with the other person—more like an "I-Thou" relationship than the almost adversarial stance of separate knowing and "the doubting game."

Perry's scheme outlines a framework of development through objective knowing, where Truth and knowledge are conceived of as separate from the knower, objectified and detached. With procedural, objective knowing it is only at the highest levels of development that the knower owns his knowing and is personally committed to it. In contrast Belenky's descriptions are of ways of knowing which are much more personal, clearly subjective in the

7. Rogers, cited in Rowan and Jacobs, *The Therapist's Use of Self*, 12.

8. Magolda, *Knowing and Reasoning in College*, 114.

9. Elbow, *Writing without Teachers*, 147.

earlier stage, but then as procedural connected knowing is learned, more relational and rigorous. While these researchers were identifying these contrasting ways of knowing as gender-related, the main point for this discussion is that both ways of knowing are valid, at the more mature levels both are procedural and thorough, and for the mature knower, both should be used and integrated in the person of the knower.

Walter Wink, a professor of biblical interpretation, added theology and biblical interpretation to the list of disciplines influenced destructively by "the fiction of "detachment,"" as he called it, which has made "vital relatedness to the content of the text impossible. By detaching the text from the stream of my existence, biblical criticism has hurled it into the abyss of an objectified past."[10]

Relational knowing identified by Polanyi, Gadamer, and Wink as essential to maturity, is described in the day-to-day experience of the women interviewed by the feminist researchers. Blythe Clinchy, one of the authors of *Women's Ways of Knowing*, has continued to develop ways of teaching which nurture connected knowing. She notes how important it is that teachers should act as midwives who allow students to explore uncertainty, encouraging an intellectual sympathy, which enables individuals to articulate and develop their "tacit knowledge." Belief predominates over doubt and teachers "promote an environment of mutual trust, in Polanyi's terms a "convivial" setting, engaging in the collaborative construction of knowledge."[11]

A further aspect of connected knowing is comparable with Polanyi's ideas of learning as an apprentice. This is not individualistic, separate, objective knowing but rather a "close personal association with the intimate views and practice" of the master.[12] Barbara Rogoff also explores relational learning as an apprenticeship of guided participation involving intersubjectivity,—personal relationship which includes "cognitive, social, and emotional interchange."[13] She challenges us to "suspend our assumption that the basic unit of analysis is the individual."[14]

When I was Dean at Christian Heritage College in Queensland we intentionally fostered Relational knowing. A recent study demonstrated a statistically significant correlation between the number of semesters enrolled and "empathically-based ways of knowing."[15]

10. Wink, *The Bible in Human Transformation*, 4.

11. Clinchy. "Pursued by Polanyi," 54–67,

12. Polanyi, *Science, Faith and Society*, 43.

13. Rogoff, *Apprenticeship in Thinking*, 9.

14. Ibid., 209.

15. Meteyard and Andersen, "The Relationship between Counselling Training,

Relational Knowing in Day-to-Day Reality

The process of relational learning, until recently sidelined in our university systems, is gaining more and more credence. Researchers are now recognizing the physicality of our learning—the neurobiological processes in relational learning. Recent neurological research is highlighting the relational attachment processes of early childhood as essential for neurological growth.[16] Neurobiology researcher, Daniel Siegel, talks of the "mirror neuron system that enables us to take in the intentions and emotions of others and create those states in ourselves as part of a larger 'resonance circuit.'"[17] Clinicians "now refer to a 'relational unconscious,' whereby one unconscious mind communicates with another unconscious mind."[18] Research is showing the presence of mirror neurons in our brains, which "mirror" the brain activity of the person we are relating to, picking up "intuitively" their thoughts and intentions, and even their unconscious thoughts. In everyday relationships human beings are physically—and emotionally—"reading" the thoughts and intentions of others and thus learning relationally, whether they are aware of this process or not.

Connected knowing emphasizes the relational process that is contextual for all learning. It also accentuates the relationship of individuals to their knowing, that knowing is not simply an absorption of knowledge added to one's memory, but rather a transformation of the knower.

The recognition that our lives are shaped more by very early relational formation, that almost becomes neurological "hard-wiring," has helped us to see that humans are not the rational beings we prefer to believe ourselves to be. In his argument that we are lovers rather than thinkers, that consumerism is a religion driven by an almost visceral imagination, James Smith claims, "That's the kind of animals we are, first and foremost: loving, desiring, affective, liturgical animals who, for the most part, don't inhabit the world as cognitive machines."[19] When we understand that humans need formation and transformation of our deepest selves, rather than cognitive information, our whole perspective on education changes.

Differentiation of Self, Religious Quest and Epistemological Development."

16. Siegel, *The Mindful Brain*, 26.

17. Ibid., 36.

18. Schore, *Affect Regulation and the Repair of the Self*, xvi.

19. Smith, *Desiring the Kingdom*, 34.

A Third Way of Knowing

To this point I have been outlining the pathways of maturity and wisdom within the contexts of relational knowing and of academic separate knowing. Both connected knowing and separate ("objective"/academic) knowing are valid and effective. Both have immature versions, traps for young players—the black and white "one-Truth" of the objective knower, and the idiosyncratic subjectivism, closed to negotiation, of the subjective knower. Both also can progress, and in so doing, become inclusive of other ways of knowing, gradually developing to wisdom and maturity. This mature position overcomes the false dichotomy of these ways of knowing, transcending them and including the best elements of both. The place of wisdom interweaves these ways of knowing with a third way—inner knowing.

Inner knowing is the increasing self-awareness and intuitive knowing that is part of spiritual and emotional maturity. Inner knowing is the willingness to engage with one's inner experience, one's deeper self, and the challenges of the unconscious, of projections, and blind spots. While implicit in the other two ways of knowing—especially at the mature levels, this pyramid face focuses on the transformation of the self as knower. Polanyi speaks of "indwelling," an ability for self-reflection, for commitment and the humility to change, of personal knowledge as intellectual commitment. "Such granting of one's personal allegiance is—like an act of heuristic conjecture—a passionate pouring of oneself into untried forms of existence."[20] This is a transformative process, an irrevocable change in our very being, a submitting of one's self to the metamorphosis of knowing.

C. S. Lewis explains his version of indwelling in a down-to-earth example. In his essay "*Meditation in a Tool Shed*," he recounts:

> I was standing today in the dark toolshed. The light was shining outside and through the crack at the top of the door there came a sunbeam. From where I stood that beam of light, with the specks of dusts floating in it, was the most striking thing in the place. Everything else was almost pitch-black. I was seeing the beam, not seeing things by it. Then I moved, so that the beam fell on my eyes. Instantly, the whole previous picture vanished. I saw no toolshed, and (above all) no beam. Instead I saw, framed in the irregular cranny at the top of the door, green leaves moving on the branches of a tree outside and beyond that, 90 odd million miles away, the sun. Looking along the beam, and looking at the beam are very different experiences. . . . You get one experience of a thing when you look along it and another when

20. Ibid., 209.

> you look at it. . . . The people who look at things have had it all their own way; the people who look along things have simply been brow-beaten. It has even come to be taken for granted that the external account of a thing somehow refutes or "debunks" the account given from inside.[21]

Indwelling is giving an account "from the inside." It is as different from objective knowing as is looking at a sunbeam is to looking along the sunbeam—giving oneself to the light in order to see. "God cannot be observed, any more than truth or beauty can be observed. He exists in the sense that he is to be worshipped and obeyed, but not otherwise; not as a fact—any more than truth, beauty or justice exist as facts. All these, like God, are things which can be apprehended only in serving them."[22]

Inner Knowing and Transformation

Walter Wink, in his criticism of Bible study as a detached academic process invites the reader to the transformative experience of encounter "from the inside." "Increasingly," he says, "scholars are recognizing that we cannot change our scholarship unless we change our lives. . . .My deepest interest in encountering Jesus is not to confirm my own prejudices . . . but to be delivered from a stunted soul, a limited mind and an unjust social order. . . .I listen in order to be transformed."[23] He goes on to describe the process as anything but passive:

> I listen intently to the Book. But I do not acquiesce in it. I rail at it. I make accusations. I censor it for endorsing patriarchalism, violence, anti-Judaism, homophobia, and slavery. It rails back at me, accusing me of greed, presumption, narcissism, cowardice, and an addiction to war. We wrestle. We roll on the ground, neither of us capitulating until it wounds my thigh with "new-ancient" words. And the Holy Spirit is right there the whole time, strengthening us both.[24]

In earlier writing Wink calls us to this transformation: "We must pass through a fiery river of social and self-analysis in order to make possible what Ricoeur calls an 'archaeology of the subject.'"[25]

21. Lewis, *God in the Dock*, 212.
22. Polanyi, *Personal Knowledge*, 279.
23. Wink, *A Personal and Social Transformation through Scripture.*
24. Ibid.
25. Wink, *The Bible in Human Transformation*, 34.

The third face then, of the pyramid of knowing is a knowing of self—a willingness to submit the self to ongoing wrestling, to ongoing transformation. The knower who gives him/herself to the transformative knowing process is indeed a different person from the one who comes in cool objective assessment, or even one who comes in empathic understanding.

Earlier in this chapter I imagined Nicodemus as a man of the Word, rather than, as yet, a man of wisdom, a man who has welcomed the transformation that comes with the Living Spirit of God. At his first appearance in the Gospel of John, Nicodemus was rational, bounded, prescriptive. By John 7 he has shifted enough to defend Jesus—and to therefore receive a rebuke from his colleagues. As I put myself into the story of Nicodemus, as I allowed myself to identify with this teacher of Israel, I too encountered a man who challenged me to another way of knowing. I wept as I imagined myself at the tomb of Jesus. In this story Nicodemus appears with thirty kilograms of spices, myrrh, and aloes. Perfume for death and for lovemaking, expensive perfume. A male equivalent of Mary's broken alabaster box of nard—anointing Jesus' body for burial. We can guess that Nicodemus had taken huge steps towards a place of wisdom. His presence at Jesus' burial was not the act of a dry, rational, and secretive man. It was the offering of a heart broken for his friend, a man whose spirit knew his God, and who lived in deep relational knowing, demonstrated in creative experiential faith. Here is a man who has allowed the transformative process to bring him to a broad way of knowing and being, in relationship with the Divine.

Relationship with God uncovers our self-deceptions, our barriers to living truth. Or as Saint Gregory expressed it, "The soul, illuminated by God's light, the soul which knows God, perceives in itself all that is impure and contrary to God."[26]

Unconscious Truth—Openness and Listening

Wisdom which involves real relationship with God, necessitates an openness to confrontation, to self-knowing, and to transformation. "Truth is tied not so much to the way things are as to the always surprising and challenging encounters with the divine Other. For that reason nobody can create a secure storehouse of truth."[27] Our conception of truth as knowing the facts, and having the right beliefs, has set us up for a relationship with God which obliges us to focus on having the right mindset, rather than living wisely. As Rieger tells us, "What is lacking in much of contemporary

26. Leclercq, *The Love of Learning and the Desire for God*, 42.

27. Rieger, *God and the Excluded*, 184.

theology, whether liberal or conservative, is an understanding of how our lives are often shaped not primarily by the truth claims that we profess but by the doctrines operative in our lives, often at an unconscious level."[28] It is this unconscious knowing, which deeper wisdom addresses, bringing beliefs into consciousness and confronting us with ways of life which are less than what we thought we have known and believed. Rieger names this explicitly, "Truth has to do with an openness and listening, with being shaped by rather than with being in control over the subject matter."[29] Real transformation occurs, and wisdom is lived out, "when the self encounters its unconscious truth."[30]

Wisdom and Love

When wisdom, rather than knowledge, is sought as the highest outcome of learning, we are transformed to become men and women who live out the ethic of love. Despite the modern privileging of rationality, the naming of love as a higher knowing than the intellect alone, has a long tradition in Christian thought. The unknown author of *The Cloud of Unknowing*, dating from the fourteenth century, claimed that our human intellect is too small to comprehend God. This mystic points us to love as the way of deeper understanding. "He whom neither men nor angels can grasp by knowledge can be embraced by love. For the intellect of both men and angels is too small to comprehend God as he is in himself."[31]

This is a way of being which not only knows through wisdom and love, but lives out the ways of knowing which bring healing to ourselves and others. Parker Palmer calls us to the wisdom of lived-out truth, wisdom that seeks consensus with others' reality, in "the patient process of dialogue. . . . Such a way of knowing is more likely to bridge our gaps and divisions than drive us further apart. Such a way of knowing can help heal us and our broken world."[32]

28. Ibid.

29. Ibid., 185–86.

30. Ibid., 183.

31. *The Cloud of Unknowing and the Book of Privy Counseling*, 50.

32. Palmer, *To Know as we are Known*, 68.

Bibliography

Belenky, Mary. F., et al. *Women's Ways of Knowing: The Development of Self, Voice, and Mind*. New York: Basic, 1986.

Clinchy, Blythe. "Pursued by Polanyi." *Tradition & Discovery: The Polanyi Society Periodical* 34 (2007–8) 54–67. Online: http://www.missouriwestern.edu/orgs/polanyi/TAD%20WEB%20ARCHIVE/TAD34-31/TAD34-31-basic-pg.htm

Johnston, William, editor. *The Cloud of Unknowing and the Book of Privy Counseling*. New York: Image, 1973.

Elbow, Peter. *Writing without Teachers*. London: Oxford University Press, 1973.

Gadamer, Hans-Georg. *Truth and Method*. New York: Continuum, 1994.

Leclercq, Jean. *The Love of Learning and the Desire for God: A Study of Monastic Culture*. Translated by Catharine Misrahi. 2nd ed. London: SPCK, 1974.

Lewis, Clive. S. *God in the Dock: Essays on Theology and Ethics*. Grand Rapids: Eerdmans, 1994

Magolda, Marcia B. *Knowing and Reasoning in College: Gender Related Patterns in Students' Intellectual Development*. San Francisco: Jossey Bass, 1992.

Meteyard, John, and Andersen, Kirsty. "The Relationship between Counselling Training, Differentiation of Self, Religious Quest and Epistemological Development." In *Psychotherapy and Counselling Federation Journal* (2012). Online: http://pacja.org.au/?p=1091

Palmer, Parker. *To Know as We are Known: Education as a Spiritual Journey*. San Francisco: HarperSanFrancisco, 1993.

Perry, William G. "Cognitive and Ethical Growth: The Making of Meaning." In *The Modern American College*, edited by A. W. Chickering, 76–116. San Francisco: Jossey Bass, 1981.

Polanyi, Michael. *Personal Knowledge: Towards a Post-critical Philosophy*. Chicago: University of Chicago Press, 1958.

———. *Science, Faith and Society*. Chicago: University of Chicago Press, 1964

Rieger, Joel. *God and the Excluded: Vision and Blindspots in Contemporary Theology*. Minneapolis, MN: Fortress Augsburg, 2000.

Rogoff, Barbara. *Apprenticeship in Thinking: Cognitive Development in Social Context*. New York: Oxford University Press, 1990.

Rowan, John, and Jacobs, Michael. *The Therapist's Use of Self*. Maidenhead, UK: Open University Press, 2002.

Schore, Allan N. *Affect Regulation and the Repair of the Self*. New York: Norton, 2003.

Siegel, Daniel J. *The Mindful Brain: Reflection and Attunement in the Cultivation of Wellbeing*. New York: Norton, 2007.

Wink, Walter. *The Bible in Human Transformation: Toward a New Paradigm for Biblical Study*. Philadelphia: Fortress, 1973.

———. *A Personal and Social Transformation through Scripture*. Online: *http://www.*bibleinterp.com/articles/Wink_Transformation3.htm

The Scriptures

11

Is the God of the Old Testament a Tyrant?[1]

Tim Meadowcroft

Prologue

Is the God of the Old Testament a Tyrant?[2] The claim that the answer to this question is "yes" is routinely made by those who have come to be described as the New Atheists.[3] Their answer carries a certain power, at least in the West, at the start of the twenty-first century, as it answers a question that any thoughtful Christian is troubled by in the light of the biblical story. The purpose of this essay is therefore to investigate the claims of the New Atheists and the (often unexpressed) fears of Christians that they may be right, and to substantiate my short answer to the question posed as to the tyranny or otherwise of God: it depends; maybe; sometimes.

The nature of the question is such that more than the existence or otherwise of God is being rebutted by those who ascribe tyranny to God. It also concerns the character of the God worshipped by Christians and/or the perception of that God: in this case, is that God tyrannical or not, tyranny

1. This essay is based on a paper presented at a University of Otago and Faraday Institute conference on New Atheism in Dunedin in September 2011. I am grateful for the response of participants on that occasion.

2. The title of this paper is that commissioned by the organizers of the above-mentioned conference. For the purposes of the essay, I accept that a "tyrant" is a being with power over others who exhibits capricious behavior primarily motivated by the interests of the tyrannical being.

3. Sometimes known as the four horsemen, the New Atheists are commonly identified as: Richard Dawkins, Christopher Hitchens, Sam Harris, and Daniel Dennett. See http://newatheists.org, cited 3 October 2011.

presumably being a bad thing? This may be illustrated by the final word in the main title of Christopher Hitchens' book, *God Is Not Great*.[4] In that book he is dealing with the possibility not that God is not, but with the possibility that God is not as perceived or projected.

I can illustrate further by reference to the 2008 British Humanist Association slogan for use on the sides of buses: "There's probably no God. Now stop worrying and enjoy your life."[5] The bus campaign had its genesis in the mind of comedy writer Ariane Sherine, quickly gathered momentum and was launched amidst much publicity in October 2008. A Guardian interview with Sherine and Richard Dawkins makes clear what has motivated the campaign.[6] Sherine, at least, is apparently responding to the type of God that is being conveyed by theists (at least to her): one who consigns people to hell and generally speaking is rather scary and exclusive and, perhaps worst of all, out of date (in 2008!). Christopher Hitchens describes this God of what he calls "the cobbled-together ancient Jewish books" as "an ill-tempered and implacable and bloody and provincial god, who was probably more frightening when he was in a good mood (the classic attribute of a dictator)."[7]

Implicit in both Hitchens' and Sherine's response to the Christian portrayal of God is the concern, not so much with what God is like as with the *portrayal* of what God is like, hence the question: Is the God *of the Old Testament* a tyrant? The question is therefore as much hermeneutical as theological: how may the character of the God whom we are discussing be known? To expand on this a little, Christians believe that the nature of God is revealed in Jesus, and Jesus is known through the witness of Scripture. Hence it is by means of the Bible that we develop an idea of what God is like. But the Bible speaks in a number of voices and in every age and place some or other of those voices do not appear to be particularly attractive. In the twenty-first-century post-Christendom West, the sorts of voices that we do not like are those of violence, exclusive nationalism, the promotion of warrior values, and/or what we see as excessive authoritarianism, retribution, and revenge.[8]

Accordingly, I will attempt to respond in theological and hermeneutical terms to the question of whether or not the God of the Old Testament is a tyrant. This will provide one sharp focus on the possibilities of response

4. Hitchens, *God Is Not Great*.

5. http://www.atheistbus.org.uk/highres2.jpg, cited 6 May 2010.

6. http://www.youtube.com/watch?v=b1KUOksyYcA, cited 6 May 2010.

7. Hitchens, *God Is Not Great*, 175.

8. In another place and time there might be other problems, and other times and places may be more relaxed about the particular voices that trouble us.

to the question posed in the title of this essay. And my approach to this particular question is suggestive of possibility rather than exhaustive.

A Caveat

As a caveat, my response is not going to be tidy because I am attempting to answer a difficult question that I certainly have not solved to my own satisfaction, and in the face of which some humility is in order. To illustrate, I recall sitting in a coffee shop in West Jerusalem with a veteran peace activist whom I deeply admire. When I said I was an Old Testament teacher his eyes lit up at the prospect of an unloseable argument, and he commented that the first six books of the Bible are basically a chronicle of genocide in the name of God. My response that the reading agenda for those books is set by the universalist opening chapters of Genesis was easily countered by his observation that those chapters form a small part of the whole.

Old Testament and Scripture

To deal first with the hermeneutical question: is the God *of the Old Testament* a tyrant? The first point to make is that there can be no proper distinction between the Old Testament and the New in the matter of "the God of . . ." Of course the testaments are different in a range of ways, but my argument is that there is no satisfactory way of distinguishing the theological vision of the two bodies of literature. I mention four attempts at a distinction. First, according to Irenaeus, Marcion distinguished between a "good" God and a "judicial" God, the former in the New Testament and the latter in the Old.[9] Yet it is easy to demonstrate that the boundaries are not coterminous. The New Testament speaks of judgment (e.g., Matt 25:31–46) and the Old Testament is replete with reference to the love and goodness of God (e.g., Hos 11:14). And what shall we say of the violence of Revelation 20?

Secondly, a similar distinction is made by those who speak of the Old Testament as the testament of law and the New Testament as the testament of grace. Yet there is a strong ethical strand in the New Testament (e.g., Jas 1:22–27),[10] and there are aspects of the vision of the Old Testament that are grace-filled.[11] For instance the prophetic emphasis on ethical congruence

9. Irenaeus (died 202), III.40.2, cited in Stevenson, *A New Eusebius*, 99.

10. As illustrated by Hays, *The Moral Vision of the New Testament*.

11. As Hitchens, *God Is Not Great*, 175, points out, "This distinction [between the Old and New Testaments] is more apparent than real, since it is only in the reported observations of Jesus that we find any mention of hell and eternal punishment."

with cultic observance pushes in that direction (e.g., Isa 1:13–17), and the very giving of the law is itself an act of divine grace or condescension in entering into covenant with humankind.[12]

Thirdly, there has been a distinction made since the time of Origen (c. 184–253) between ceremonial and moral law in the Old Testament.[13] Yet this distinction is not as tidy as it looks on the surface. It may be obvious enough to a Western Christian that cormorants and insects with unjointed legs may now be eaten (Lev 11:13–20), but there are other aspects of the purity laws that may still speak into cultures that work with purity/impurity and sacred/profane boundaries (such as the indigenous Maori culture in Aotearoa/New Zealand, my own country).[14]

This is one aspect of a fourth and more generally applied notion that the story of the Bible progressively unfolds a revelation of God such that some parts of the earlier revelation have to be left behind. This is a convenient notion, and even helpful as a broad generalization, but very hard to apply. When it comes to the point, there is a fuzzy boundary between what should be retained and what should be abandoned. A mention from my own tradition of what I think are three key evangelical heresies of the twentieth century shows the danger, as each builds on a distorted notion of how the New Testament has overtaken the Old. They are: the promotion of an individual faith as opposed to a personal faith; the wedge driven between concepts of justice and righteousness such that false distinctions are made between personal morality and matters of the public good, with the implication that God is more interested in the former; and a reduced commitment to the stewardship or guardianship of creation in favor of a focus on an other-worldly redemption-based spirituality. The sustenance of these distorted perspectives, while not arguable from a careful reading of the New Testament, is considerably aided by the leaving behind of the Old Testament.

All of this adds up to a negative argument, which essentially says that because a clear distinction between the Old and New Testaments cannot be sustained, they should be taken as cohesive. More positively we might note the determination of the Matthean Jesus that no aspect of the law is abandoned; rather, its essence is glimpsed and eventually achieved by means of the person of Jesus (Matt 5:17–48).[15] Therefore, if I am to respond to the accusation that the God of the Old Testament is a tyrant, I cannot just use

12. Wright, *Living as the People of God*, 21–24.

13. Wright, "The Ethical Authority of the Old Testament," 102–3.

14. See for example Shirres, *Te Tangata*; and Barlow, *Tikanga Whakaaro*.

15. For further on the so-called Antitheses in the Sermon on the Mount see Meadowcroft, *The Message of the Word of God*, 175–86.

Jesus as a trump card to let God off the hook. I must respond in terms of the possibility that the God revealed in the Christian Scriptures is a tyrant. And I now do so with three types of argument: sociological/political, literary, and christological/theological. The first two constitute what I am suggesting is a hermeneutical response to the question: is the God of Scripture a tyrant?

Sociological/Political Response

For the sociological/political, I am helped by Walter Brueggemann. In a short monograph on the book of Joshua, he confronts the genocidal/retributive activity of God with respect to the Canaanite occupants of Palestine prior to the arrival of the exodus people and also with respect to the exodus people themselves.[16] His treatment is not entirely satisfactory.[17] But he brings a timely reminder that the context in which these texts have been produced must be taken into account. The texts speak of a time when the people of Israel—although they were barely even that—were struggling for a tiny foothold in a land whose current inhabitants possessed a superior technology and a strong determination that there should be no home for a homeless people west of the River Jordan. Brueggemann notes, for example, the iron chariots of the Philistine people (Josh 11:4). And they speak probably from a time much later than that being recounted, when the notion of Israel has been considerably reduced by the experience of exile brought about by the people's encounter with the later "iron chariots" of Babylon.

Reading of the period of Joshua and the settlement of Palestine has become distorted, though, under the twin influence of the Christendom paradigm and the status eventually, albeit briefly, achieved by the Kingdom of Israel under Solomon. As a result contemporary readers tend to read the Solomonic period back into the settlement period as if it were the norm for "Israel." It was an era marked by increasing privilege for the few and indebtedness for the many within Israelite society. We know this both from some of the material evidence and from the messages of the writing prophets. Putting these together, we who read from within the Western "empire" or hegemony have tended to transfer that picture of Israelite society back onto our reading of Joshua and Judges and hence have read the people entering the promised land as the aggressors. We have read the stories of the conquest and the judges as if the tribes of Israel were the ones with the power, that is, the ones with the iron chariots.

16. Brueggemann, *Divine Presence amid Violence*.

17. See Meadowcroft, review of W. Brueggemann, *Divine Presence amid Violence*, 102–3. Note also the hesitations from Wolterstorff, "Reading Joshua."

But there is another paradigm that is hinted at by the text itself, namely, that their story of God's activity was from the perspective of the oppressed. In that light, the activity of God becomes less that of an avenger and more that of a warrior on behalf of an oppressed people. From that viewpoint, Brueggemann finds that the divine commands to violence received by Joshua are a response to human domination which threatens the survival of the people who depend on God for their wellbeing. In the light of that perspective he poses the question again: "Would the God of the Bible mandate such violence?" And his answer is "yes, in the interest of Israel's survival as a holy people."[18] The methodological point is that the question of the violence of God needs to be posed in context. In this context, as an expression of the God who "is passionately against domination and is passionately for an egalitarian community," the answer to the question posed by Brueggemann is "yes, in certain circumstances the God of the Bible does mandate violence."[19] However, this is not the same thing as saying that God is a tyrant, since tyrannical behavior is inherently self-interested.

I do not claim that this solves the problem. Indeed, Brueggemann himself laments: "It is maddening that at the crucial places, the text mumbles about how the power of Yahweh could work against such hardware and such technique."[20] But at least the problem of the apparent tyranny of God has been somewhat ameliorated.

Literary Response

In any case, Brueggemann has led us towards a literary perspective on such material that is further developed by John Goldingay in a variety of places but which I am accessing by way of his comments in the third volume of his Old Testament theology, *Israel's Life*.[21] At this point I move on from the conquest as a potential vehicle for God's tyranny to the ongoing life of Israel as a special people on a special piece of land. In the context of reading the book of Deuteronomy, Goldingay first makes the basic interpretational point that historical accounts in Scripture should not necessarily be taken as models of action to be undertaken by later readers.[22] It therefore does not follow that the command to conquer the Canaanites is a prescription

18. Brueggemann, *Divine Presence amid Violence*, 39.
19. Ibid., 39.
20. Ibid., 65.
21. Goldingay, *Israel's Life*.
22. Goldingay, *Israel's Life*, 580–82.

for later generations of believers.[23] The most that can be said is that this was something that happened once long ago under the sovereignty of God. The first readers/hearers, on whom I comment below, probably read or heard some centuries after the events of record, and were no more likely than we are today to suspend the moral requirements of a just and merciful God in order to justify the activities called for in the conquest.

How can I justify that statement? First, both Deuteronomy and the book of Joshua mentioned above are located in what is generally acknowledged to be a block of material known as the Deuteronomist history that runs from Deuteronomy to the end of 2 Kings.[24] The provenance of that material must therefore be after the collapse into exile recorded at the end of 2 Kings 25. This was some three hundred or more years after the time of the events being recorded: perhaps as far away from the first readers as Shakespeare's MacBeth is from us, or indeed as Shakespeare himself was from the Scottish king in question. Indeed the words of the prophets, uttered probably in the same era as that in which Deuteronomy was formed and in whom a universalist vision keeps breaking through (e.g., Amos 6:2; Jonah 4:11) make it impossible to replicate the possession/dispossession of land and peoples as integral to a covenant inheritance.[25]

Accordingly, Goldingay would say, Deuteronomy should be read for what it is, a story about an inheritance from God, enshrined in and remembered and re-implemented by means of the text. The inheritance of land had to be appropriated, but this was only possible because it was ultimately a gift from God. And it was an inheritance that only remained in place at the pleasure of God and conditional on the faithfulness of the people.[26] That is why there was an exile.[27] Integral to that inheritance was the covenant

23. Or indeed for manifestations of nation states called "Israel." Tangential to our current concerns, a reading that draws parallels between the conquest of the Canaanites and the rights of the state of Israel today—whether the reading be pro or anti the state of Israel—makes a false assumption that modern Israel is equivalent to the people formed by God around the covenant in those far off days on the Sinai Peninsula. Furthermore, it is patently not the case that the modern state of Israel equates to the Jewish people *per se*. Therefore great care should be taken in reading: for those who want to justify current Israeli conquest or colonization, not to assume that support can be drawn from the book of Deuteronomy for the contemporary dispossession of land and housing; and for those who are reacting against this, not to reject Deuteronomy on the equally mistaken assumption that it somehow supports injustice against disenfranchised peoples. For further see Awad, *Palestinian Memories*, 51–59.

24. Marshall et. al. *New Bible Dictionary*, 650.

25. Isa 56:18, for example.

26. Goldingay, *Israel's Life*, 580–82.

27. 1 Kgs 9:69; 2 Kgs 24:20; Ezek 36:18–19; Jer 22:89.

made between God and God's people, and the ongoing remembrance of that covenant. In literary terms, therefore, to attribute tyranny to the God of Scripture is problematic on two counts. First, on the assumption that the texts in question bear some relationship to the way things are, it is a reductionist reading of a much more complex portrait of God. Secondly, it fails on the level of appreciation of the nature of the texts in question and of their relationship to one another.[28]

Theological Response

This brings us to the third and final part of my response to my self-imposed question. This is the theological response, and it pushes me towards the question: what is God like? So far we have been thinking hermeneutically about how God is conveyed. Underlying that, though, has been an assumption that, if we could get the hermeneutics right, we might uncover a God of whom we would approve. That is a huge assumption or hope. But first, a methodological comment is in order. What I am about to suggest is posited on a key assumption, namely, that somehow the nature of the text and the purpose of the text is such that we come to know more of God than the individual parts of Scripture themselves know or at least express of God. This raises the possibility that any given piece of Scripture calls for a theological critique.[29] It also raises the possibility that, insofar as it is a human construct, Scripture on its own is not able fully to comprehend God. This means that our reading is always, and appropriately, influenced by our perceptions of what God is like. The reading of Scripture may thus necessarily be described as theological.[30]

Reading theologically, what sort of God forms the framework to our reading of the parts in which God seems to be behaving tyrannically? There are a variety of potential approaches to this, each of which has something to offer. I will speak of three of them and then suggest that a conversation takes place between the three.[31]

28. Relevant but beyond the scope of this article is the historicity of the conquest as painted in Joshua. See Anderson, "What about the Canaanites?" 269–71.

29. For further on this line of thought, see Meadowcroft, "In Whose Interests Do We Read?" 161–70.

30. What that exactly may mean is beyond the scope of this paper. Broadly speaking, by "theological reading" I mean a reading which is undertaken under the assumption that God speaks in the text of Scripture.

31. For a more detailed account of this conversation see Meadowcroft, "Introduction: An Interpretive Conversation," in *Ears that Hear*.

Christological

First, one approach to the reading of Scripture theologically is to do so in the light of Christ, in whom is expressed all the fullness of God and to whom Scriptures bear witness. One form of this approach has been articulated by Murray Rae in his monograph on *History and Hermeneutics* and I am taking my lead from him.[32] He writes:

> This is the point of the incarnational narrative. In the incarnate life of Jesus Christ, the Word of God and second person of the Trinity graces our history with his own presence, thus confirming its goodness, and showing it to be the medium through which God's loving purpose is worked out. In Jesus Christ, God's relation to the world takes the form of his becoming a subject within it.[33]

Rae then goes on to make the point that it is "through Holy Week and Easter most especially that God's love for his creation is made apparent."[34] On this reasoning the culmination of the revelation of Godself to humanity is in the incarnation of God in Christ and in his death and resurrection. All else is understood in the light of that person and those events, for it is in them fully and finally that we see what God is like. All aspects of God's story are then read against an assumption of God's fundamental goodness and loving relatedness to God's creation, as demonstrated in the life and work of Jesus. Therefore it is in the light of that goodness and love that we are able to read theologically.

There is more than one way to go about this. One approach is to say with Rae and others that the task of Scripture, from beginning to end, is to bear witness to Christ. The tyranny of God is then read christologically, and usually through the lens of the New Testament. Another approach is to say that Scripture is read in the light of Christ, which is not quite the same thing as Scripture bearing witness to Christ. This potentially involves a theological critique of aspects of Scripture as part of the evolving story of God with respect to humanity and the cosmos. In that respect there are aspects of that story that need to be read as culturally conditioned and/or limited in perspective and so needing to be re-appreciated in some way.[35] And, as we have seen in our hermeneutical comments above, this

32. Rae, *History and Hermeneutics.*

33. Ibid., 59.

34. Ibid., 59.

35. I suggest that to read the Scriptures christologically, in the manner just described, is potentially to express one or more of three things: that the word of God in

re-reading in the light of Christ includes the genocidal aspects of the early life of the people of Israel.

Tradition Or "Rule of Faith"

Even as we do so, in practical terms there is a danger that a christological reading becomes subject to the human tendency to read a "canon within a canon." It is at this point that the notion of a "rule of faith" becomes useful. Although this phrase has a technical usage, I am taking it as broadly expressive of the idea that we read in the context of the church and may usefully and legitimately be guided by how the community of faith has read and interpreted, through the centuries and in the present. This is where the concept of tradition becomes useful. There are various ways of describing tradition, understanding its function and relating it to Scripture itself. James McClendon focuses on particular creeds and statements that have punctuated the life of the church and taken on an ongoing significance.[36] He describes them as "cairns, trail-marks that indicate where the people of God have been on their journey through time. In this sense," he continues, "they tell us how Scripture has been (then and there) read, and invite us to read it that way if we can."[37] Traditions are valuable in that they draw the reader into a comprehensive reading community that helps to make sense of Scripture as it has been experienced over time. That community lends a confidence that there is much more to say of God than that God is tyrannical.

But McClendon goes on to caution against too heavy a reliance on tradition. In a similar vein, John Webster insists on a differentiation between "Holy Scripture" and tradition in the sense that tradition can only be a hearing of Scripture and does not in any sense participate in the speaking of Scripture.[38] There is also a danger that theological tradition gives permission not to do the hard work of reading and interpreting into the questions of the present age, such as those posed by the New Atheists and also felt by Christians.

Scripture is a witness to the revelation of God in Christ; that Jesus provides a model for interpretation of the Scriptures; and that the Scriptures are best understood and interpreted in the light of Christ. For further on this see Meadowcroft, *The Message of the Word of God*, 24–25.

36. McClendon, *Doctrine*, 470–71.

37. Ibid., 471.

38. Webster, *Holy Scripture*, 51.

Vox Dei

If tradition can lead into too easy a disengagement from the questions of our age, so a christological reading may lead into too easy a jettisoning of aspects of God of which we do not approve. Both types of reading need to take place in conversation with one another. The tradition forces us to read parts of Scripture that are perceived to be out of tune with our understanding of God, and the person of Christ enables us to put those parts of Scripture into a wider perspective. And the conversation may be conducted by means of a lively appreciation of the living word of God wherever in the Bible it is encountered. Accordingly, and as a third comment on the theological reading of Scripture, I assert with Webster in his reading of Bonhoeffer that "Holy Scripture is the *viva vox Dei*, and that this living voice demands an attitude of ready submission and active compliance,"[39] even at points where it is difficult or even indefensible to do so.

But I make that assertion mindful of the difficulties inherent in doing so at least in the matter before us. Both the community of faith and the life and work of Christ suggest to me that the God of Scripture is not a tyrant. But I must confront the undeniable witness of Scripture to what Howard Wettstein calls "the dark side of God's world,"[40] a side hinted at in Isa 45:7: "I form light and create darkness, I make weal and create woe; I the Lord do all these things." In the Scriptural vision there is nothing that lies outside God's providence or sovereignty.[41] At the level of the creative activity of God this demonstrates itself in the tragedies of ironically named "acts of God" such as earthquakes and tsunamis which themselves are part of the creative process. At the level of the morality of God and the humanity created by God, there are actions of God that are simply impossible to see as good, but which nevertheless are part of God's story.[42] Even those moments when the actions of God seem indefensible somehow "reek of truth," as Wettstein puts it.[43] At this point, we note the importance of maintaining a conversation between this perspective and the various traditions of the faith that have grappled

39. Ibid., 80.

40. Wettstein, "God's Struggles," 322. This might also be expressed with the vivid phrase "a kind of ontological wasting disease" used of evil by Hart, *The Doors of the Sea*, 73, although Hart is working with a somewhat different notion of providence from that of Wettstein.

41. I am not sure what the difference is between providence and sovereignty, but see Wright et. al., *New Dictionary of Theology*, 541: "Providence is the beneficent outworking of God's sovereignty."

42. That is, the story both of and by God.

43. Wettstein, "God's Struggles," 332.

with them, as well as with a christological reading that sees all of this as somehow wrapped up and resolved in the Christ event. But we must exercise caution lest either of those theological approaches too easily silences the voices within the chorus of Scripture that are particularly discordant in a post-Christendom Western academy and church, and which are therefore voices that may need to be heard.

Concluding

I am challenged by John Goldingay's commentary on the Psalm that has one of the most memorable openings of all the Psalms and probably the most repelling ending, Psalm 137: "By the rivers of Babylon—there we sat down and there we wept" (Ps 137:1); "happy shall they be who take your little ones and dash them against the rock!" (Ps 137:9). With respect to that Psalm, Goldingay cites a piece of dialogue in the novel *Original Sin* by P. D. James. One character says: "If I had a God, I'd like him to be intelligent, cheerful and amusing." Her Jewish colleague replies: "I doubt whether you'd find him much of a comfort when they herded you into the gas chambers. You might prefer a God of vengeance."[44] Is the God of Scripture a tyrant? It depends; maybe; sometimes. But a God made in my image would hardly be an improvement.

At the end of the day New Atheism might be challenging us to be clearer than we are on the nature of God and why we think as we do. But I am pushed by the question of God's tyranny to a stance that is unlikely to satisfy the atheist and is also counter-cultural within the academy and probably also within the contemporary church. And that is the stance eventually adopted by Job, who, after all the theologizing, hermeneuting, and ameliorating, stood before God in the silence of submission and incomprehension and said: "Therefore I have uttered what I did not understand, things too wonderful for me, which I did not know" (Job 42:3).

Bibliography

Anderson, G. A. "What about the Canaanites?" In *Divine Evil? The Moral Character of the God of Abraham*, edited by M. Bergmann, M. J. Murray, and M. C. Rea, 269–82. Oxford: Oxford University Press, 2011.

Awad, Alex. *Palestinian Memories: The Story of a Palestinian Mother and Her People.* Bethlehem: Bethlehem Bible College, 2008.

44. Goldingay, *Psalms: Volume 3*, 612.

Barlow, C. *Tikanga Whakaaro: Key Concepts in Maori Culture*. Oxford: University Press, 1991.

Brueggemann, Walter. *Divine Presence amid Violence: Contextualizing the Book of Joshua*. Eugene, OR: Cascade, 2009.

Goldingay, J. E. *Old Testament Theology, Volume 3: Israel's Life*. Downers Grove, IL: InterVarsity, 2009.

———. *Psalms: Volume 3, Psalms 90–150*. Grand Rapids: Baker, 2008.

Hart, David Bentley. *The Doors of the Sea: Where was God in the Tsunami?* Grand Rapids: Eerdmans, 2005.

Hays, R. B. *The Moral Vision of the New Testament: A Contemporary Introduction to New Testament Ethics*. Edinburgh: T. & T. Clark, 1996.

Hitchens, Christopher. *God Is Not Great: How Religion Poisons Everything*. New York: Twelve, 2007.

Marshall, I. H. et al. *New Bible Dictionary*. Downers Grove, IL: InterVarsity, 1996.

McClendon, J. W. *Doctrine: Systematic Theology, Volume II*. Nashville, TN: Abingdon, 1994.

Meadowcroft, T. J. "In Whose Interests Do We Read? A Response to Miriam Bier." In *Reconsidering Gender: Evangelical Perspectives*, edited by Myk Habets and Beulah Wood, 161–70. Eugene, OR: Pickwick, 2010.

———. "Introduction: An Interpretive Conversation." In *Ears that Hear: Explorations in Theological Interpretation of the Bible*, edited by Joel B. Green & Tim Meadowcroft, 1–10. Sheffield: Phoenix, 2013.

———. *The Message of the Word of God: The Glory of God Made Known*. Leicester: InterVarsity, 2011.

———. "Review of Walter Brueggemann, *Divine Presence amid Violence: Contextualising the Book of Joshua*." *Colloquium* 42 (2010) 102-3.

Rae, Murray. *History and Hermeneutics*. London: T. & T. Clark, 2005.

Shirres, M. P. *Te Tangata: The Human Person*, Auckland: Accent, 1997.

Stevenson, J., editor. *A New Eusebius: Documents Illustrative of the History of the Church to A.D. 337*. London: SPCK, 1960.

Webster, John. *Holy Scripture: A Dogmatic Sketch*. Cambridge: Cambridge University Press, 2003.

Wettstein, H. "God's Struggles." In *Divine Evil: The Moral Character of the God of Abraham*, edited by M. Bergmann, M. J. Murray and M. C. Rea, 321–34. Oxford: Oxford University Press, 2011.

Wolterstorff, N. "Reading Joshua." In *Divine Evil? The Moral Character of the God of Abraham*, edited by M. Bergmann, M. J. Murray, and M. C. Rea, 236–56. Oxford: Oxford University Press, 2011.

Wright, C. J. H. "The Ethical Authority of the Old Testament: A Survey of Approaches, Part I." *Tyndale Bulletin* 43 (1992) 102–3.

———. *Living as the People of God: The Relevance of Old Testament Ethics*. Leicester, UK: InterVarsity, 1983.

Wright, David. F., et al. *New Dictionary of Theology*. Leicester: InterVarsity, 1997.

12

Making Meaning from Genesis

Yael Klangwisan

It is not a flawless process, coming to a text; especially when the text is one so ancient and yet so embedded in Western memory such as the "In the Beginning" text(s) and the Garden of Eden text(s). These contain the echoes of the primordial beginnings of the world, and humanity, according to the tenets of Christendom, and have inspired and awed countless generations. When we come to such a text we bring this cultural memory of the text with us, in a splendid array of adaptations and mutations, shaped by culture, values, and traditions as well as popular beliefs.

This is not a modern phenomenon. The impact of culture on making meaning from the ancient text is readily apparent. The Renaissance painters of Genesis scenes provide a fascinating illustrated history of how the contemporary culture of the reader impacts meaning. Of course, rather than presenting the reading as a commentary (another text), the painters displayed their reading in images, snapshots of key scenes. It is apparent how, in the absence of "primary audience" understandings of landscapes and contexts, that the European painters found their links to the text from their own worlds.

For example, one might take the famous *Fall of Man* oil on panel by the fifteenth-century Flemish master Hugo van der Goes.

This painting is one panel of *The Vienna Dyptych* that is housed at Kunsthistorisches Museum in Vienna.[1] Painting around 1479, van der Goes captures in oils his reading of Garden of Eden. In this rendition, the foregrounded Adam and Eve have the skin colorings, facial features, physique, and coif representative of van der Goes' Europe. Add the customary apparel of the Netherlands during the Northern Renaissance and *the primordial couple would be instantly indiscernible* from the crowds in the streets of Ghent. The landscape forming the background of his scene is also expressive of a thousand country vistas of fifteenth-century Europe. The rolling green hills, deforested for pasturing, dotted with the shrubs and trees that thrive in the Netherlands' cool temperate climate, the Tree of Life itself portrayed in the form of a young apple. Eve's nudity is minimally but politely obscured by a purple iris that further associates the contextual imagery to the cool temperate habitat of northern Europe. This *mise-en-scène* could not be further from the arid to semi-arid geographical context of Ancient Israel that gave birth to the ancient Genesis text and its lush dreams of water.

The depiction of the Gen 3:1–6 in van der Goes' art is an illustration of how the reader makes meaning from a text. Van der Goes presents the primordial pair together with a serpentine humanoid casting its shadow under the tree—an unholy trinity of sorts that pairs with the other panel of Van der Goes' dyptych, *The Redemption of Man* that presents Christ brought down from the cross, and surrounded by his faithful. The human couple, for Van der Goes, are mute, naïve, their dreamy gazes held off-scene, something to the east, perhaps that future gospel event made visible on the second panel. In the same moment the humanoid serpentine creature is clearly engaged, "his" gaze focused away from the object of the couple's gaze, and invested on the woman, as she plucks, in a trance, the forbidden fruit. Adam's hand is also outstretched for his share.

1. "Diptychon mit Sündenfall und Erlösung (Beweinung Christi)," *Eichenholz*, (Vienna: Kunsthistorisches Museum, Gemäldegalerie), Used with permission.

The scene as depicted in Genesis focuses on two characters: the woman and the serpent, with the third, Adam, silent and not made visible in the scene until Gen 3:6. The serpent in the text is not described as humanoid. *Nachash* (snake) is a common enough word in the Hebrew Bible. Only the snake in Genesis is ascribed some special abilities, such as speech in Gen 3:1. Though, with the application of a little logic the serpent could acquire legs, so that with the curse of Gen 3:14 to "go on its belly" it might appropriately loose them again; a cunning etiology, but not fully supported. Van der Goes' disproportionate depiction of a humanoid serpent replete with legs, arms and also face (eyes, nose, mouth, even eyebrows) arises from the painter's endeavor to make meaning of the text, and not what the text itself designates. It is likely the painter bolsters the reading of Genesis 3 that he exhibits in *The Fall of Man,* from the long Christian tradition of interpretation that associates the character of the serpent with the typically anthropomorphized character of *Ha-satan* (the Devil), in this particular vignette. Again, this association of Satan and Serpent is not inherent in the Genesis text.

Van der Goes is not alone in his use of license to make meaningful his reading of Genesis. Heironymous Bosch (1450–1517) in his tryptych, *Garden of Earthly Delights*, makes meaningful his reading of Genesis by another reading, that of the whole canon, which crystallizes in Bosch's mind as that of creation, corruption and hell. The two exterior shutters contain a split image of God's creation of the world in Genesis 1. The creation, for Bosch, is a dark, monochrome work of oil on oak, a flat European earth under a broiling heaven of storm clouds, encased in a filmy sphere. The left panel inside the tryptych contains a scene of sexual innocence from Genesis 2. God, who appears as Christ, takes the newly created Eve by the arm to present her to Adam. It is a bright, colorful paradise. The introduction of sexuality heralded by the union of Adam and Eve undergoes a change in the second panel which, while maintaining the colors and background imagery of the first panel, introduces images of sexual corruption, and sin in the pre-flood world that teems with people who have the features of Bosch's Europe. The final panel, whose theme colors now move to blacks and reds, illustrate the horrors of hell. For Bosch, the demonic is everywhere and sexuality is the root of all evils. He paints these beliefs into his reading of Genesis.

Adam and Eve, the oil on panel by Dürer (1471–1528) evidences the influence of the humanism of Greco-Roman style idealized by many renaissance painters, an idealization of the human body. Humanity, tree, and snake are glorious in their earthiness. The snake is no longer anthropomorphized. Lucas Cranach the Elder (1472–1553) merges Genesis 3 with Isaiah 11 (the peaceable kingdom) for his 1526 *Adam and Eve;* again the influence of European images is apparent. The influence of Dürer's work on Cranach might also be perceived in the piece. The presentation of the roles of male and female in the story is a focus for Cranach. Here Adam is scratching his head, postured in such a way as to convey his confusion while Eve's body and expression display certainty and thoughtful intentionality. Cranach painted further "Adam and Eve" works of the same scene in 1528, 1533, and 1538, each one a slight variation on the former. Cranach appears to have evolved in his reading of Gen 3:6 over time. Michelangelo (1475–1564) also paints his "European" *Adam and Eve*, their bodies, proportions, and allure more reminiscent of his works immortalizing the Greco-Roman pantheon rather than Hebrew cultural heritage. The human form is idealized for Michaelangelo. He sees beautiful humanity in the text's lines.

For Titian (1485–1576) the role of the Adam undergoes a change probably in response to (Titian's) social views on the place of women, and his theological views of woman's culpability for the Fall. In several of the aforementioned paintings Adam appears with ambiguity, passivity, and marginalized. In Titian's reading, as illustrated by his painting *Adam and Eve,* Adam is foregrounded, in a heroic and virtuous light, forbidding Eve's actions. Similarly for Rubens (1577–1640), gender relations between the primordial pair are foregrounded. Here Adam seems aggressive and accusative while Eve's carriage suggests a capricious, hedonistic presence.

In modern art the presentation of Genesis themes continues to be popular but changes drastically from the Renaissance. Modern painters exhibit strong engagement and contestation of the Genesis scenes. Gustav Klimt (1862–1918) re-inscribes the text with his symbolism of Tree, Lovers, and "the-other-woman" as serpent (perhaps influenced by the legend of Lillith) in his 1909 painting, *The Tree of Life*. He expresses a reading of the text that privileges metaphor rather than historical reality. The Tree of Life is covered in all seeing eyes. While the Italian avant-garde painter Enrico Baj (1924–2003), in his 1964 *Adam and Eve,* has a sensual primordial couple posed as the victims of myth, engaged in dialogue with an *animé-esque* caricature; a provocative and challenging postmodern and critical reading of Genesis. Baj shows how readily cultural beliefs and values shape how the reader receives the text and responds. These are the resources on which the reader is so dependent. Reading is embedded in a socio-cultural frame.

How the reader reads this ancient text will be influenced by how the reader perceives the book was gifted/written. Whether the reader believes God gave Scripture and how that process occurred also shapes the reading. From the traditional, literalist perspective, the transmission of this text occurred in a sacred vacuum with no outside or human influences. God's thought was encoded by Moses, as the inerrant book of Genesis, which is then decoded by the faithful reader, arriving at the same thought as God's.

Modern language theory such as Relevance Theory[2] on the process of communication recognizes a far more complex process. The world of the author and presupposed understanding of the world of the author's audience shapes their communication. The author writes in a milieu of worldview, history, rule, in the presence of other texts and literature, with views on the Sacred, with concerns, having experienced tragedies and also victories, with certain enemies, and also opinions on what is wrong or right with the world, opinions regarding who or what is God and how this God should be served. The author writes in a language of their own time, from unique geo-political, geo-social locations, to an audience that he or she presupposes will understand the nuances of the communication. The author fills their writing with allusions and cues to meaning readily apparent in their world, that they are ready and able to understand. They write using expected genre, convention, according to the state and structuring of knowledge of the time. The author writes from the midst of an immediate context, writing what they believe will be of relevance to their audience. The author writes in relevant genre, convention and tone, employing stylistics and plays that the they believe will hold their audience's attention and bring them into agreement with their arguments.

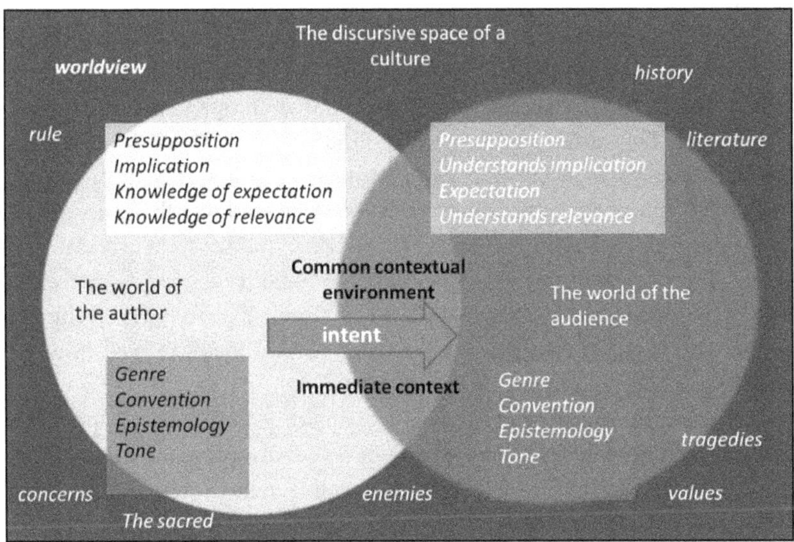

2. Sperber and Wilson, *Relevance: Communication and Cognition*, and more recently Wilson and Sperber, *Meaning and Relevance*.

This does not mean that Scripture cannot be God-breathed. Martin Buber's notion that God is in between every letter of the Holy Writ, pervading every space from sub-atomic worlds to the vast reaches of the cosmos is evocative. Our views of God are often patently too small, too restricted, too narrow, too evident of human inability to comprehend the divine without humiliating it, levelling it to satisfy human insecurities around truth. Reading a text, being honest about how texts are read, how readings are shaped (particularly when from an ancient and sacred text) is a complex, emotive and doctrinally charged endeavour.

The reader gains meaning from Genesis when he or she understands its genre. Genesis 1–3 is not a simple telling. It is complex and elegant poetic narrative, described by Westermann as a unique "fusion of poetry and prose."[3] The Genesis "Beginnings" text is highly stylized particularly in the first chapter with the repeated refrains of making, naming, and blessing. The language is ornate, ornamented with Hebrew words that are replete with allusions and poised to generate further reflection. For example, the author makes use of words and phrases with complex or associative meanings such as *tehom* or "deep" in Gen 1:2, which evokes in the Hebrew imagination both the mythical, primordial deep, but also the curled sea monster ready to pounce.[4] *Merachafet* also in Gen 1:2 conjures up the imagery of a womb-like, brooding embrace with its alliterative connections to *ruach* (breath) and *rechem* (womb) and *racham* (compassion). The author was concerned to integrate a structure through which to arrange these redolent words and their arrangement as poetic prose, providing such a platform through repeated patterns of action, strengthened by use of formulae. The author employs a macrostructure through the text that is complex and spectacular.

Jewish-Belarusian painter Chagall (1887–1985) embodies in his 1961 oil on canvas *Adam et Eve chassés du paradis*, a reading of Genesis that attempts to capture the impression of beauty, spirit, and loss that was evoked by his engagement with the text. He transfers this sense of wonder and beauty skillfully in his art. The spiritual-emotional response arising from a viewing of this painting is immediate and irrepressible. The same feeling of connection with the Divine would be much more difficult to awaken when reading a scholarly commentary on Genesis 1–3.

The poetic narrative of Genesis 1–3 could be described as opening a window into heaven. It is the function of this evocative genre to transport the reader into a realm where the reader will feel; feel touched. The genre

3. Westermann, *Genesis 1–11*, 90.

4. There is an association with the sea-dragon Tiamat. See Sarna, *The JPS Torah Commentary*, 6.

artfully applied, lines the events poetically described with a sense of immediacy; the sense of the always already present. Artistic, creative media, more than any other medium, enhances the sensory reception of a message and thus the poets might speak of their work as writing towards the "glimpse of the divine." The reader is moved, far more by the prose than by any encyclopedic sets of facts. The reader of Genesis, especially when reading in the original language, experiences beauty, awe and fear, and the intense desire to hear more, to hear how the story ends. The reader experiences the allusion of access to that which is intangible; that can never be fully apprehended (such as the Divine). The polysemy of such texts allows for diversity of meaning. It is experienced in reading as generative and fertile. Prose allows for epiphany, the experience of many a reader of Genesis 1–3. The poetic brings the event into the present.

Genesis 1 is filled with subtle and poetic allusions to the Temple of God.[5] The whole universe is God's temple and Jerusalem, his footstool (Isa 66:1). In rhythm with the seven day week, the rooms/courts are erected and filled. The vastness of space, the seas and the heavens, and the dry land form the temple plan. Within these temple courts are wondrous artifacts that awe the worshipper: the heavenly bodies that fill the sky, birds and fish filling the sea, and animals and humans ornamenting the earth. The principle artifacts in any ancient Near Eastern temple are the god-images and in the Garden of Eden these god-images are man and woman; the crowning achievement of God's creation activities. The stop-rest inauguration of the temple follows on the seventh day.

On a second level, repetition is a literary stylistic employed by the writer. Genesis 1 is constructed (among other things) via artful repetition, each repeated formula is like the placing of a column, in God's temple; a poetic temple under construction. Each piece stunningly fitted and worked until a masterpiece of poetic architecture is performed.

- "and God said" (1:3, 6, 9, 11, 14, 20, 24, 26, 28, 29)
- "let there be" (1:3, 6, 9, 11, 14, 20, 24, 26)
- "and it was so" (1:3, 7, 9, 11, 15, 24, 30)
- "and God made" (1:4, 7, 12, 16, 21, 25, 27)

5. This is not a new idea. Westermann notes this association in his commentary *Genesis*, 29, as a natural conclusion related to the vastly older and well known lyric poetry of the Babylonian tradition. Watts emphasizes strongly on this view of Genesis 1 and 2 in Watts, "Making sense of Genesis." Further evidence in the text may be found in the etymology of the word *rakia* in Gen 1:6 describing "the expanse" which is a word associated with building, a "hammering out of metal." See Sarna, *Genesis*, 8.

- "and God saw that 'x' was good" (1:4, 10, 12, 18, 21, 25, 31)
- naming or blessing (1:5, 8, 10, 22, 28)
- "there was evening and there was morning" (1:5, 8, 13, 19, 23, 31)
- First day, second day . . . (1:5, 8, 13, 19, 23, 31; 2:2)

McKenzie, in his book, *How to Read the Bible*, discusses the history writing genre of the ancient Near East in relation to reading Genesis.[6] He describes its generic expression as a "corporate" kind of literature, unique to the ancient world that must be distinguished and separated, in the reader's mind, from the aims that are privileged by modern writers. The ancient writers were not concerned with evidence-based, encyclopedic exactitude but were focused on the exploration of cause and effect. Etiology is a form of story-telling that explains "why" the world is as it is—from the most ordinary of human activities such as marriage, to tragedies on the national scale: "An etiology is a story that explains the cause or origin of a given phenomenon—a cultural practice or social custom."[7] Genesis 2:21–24 is an excellent example of a mini-etiological story within a larger one. Genesis 2:24 describes how the social custom of marriage came about. In this etiology the past serves to explain the present, but this is only a mini-etiology. The macro-etiology of Genesis 2–3 is more encompassing of the human condition.

> So the LORD God caused a deep sleep to fall upon the man,
> and he slept;
> then He took one of his ribs
> and closed up the flesh at that place.
>
> The LORD God fashioned into a woman the rib
> which He had taken from the man,
> and brought her to the man.
> The man said,
> "*This is now bone of my bones,*
> *And flesh of my flesh;*
> *She shall be called Woman,*
> *Because she was taken out of Man.*"
>
> For this reason:
> a man shall leave his father and his mother,
> and be joined to his wife;
> and they shall become one flesh.[8]

6. McKenzie, *How to Read the Bible*.
7. Ibid., 30.
8. Gen 2:21–24 Jewish Publication Society translation.

Genesis 2:21–24 thus gives meaning to the social question "Why marry?"

Recognizing symbolism is important for locating meaning in Genesis. Reading symbolism adeptly helps unlock the implications, intimations, and connotations in Scripture. This enables the reader to embed a great deal more pertinent information into the text. For the initial audience this "reading between the lines" would have occurred as a natural process of listening to the text read aloud but readily earthed into their social and temporal context. The primary audience not only drew on the words of the author but also the significance and implication of his words in their historical, social, geo-political setting. In order to do this with some objectivity, the reader must understand this context and read not as "modern reader" (eisegetically reading the modern world into the text) but imagining in an educated way what it might have been like to hear the text read originally. For this reason the reader must not only read the text but also read the ancient world back into the text; the world for which the text was originally meant.

Names in Scripture carry significant meanings. They are monikers with a further and subtle task to engage the reader on another level. Often these meanings are not conveyed in translations of the text, certainly not the English translation. Thus potential meaning is lost to the English reader. For example, Adam and Eve are not simply Hebrew personal names as popularly understood. In fact, the Hebrew names of Genesis 2 are not personal names at all. *Adam* in its first appearance in Scripture is preceded by the definite article (*ha-*) meaning "the earthy one," associating Adam to the clay, earth, or dirt with which God made him.[9] It comes to mean "human" or "man" in the story and can refer to the first man, or later all men (humankind) i.e., sons-of-adam (Deut 32:8). This is a clever stylistic that brings the story from a third person narrative, to a story that comes to involve "me," the reader. The reader is also *"adam." Chavvah* (Gen 3:20) means "life," representing Eve as Every Woman and her representative and critical function as a mother/bearer of children. These two names, "*adam*" and *Chavvah*, represent the primordial couple but also are representative of all human beings, representing gender difference as a primary truth of the human condition for ancient Israel.

The other and stranger symbols in the Genesis Eden story introduce a tragic truth of the human condition: that of life and its corollary, death. The snake is the central antagonist in the Genesis 2–3 story whose appearance heralds the end of innocence and the initiation of death. Death and suffering, Meyers reminds the reader, was all too prevalent in the ancient Israelite

9. Trible, *God and the Rhetoric of Sexuality*, 77–78.

world.[10] Starvation and sickness were commonplace. While in popular readings, the serpent is generally associated with Satan, scholars of the ancient Near East would immediately locate the significance of serpents in other ancient sources such as the Babylonian myths (i.e., The Epic of Gilgamesh where the serpent stole eternal life from the hero). Its prevalence exists also in Egyptian mythology of that nation and location in which the narrative of Genesis will close; the last words of Genesis (50:26) being those describing the embalming and burial of Joseph "in Egypt." The snake or "Uraeus" is of primary religious and cultural significance in ancient Egypt.[11] It is the primary representation of the divine power of Pharaoh, who is lauded as the "living god" of Egypt. The "tree of life" is also strongly represented in Egyptian mythology and stood between the thresholds of life and death.

Lacocque explores the theme of life and death with great sensitivity in his book, *The Trial of Innocence*, reminding the reader, that however forbidding, death does not finally prevail, nor does "nothingness" nor "purposelessness" of life outside the Garden.[12] Life through Eve persists and for Lacocque, the possibility and imperative of return is always already imminent. Lacocque describes Genesis and the Eden narrative as "a narrated philosophy" that "focuses on the nature and destiny of the humans, their *raison d'être*, their relations with the Creator and with other creatures, their alienation from their environment, their limitations and mortality, their work and sexuality, their aspirations and hopes . . ."[13] Genesis is a human book, written by human hands, filled with human voices, yearnings, and desires but it probes, with alacrity, the meaning of life. It identifies, with feeling and evocation, the struggles that humans endure in their "thrownness" in life—in the people who through the centuries, have struggled to find purpose and who have continually grasped towards an understanding of the Divine. God's place in this book and with those who wrote it is pervasive and deep. The poetic and artistic language give us a truer glimpse of the hand and breath of God than reductive, literalistic readings. The science of reading is in fact a blessing, and when applied to Genesis, there is epiphany and profundity and deep truth-speaking. Read in the company of an understanding of ancient Near Eastern context we see a stunning message elegantly and persuasively communicated.

10. Myers, "Food and the First Family," 141.
11. Watts, "Making Sense of Genesis."
12. Lacocque, *The Trial of Innocence*.
13. Ibid., 14.

Bibliography

Evans, Craig A., Joel N. Lohr, and David L. Petersen. *The Book of Genesis: Composition, Reception, and Interpretation*. Leiden/Boston: Brill, 2012.

Lacocque, André. *The Trial of Innocence: Adam, Eve, and the Yahwist*. Eugene, OR: Cascade, 2006.

McKenzie, Steven L. *How to Read the Bible: History, Prophecy, Literature—Why Modern Readers Need to Know the Difference, and What It Means for Faith Today*. Oxford: Oxford University Press, 2005.

Sarna, Nahum Mattathias. *The JPS Torah Commentary: Genesis*. Philadelphia: Jewish Publication Society, 1989.

Sperber, Dan, and Deirdre Wilson. *Relevance: Communication and Cognition*. Cambridge: Harvard University Press, 1986.

Trible, Phyllis. *God and the Rhetoric of Sexuality*. Philadelphia: Fortress, 1978.

Watts, R. "Making Sense of Genesis." In *Science in Christian Perspective*. Online: http://www.asa3.org/ASA/topics/Bible-Science/6-2Watts.html

Westermann, Claus. *Genesis 1–11: A Continental Commentary*. Translated by John J. Scullion. Minneapolis: Fortress, 1994.

Wilson, Deirdre, and Dan Sperber. *Meaning and Relevance*. Cambridge: Cambridge University Press, 2012.

The Ending

13

Tracing the Way Home

The Kingdom of Heaven on Earth

JUDITH BROWN

Introduction

THERE IS A POEM by the German writer Heinrich Heine, which has long been popular among the literate enemies of religion. Here is a stanza from it:

> *A newer song, a better song,*
> *My friends, let's bring to birth now!*
> *We shall proceed right here to build*
> *The Kingdom of heaven on earth now.*[1]

Heine died in 1856, the mid-point of a century of significant individuals[2] whose legacy has made possible the bringing of the horizon of heaven

1. From *Germany: A Winter's Fable,* in Heine, *The Complete Poems of Heinrich Heine,* 484.

2. Charles Darwin was born in 1802 (d. 1882), Ludwig Feuerbach was born in 1804 (d. 1872), and Karl Marx in 1818. Arthur Schopenhauer, though born a generation earlier in 1788, did not die until 1860. And Friedrich Nietzsche was, only just, a living

down to earth, who reduced theology to anthropology (but as Feuerbach said; at the same time exalting anthropology to theology).[3]

As such they are all part of the inheritance of the Marxist utopian philosopher Ernst Bloch. It is the development of this critical atheism which this paper will consider. Bloch's turn of mind has concerns that differ from those of the contemporary critics of religion. But in its interrogation of the basis of our knowledge of self and the world it is the doorway to contemporary atheism. Yet in comparison to contemporary critics of religion, what makes Bloch especially important is that his atheism never repudiated the religious heritage. Rather, he sought to recover positive, developmental elements in it as a resource for living "unbounded" in mature humanity. Bloch undertook an investigation into the essence of religion that can be, I argue, a productive corrective to the notion that it is a delusion and one detrimental to the flourishing of human being. That is, an investigation that makes constructive appropriation of the religious tradition without compromising an essential rejection of supernatural postulates.

Positioning Bloch

Bloch was born in Ludwigshafen in 1885.[4] Before his turn to Marxism, around 1920, Bloch had earned a name for complex writings drawing heavily on the messianic and left-wing thought of both Judaism and Christianity.[5] In the early 1920s he began forging a unique blend of this tradition with the emerging discipline of sociology[6] and Marxism.[7] As an observer of the

---

contemporary of Heine's (born in 1844, dying in 1900).

3. See Feuerbach, *The Essence of Christianity*, xxxviii. Feuerbach proclaimed that religious beliefs were "projections" of human states. In *The Essence of Christianity* "he argues that religious language must be a form of human language, and must therefore be a form of conversation humanity holds with itself." "'God' can in this sense never be higher than the underlying humanity." Vincent Geoghegan "Religion and Communism," 586.

4. His family were lower middle class assimilated Jews. For this and the following biographical details see Jack Zipes' introduction in Ernst Bloch, *The Utopian Function of Art and Literature*. Hereafter *U.F.*

5. Bloch's marriage in 1913 to the Christian mystic and sculptor Else von Stritzky was very important for his work and Else's early death in 1921 was a loss Bloch himself said he never truly recovered from.

6. He had undertaken study with George Simmel in Berlin from 1908–11, and was a marginal figure in Weber's circle. Simmel is regarded as the source of Bloch's notion of the "lived moment" and the opaqueness of this for us.

7. The major product of this period is the remarkable *Geist der Utopie,* dedicated to von Stritsky. The work was first published in 1918 and revised, after his turn to Marxism, in 1921.

Russian revolution and the failure of revolutionary socialism in Europe, notably in Germany, he became a vigorous critic of what he termed "cold-stream" Marxism, and began developing his key ideas into a philosophy of hope. Bloch's Marxism is a distinguishing aspect of his thought and both his dialogue with Marx's own attitude to religion and the particulars of his own reading of it will be addressed in what follows.

Many complexities, indeed ambiguities, are apparent in Bloch's life and thought: He never joined the Communist party; but was a supporter of the Stalin show trials.[8] Late in life he became a teacher of philosophy at Leipzig University, keeping his position because of his profile but subject always to the hostility of the State. In 1961, during a guest lectureship in West Germany the Berlin Wall was built and Bloch chose to remain in the West. But he never found the capitalist West a congenial environment (he was dismayed by the materialism of America during his exile there in WWII). Bloch lived long enough (dying in 1977) to become something of a hero to the radical New Left in the West and the protest movements of the 1960s. And this atheist of impeccable integrity influenced a number of twentieth-century theologians.[9]

Bloch and Marx

First among the Marxist methodologies that Bloch appropriated[10] is the dialectical method, the only true means of investigation of the world. Marx believed that his inquiry into the meaning of the world was the, as yet, only truly scientific investigation. Study of the problems of humanity and the world should begin with facts—not *a priori* philosophical or religious principles. Truly scientific inquiry is committed to "real men in their actual, empirical process of development under definite conditions."[11] For Marx there is no human nature *per se*. Human *nature* is its history. We are formed by "conditions in the social production of our place and time,"[12] the prevailing organization

8. See "Jubilee for Renegades" first published in *Die neue Weltbuehne*, December 1937, republished in Ernst Bloch *Vom hazard zur Katastrophe*. First English translation David Bathrick and Nancy Vedder Shults, *New German Critique*, 17–25.

9. Primarily Jürgen Moltmann, also Ernesto Baldacci. His thought has a general resonance in the theology of Johann Baptist Metz and other Liberation theologians. Paul Tillich played a vital role in the translation of his work into English.

10. I use this word acknowledging that his Marxism was sincere and central to his philosophy—yet for Bloch its critical apparatus was never deterministic (a very important aspect of his thought itself).

11. Venable, *Human Nature*, 19.

12. Ibid.

of labor. Indeed, we can be no more than what we actually do in our concrete historical environments: an "ensemble of the social relations."[13]

For Marx history is the history of competing classes, which are expressions of a basic incompatibility of human interests. Throughout history classes have arisen from the particular division of labor in any given era. The reason for Marx's radical objection to capitalism is that the type of human being created in the class-controlled manufacturing division of labor is especially unable to execute purposive labor. Capitalism has alienated the laborer from the work of their own hands. Capitalism has made our life activity merely a means of existence.

As we are constituted by our behavior and powers within our actual physical and historical environments we in turn alter these in an ongoing process. This is the engine of history itself. Humanity's relations, capacities, and behavior are what constitute society and society in turn modifies us. Marx himself speaks of "potential human being," and stresses the need to direct the change that occurs in humanity into beneficial avenues. Needs and capacities are fundamental: "To know what is useful for a dog, one must study dog nature . . ."[14]

Marx believes this is the methodology that best serves humanity—first dealing with human nature in general by which he means for example our *actual* need for food and then with human nature as modified in each historical epoch, that is the particular forms of *expression* of that need in the different periods of our history.

The subordination in capitalism to the commodity fetish is a distortion of our species character: what sets humanity apart from the animal world is that we produce our very lives through our critical intelligence:

> A spider conducts operations that resemble those of a weaver and a bee puts to shame many an architect in the construction of her cells. But what distinguishes the worst of architects from the best of bees is this: that the architect raises his structure in imagination before he erects it in reality. . . . He not only effects a change on the material on which he works, but he also realizes a purpose of his own that gives the law to his modus operandi . . .[15]

Under capitalism the institutions of society such as government, culture and religion are all forms of the dominant ideology of the ruling class. The State, private property, alienation and religion are the practices

13. Marx, *Theses on Feuerbach*, Thesis VI. This was originally published in 1845. See McLellan *Karl Marx: Selected Writings*, 157.

14. Marx, *Capital*, 668.

15. Ibid., 179

and forms that Marx explicitly said would be absent from the future Communist society. Marx's detestation of religion was expressed very early. While still in his twenties he stated that "criticism of religion is the premise of all criticism."[16] Religious alienation was the first to be unmasked. How radical this rejection was is shown by Marx's assertion that even atheism is inadequate. Atheism has to be overcome because it posits humanity only through a denial of God: "But socialism . . . no longer stands in any need of such mediation. . . . Socialism is man's positive self-consciousness, no longer mediated through the abolition of religion."[17]

Bloch's attitude to religion is not that of Marx's. Bloch is more than a "mere" historical materialist. His sophisticated approach to religion affirms much of its material, particularly, as we shall see its "heretical" tendencies. Bloch's philosophy is a supreme example of the valorization of human autonomy, the belief that we have what it takes in ourselves. But this competency, or sufficiency, *needs* the religious traditions as a resource, a repository of images and stories. In Bloch's writings there are great swathes of pages filled with religious language and resonances: terms such as "the Kingdom of God," "the age of the Holy Spirit," and the *Parousia* are common.

However, in Bloch's philosophy of hope the goal, legitimately in Bloch called salvation, is entirely other to that of the Gospel. In his writing transcendent referents are replaced by human capacities. The religious material is always refunctioned in order to support his contention that even the most unpromising material can be mined for nuggets of the "essence content of our striving."[18] But for Bloch, religion is not just tolerated for what it could contribute to a project that would naturally lead to its own abolition. Religion has its own "veins of gold" that are utopian elements expressed in its own distinct and unique ways. This atheist of uncompromised integrity finds in religion supreme examples of our emancipatory yearning.[19]

As has been mentioned Bloch is highly critical of "coldstream Marxism," the belief that the revolution (a word which Bloch seldom uses, rather speaking of the changing of the world) is the inevitable result of the dialectical class movement that is the engine of history. Bloch did prioritize dialectical

16. Marx and Engels, "Contribution to the Critique of Hegel's Philosophy of Law," 175. The early nineteenth century was in a ferment of debate about the role of religion in German Hegelianism. Those involved in the debate included notable thinkers such as F. W. J. Schelling, Moses Hess, Friedrich Julius Stahl, and Ludwig Feuerbach.

17. Marx and Engels, "*Economic and Philosophical Manuscripts of 1844*," 306.

18. Bloch, *The Principle of Hope*, 3:1374. Hereafter *P.H.*

19. We must note here that this repository of our hopefulness is not confined to Christianity or Judaism but is found in ancient Greece or Egypt or Persia as well as the religions of the East.

processes, and he did think that the "seeds of its own destruction" were inherent within the very structure and nature of capitalism itself. But Bloch is not a determinist. It is absolutely vital that we seize the moment. The inevitable crises of capitalism are *kairos* moments. Human activity is decisive. For Bloch the world *is* open-ended and process,[20] a laboratory of the possible. But this open-endedness is *never* formless. It is not a disincentive to action. It indicates that our path is out ahead, and that only when we have attained our full maturity will we begin to be fully human. One of his most famous aphorisms thus goes: "true genesis comes not at the beginning but at the end."[21]

The Human Project

For Bloch, humanity is a project—our task is our completion of ourselves and the world. As we shape the world, so we form ourselves. All about us are traces (*Spuren*) which contain utopian pre-appearances, fore-tellings, or intimations. They are nothing less than revelations of the content of the redemptive trajectory of human subjectivity.

Humanity is shaped by a summons that is already within us—the utopian spark. Just as the world's condition is an unfinished one, so we are also incomplete, an "incognito," a not yet (*noch nicht*). This category of "not yet" is a signifier, first introduced into Bloch's writing as early as 1907. The term refers broadly to the tension that inheres in the world's development in light of the fact of its incomplete state. In this sense it is part of the structure of the world. It is ontologically restless. What is "not yet" is a condition of anticipation, a utopian pre-shining (*Vor-Scheins*).[22] It designates a quality of truth, a shedding of light on our self's false consciousness. It cannot be realized in the ideology of the status quo.

So Bloch's philosophy seeks to motivate us, to enact Marx's dictum that the philosopher's task is to change the world, to affect *praxis*. The goal of this is our homecoming. Indeed, a very important term in Bloch's philosophy is *Heimat* or "home."[23] A notion with deep roots in Austro-Germanic culture

20. *U.F.*, 72.

21. *P.H.* 3:1375.

22. The translation of this term is a subject of debate. The verb *Scheinen* means "to shine." *Vor* is "before" or "in front of." Attempted translations include "anticipatory illumination," (Jack Zipes), pre-appearance (Wayne Hudson, the Plaice brothers), or even "utopian pre-telling."

23. As a consequence of his marriage in 1934 to Karola Pietrkowski (Pychtrovkovskee), who was an architecture student and then a courier (from 1932) for the Communist Party, Bloch learned that his name was on a list of the National Socialist's opponents. This led to an extended flight from the advancing German army. Details on

it means much more than the English "home". It involves the full spectrum of the human sense of belonging and completion, the full realization of the subjectivity of humanity. Bloch often quotes a specific passage from one of Marx's letters to Ruge: "It will . . . become evident that the world has long dreamed of possessing something of which it only has to be conscious in order to possess it in reality."[24]

And he concludes his vast *Principle of Hope* with these words:

> Once the [working creating human being] has grasped himself and established what is his, without expropriation and alienation, in real democracy, there arises in the world something which shines into the childhood of all and in which no one has yet been: homeland.[25]

But this goal, this "homeland" is utterly opaque—it is hope that opens the long common road into this future.

As part of his reclamation of religion Bloch engages with Feuerbach's critique of the religious function. Feuerbach had a profound influence on Marx in his negative manifestation—but Feuerbach also upheld the value of religion. Hence Bloch is both critical—Feuerbach fails to take into account the element of temporal transcendence implied in the incomplete nature of the world and our condition of "not yet"[26]—and laudatory: Feuerbach also maintains a concern with our religious heritage that means he was not "merely a gravedigger."[27] In his *Atheism in Christianity* Bloch remarks that "one can even say, with some exaggeration, that no one, so far as method was concerned, was as indebted as [Feuerbach] to the radically human line in Christianity."[28] On the other hand Marx, for whom all religious traditions are false, simply throws the baby out with the bathwater.

Bloch and Christianity

To support his arguments for the reclamation of religion Bloch posits a double strand within Judaism and Christianity that incorporates a secret

this can be found in the introduction by Jack Zipes to Bloch, *Utopian Function*, xviii. It is not too fanciful to suggest that the continuous and largely enforced journeying that marked much of Bloch's life influenced his concept of "Home" (*Heimat*).

24. Marx. *Letter to Ruge*, 38.

25. *P.H.* 3:1376.

26. *P.H.* 3:1196.

27. *P.H* 1:273.

28. Bloch, *Atheism in Christianity*, 209.

resistance. Yes, God *is* an image of the conflicts in our human social world. Productive reading of the Bible is done with "the eyes of the Communist Manifesto."[29] Class conflict is imported into the notion of God: but there is a distinction. Within Christianity there is a tension between God who is become (the Creator God, the one who said "behold it was very good") and the God of becoming, the Exodus God, the one who says "behold I make all things new." It is this deity who is an image of the struggle of the oppressed. Bloch posits a theocratic orthodoxy; a Priestly tradition allied to the ruling classes whose God is the Creator God, a static timeless God; and a counter tradition whose God is the Exodus God. This God is an image of the revolutionary principle. It is a heritage that Bloch calls "Promethean" that is above all a record of humanity's "venturing forth." This is the God who said "I will be who I will be." The God of the Priestly class is, further, the maker of an imperfect world, the source of injustice and of dualisms the Exodus God actively struggles to overcome.

In defence of his exegesis[30] Bloch appropriates passages such as the story of the Tower of Babel (Gen 11:1–9). This myth preserves the truth of human creativity emerging in rebellion against the God of the priests, in our dream of making a name for ourselves. This is the real positive element of human hubris, the spirit of rebellion, the desire to create like God. When expelled from the garden humanity attempted to enter heaven. But the practical outcome of the fall of the Tower is that we live in a world in which this self-directed creative impulse is fragmented. Yet in the scattering after the fall of the Tower there arose the many fragments that are a heritage and signpost to our authenticity.

Bloch links the Old Testament Exodus God with Jesus as "Son of Man," who identifies with the poor and oppressed without condescension and who rejects the Priestly status quo, as in his anger against the money-lenders.[31] The creator God, according to Bloch, gives up his glory to the Messiah, who identifies himself as the Son of Man. Bloch also cites Jesus' words in John 3:14: "Just as Moses lifted up the snake in the desert, so the Son of Man must be lifted up" to connect the Son of Man to the serpent; for it was the serpent in the garden who enacted the first rebellion against God. This identification symbolizes the Promethean rebellion against the Creator God: it legitimates our "truly human" desire to be as God. Lucifer is the exemplar of the Promethean ideal in his rebellion: he symbolizes our fallen reality. Job

29. Bloch, *Atheism in Christianity*, 69.

30. Bloch bases his contention on the biblical scholarship of Julius Wellhausen and Eduard Meyer, who have an evolutionary perspective.

31. *P.H.* 3:1260.

is also a Promethean type. Job's faith encapsulates the anti-Yahwist strand in Judaism. Those who are Luciferan are "makers of consciousness, creators of light, makers of the world."[32] This utopian element is this-worldly and forward-looking. In contrast, the Creator God, who demands sacrificial death as the only possible payment for a debt he has arbitrarily created, is revealed as indistinguishable from the demonic, from Satan.[33]

Culture and Hope without God

So what is the underlying interpretive framework that enables Bloch to so describe Christianity, and religion in general? In his analysis of the function of culture, of which religion is a component, Bloch subverts many of the orthodoxies of Marxism. At the outset he states that the superstructure has functional value.[34] In classic Marxist theory legal systems, bureaucracy, government, educational and cultural institutions arise subsequent to economic organization. It is events in the economic base, the organization of the means of production, that matter, and they are held to contain inevitable tendencies, contradictions, that *in themselves* are sufficient to bring about the revolution (the collapse of capitalism).

Bloch contends that advocates of economic sufficiency are actually mimicking the bourgeois division of labor. Their isolation of the economic base sunders *humanly* significant connections. Hence Bloch uses as an image of the relationship of base to superstructure that of the relation of a mast to the deck of a ship: connected but moving independently according to their functions. As Bloch says "economic schematism does not explain Pushkin."[35] This is the problem in Marxism of the production of culture: the difference in mediation between "Athens as a place of commerce and as a place for the Parthenon."[36]

32. *P.H.* 3:1054.

33. There is an unoptimistic appropriation of the Cabbalist Isaac Luria. Luria viewed the "beginning" word in Genesis not as the beginning of a vital and independent creation but of an imprisonment, as creation came about through the contraction of God. Humanity, the creation, is in a condition of exile. God's creation holds captive the spiritual sparks of all men and even God, who is therefore homeless in this creation. See *P.H* 3:1237.

34. This important idea is presented in "Ideas as Transformed Material in Human Minds, or Problems of an Ideological Superstructure (Cultural Heritage)" in *U.F.*, 18–70.

35. Bloch "Ideas as Transformed," 30.

36. *U.F.*, 29–31.

According to Bloch it is both elements together in a dialectical movement which are the engine of history. Our own reflection on this "totality of subject-object relationship"[37] is a part of the process. The superstructure is both product and place of our self-reflection. In the conditions that prevail under capitalism our self-reflection can only be an idealization. It is a sublimation *of the capitalist work relationship* that produces premature solutions to social contradictions.

However, within the superstructure there is always a *surplus* (*überschuss*). The surplus may still be tied to the contradictions of the superstructure but such contradictions are not fundamentally its nature. This *surplus* is the utopian element so disastrously ignored by Marxist orthodoxy. (Indeed, the neglect by European Marxism of the dreams and longings of ordinary people is one of the explanations Bloch offers for the rise of fascism in the 1920s and 30s).[38]

This surplus is the Utopian "hidden essence."[39] It is what has not ossified, nor mere ideology. It is open, not, as Bloch puts it, "thwarted in existence."[40] Here Bloch praises Hegel for his insight that what we make with our culture is an heirloom. Tradition and producing the future is one and the same thing. The surplus is Marx's "dream about a thing"[41] and it turns history from a "temple of memory" into an "arsenal."[42]

The surplus arises because all parts of the social totality do not develop at the same pace: this is "non-synchronomous development" (*Ungleichzeitigkeit*).[43] Archaic elements are present in society, and logically this implies the presence of what has not yet been fully realized. In other words some ideas exist out of their time and must await the right social conditions. Following Marx, the oldest of these elements is mythology. In mythology there are archetypes, expressions of remnant awe, an understanding not reduced to product but, especially in rebellious archetypes—for example, Prometheus or Lucifer—embodying a pre-shining, an "anticipatory illumination," of utopian longing.

37. *U.F.*, 32.

38. See Bloch, *Heritage of the Times.*

39. *U.F.*, 49.

40. *U.F.*, 49.

41. *U.F.*, 51.

42. *U.F.*, 51.

43. An example of Bloch's application of this idea is found in his 1935 critical analysis of the rise of fascism: Bloch, *Heritage of Our Times.*

The Ending

The moral quintessence of the utopian spark is *hope*. Hope awakens the "world from the dream about itself."[44] Hope is the condition in which free imagination, ethics without ideology and property, can take root. In this the "I" and the "we" are the one and the same problem: "I am. We are. That is enough. Now we have to start."[45] The "self" and the "We" (*Wir*) are mutual terms, that is, "we ourselves," not conflicting values. Self-possession is a collective possession. Our maturity is a species project.[46]

The problem for us is that we are too close to ourselves. We live in the "darkness of the lived moment."[47] This condition hinders our coming to one another and the world. The lived instant, the moment, is inaccessible, too lived in and so not experienced. For Bloch atheism therefore is the necessary ground to our salvation. The death of the gods has left a hollow space (*Hohlraum*) which is God's locus and survives him. This newly void space is really the *topos* of humanity-out-ahead. By taking possession of it we gain our self-consciousness and move beyond our limited nature to our infinite nature, which is our species being. It is a turning-point when Christianity comes to itself by putting on its inherent atheism: when the "elements invested in the external divinity are repatriated to their true home."[48]

But, though we hope we do not do so in possession of ourselves, and so do not recognize our desire. The darkness we begin in is the same in character as the state of the world: and like that it is a condition of rich possibility, of creative ferment. In a critique of the classic Hegelian dialectic Bloch approvingly cites Nicholas of Cusa's notion that "things come into existence when God unfolds himself in nothingness."[49] It is this nothingness or darkness that the world is formed from: the *ex nihilo* is the original creative night and is the source of fragmentation and diversity, and death. It is not chaos, but "productive death,"[50] and is the engine of dialectical momentum, always having a difference to it in each appearance: "The negative is . . . medial. . . . Nothingness becomes an objective Mephistopheles who agitates and creates the world."[51]

44. Bloch here is paraphrasing Marx's famous 1843 letter to Ruge.

45. Bloch, *Spirit of Utopia*, 1.

46. Obviously here Bloch is extending Marx's view that our self-possession is a process of work in which we overcome the alienation of capitalist reification and "come to" ourselves.

47. A phrase Bloch lifts from Jakob Boehme. See *P.H.* 1:290–99.

48. Geoghegan, "Religion and Communism," 592.

49. Bloch, "The Dialectical Method," 310.

50. See Bloch's comments on music in *P.H.* 1:1098.

51. Bloch, "The Dialectical Method," 311.

This dialectical movement is also one of the elements to be commended in Jacob Boehme, who Bloch states "discovered the dialectically necessary relation that light must have to darkness in order that it become manifest as an object."[52] Boehme and de Cusa are both part of a pre-Utopian tradition that sees the world in terms of a process of illumination. In this the "dark original ground," the essence, (*Ungrund* in Boehme) proceeds by dialectic to manifest the Kingdom of light: the "root of a Kingdom in which there is no longer any other element than the Son of Man."[53] Human action and hopes are steps in a "process of cognition."[54]

Concluding Remarks: Reclaiming Ourselves

So what in conclusion should we say of Bloch's understanding of the meaning of the world? As noted above, in his discussions of Hegel, Bloch locates the vitality of the dialectic in the element of negation (contained in the antithesis). This is the element that makes the dialectic a "process of breakthroughs."[55] For Bloch what Hegel lacks is the confrontation with existence, with suffering that calls a person to action. Where, asks Bloch, is the reassurance in the idea that in human consciousness, which is recapitulated history, God comes to himself?[56]

Bloch valorized our ontological restlessness. He sought a meaning in it that is more than a rubbing against the grain of material realities:

> Matter in this our modern age is burdensome, and souls have become increasingly unpitying and ungenuine, so that Christmas, Easter, and Pentecost seem like one long Good Friday, like merely the insubstantial knowledge that the redeemer has died . . .[57]

Our concrete situation engenders an experiential condition in which many diverse things are present but unintegrated. There is the feeling "that in our strangely weary and obscure life something important [is] not right."[58]

52. Bloch, "The Dialectical Method," 292.

53. *P.H.* 2:643. Bloch is speaking of Boehme's praise of the philosopher's stone.

54. *P.H.* 2:954.

55. Bloch, "Dialectical Method," 285.

56. Hegel's belief that the Spirit has come to maturity in his own time, is, as with all forms of thought, including the Platonic, that advocated or facilitated closure, rejected by Bloch.

57. Bloch, *Spirit of Utopia*, 68.

58. Ibid., 168.

The term Bloch gives to this, for him the profoundest element of our being, is hunger.[59] He raises this to a metaphysical principle in the form of appetite. It is the first cause even of our incorrigible will to hope. It manifests in our daydreams (rather than the night dream as in Freud) and cultural creations, even the least sophisticated (such as the circus; the detective novel; the many contents of colportage). The day-dream is formed consciously, it is an act of freedom—it is "within our power."[60] By implication, society is not built on repression, as with Freud, but by the striving to end a state of deprivation (whether articulated or not).

Such is the state of the age that the only substance, the only salvation, is in subjective spontaneity. We must be ourselves in "order to see what shall be."[61] We cannot become ourselves alone—true "Christian charity"[62] says Bloch is orientation to the We, living completely into the salvation of the fellow human such that this interdependence is unmarked "by anything alien to us."[63] This is why the Gospels do not, as other myths do, proclaim the sun but the Son of Man. Christ the man is the "unveiled face of us."[64]

We must rethink the world in terms of the human image in it, recognizing "ourselves as the principle guiding every transformation in this world, and without which there would be . . . no hope."[65] Though to what extent we shall be resurrected is unknown, what we shall be after the final self-elucidation is a solved mystery transcending the "untrue world subject to the Apocalypse."[66]

For Bloch there is an *a priori* humanity that is yet undiscovered but is the ceaseless object of human journeying. The journey is the validation of the premise. This is so because there is a destination that we cannot yet know absolutely, but is our truest selves. The kingdom of God is both realized in history yet resisted continuously in history. It is its endurance despite defeat that sustains the truth of this symbol and validates the commitment necessary to the utopian project. "The Kingdom was preached not to the

59. This is too large a topic to be examined here. Bloch offers a critique of the Freudian analysis of the (night) dream and the influence of the unconscious in us. Bloch regards hunger not the sex drive as constitutive of our human activity. Such longing or desire is a structure constituting our psychology. See *P.H.* 1:51–113.

60. *P.H.* 1:88.

61. Bloch, *Spirit of Utopia*, 173.

62. Ibid., 212. This phrase precedes a section entitled "Christ, or, The Unveiled Face."

63. Ibid., 212.

64. Ibid., 212.

65. Ibid., 228.

66. Ibid., 228.

dead but to the living."[67] As said, it is hope which gives impetus to the having of a world. Hope is a mode of our subjectivity. Because of hope both our estrangement and incompleteness have meaning. Hope is the ground of desire; hope is the "mainsail into the other world."[68]

Salvation *is* the incarnational coming of the other, who is our alienated self. Salvation is the consequence of necessary human action making history, of the struggle with the given by concrete beings who have no greater metaphysical identity. We have a teleology, one that is such that: "What yesterday was still religion is no longer such today; and what today is atheism tomorrow will be religion."[69]

Bibliography

Bloch, Ernst. *Atheism in Christianity: The Religion of the Exodus and the Kingdom*. New York: Herder & Herder, 1972.

———. "The Dialectical Method." Translated by John Lamb. *Man and World* 16 (1983) 281–313.

———. *Erbschaft deiser Zeit* in *Gesamtausgabe* Vol. 4. Frankfurt am Main: Suhrkamp, 1977.

———. *Geist der Utopie*. Rev. ed. München: Duncker & Humblot, 1921.

———. *Heritage of Our Times*. Translated by Neville Plaice and Stephen Plaice (Translation of *Erbschaft deiser Zeit*). Berkeley: University of California, 1991.

———. *New German Critique*. Translated by David Bathrick and Nancy Vedder Shults (Translation of *Vom Hazard)*. Ithaca, NY: Cornell University Press, 1989.

———. *The Principle of Hope*. 3 vols. Translated by Neville Plaice, Stephen Plaice, and Paul Knight. Cambridge: MIT, 1995.

———. *The Utopian Function of Art and Literature: Selected Essays*. Translated by Jack Zipes and Frank Mecklenburg. Cambridge: MIT, 1988.

———. *Vom hazard zur Katastrophe*. Frankfurt am Main: Suhrkamp, 1972.

Feuerbach, Ludwig. *The Essence of Christianity*. New York: Harper & Row, 1957.

Geoghegan, Vincent. "Religion and Communism: Feuerbach, Marx and Bloch." *The European Legacy* 9.5 (2004) 585–95.

Heine, Heinrich. "Germany: A Winter's Fable." In *The Complete Poems of Heinrich Heine*, translated by Hal Draper, 481. Boston: Suhrkamp/Insel, 1982.

Marx, Karl. *Capital: A Critique of Political Economy*. Volume 1, Part 2. New York: Cosimo Classics, 2007.

———. *Theses on Feuerbach*. In *Karl Marx: Selected Writings*, edited and translated by David McLellan, 156–58. Oxford: Oxford University Press, 1977.

Marx, Karl, and Frederick Engels. "Contribution to the Critique of Hegel's Philosophy of Law." *Collected Works*, Vol. 3, 3–210. London: Lawrence & Wishart, 1975.

67. Ibid., 164.
68. Ibid., 206.
69. Feuerbach, *Essence*, 32.

———. "Economic and Philosophical Manuscripts of 1844." In *Collected Works*, Vol. 3, 229–346. London: Lawrence & Wishart, 1975.

———. "Letter to Ruge." In *Karl Marx: Selected Works*, edited by David McLellan, 36–38. Oxford: Oxford University, 1987.

McLellan, David. *Karl Marx: Selected Writings*. 1977. Reprint. Oxford: Oxford University, 1987.

Venable, Vernon. *Human Nature: The Marxian* View. New York: Knopf, 1945.

Epilogue

Andrew Shepherd

Religion, the quest for transcendence is, as noted by Graham O'Brien in his chapter above, "intrinsic to human existence to the world." Whether cave drawings from millennia ago or a contemporary religious ceremony employing particular language, vestments, and rituals, the search for and expressing of meaning and purpose has always been a human trait. The New Atheists argue that the modern scientific understanding of the world makes this religious impulse anachronistic, irrelevant, and potentially down-right dangerous. The arguments employed by Sam Harris, Christopher Hitchens, Richard Dawkins, and Daniel Dennett ("The Four Horsemen of New Atheism") and by others, coalesce around three major themes.

First, New Atheists assert that our increasing scientific knowledge and understanding of the world means there is no longer any need for religious narratives. Modern science with its increasing understanding of the subatomic and micro-biological worlds can now answer these deepest questions of origin, meaning and purpose. The universe has come about through a process of chance, life has evolved over billions of year, and humanity is purely part of this evolutionary process.

Second, as part of their prioritizing of this new meta-narrative over and against alternative or complementary religious narratives, New Atheists raise a number of direct critiques of the phenomenon of religion. Essentially critiques revolve around the issues of theodicy and of violence. With regard to theodicy, New Atheists claim that the randomness, chance, and violence (predation, death and decay) evident in the natural world undermine any theological understanding of an all-loving, all-knowing, all-powerful God. With regard to violence, New Atheists claim that those who take religion seriously are wedded to out-of-date superstitions, founded upon strange sacred texts. Further, it is their assertion that both these texts and the religious traditions encourage and mandate prejudice and ignorance, all of which then lead to hatred and violence.

Some of the contributions within this volume have responded directly to these critiques. To the accusation of religious violence, Tim Meadowcroft, Yael Klangwisan, and I have suggested that the accusation that religious texts and religious belief mandate and encourage violence is a simplistic one that ignores both the hermeneutical complexity of texts and the diversity of opinions and practices within religious traditions.

To the question of theodicy, Nicola Hoggard Creegan agrees that the challenge of theodicy has to be taken seriously. Yes, the natural world is one "red in tooth and claw" and yet alongside this inherent competition and violence, it is important to recognise that biologists and ecologists are now also drawing our attention to the collaboration and relations of mutuality which characterize the community of creation. Perhaps, as Hoggard Creegan suggests, we would do well to see the natural world as one composed of "wheat and tares." Engaging honestly with such questions of theodicy may require a rethinking of our understanding of the Divine and John Bishop has offered glimpses of a theism which moves beyond an understanding of God as the "'grand cosmic controller,' an all-powerful and morally perfect supernatural personal agent," instead contending for a relational, de-supernaturalized, God, understood as the telos of the Universe. While some may be uncomfortable with the sketched outline Bishop offers, there is no doubt that advances in our scientific understanding will lead to new understandings of the Divine.

Yet alongside these direct responses to the critiques of theodicy and "religious violence" contributors have also challenged the blind spots within the arguments of the New Atheists themselves. Deepening a theme raised by John Bishop, John Owens, and Neil Broom reflected on the concept of purpose (*telos*). In their rebuttal of a naturalistic ontology they argued that seeing "life" as a "wholly material process" ignores the purpose and intentionality that is inherent within it or, as Owens puts it: "the original end-directedness of living things."

Indeed, beyond the response to the themes of theodicy and religious violence, a common theme of the assembled chapters has been the suggestion that perhaps the main difficulty with the ontological naturalism advocated for by the New Atheism, is that it fails to give an honest appraisal of how most of humanity understand and experience the world. As a number of contributors note, the reductionism of naturalistic materialism in which everything can be explained, robs the world of wonder and mystery.

Importantly, Peter Lineham has suggested that the recent renewed prominence of atheism, should not be construed as aberrant, but rather be seen as part of the long tradition of non-belief. Indeed, the work of the

New Atheists is not at all novel, but simply reiterates well-known arguments rehearsed by Voltaire and other significant Enlightenment thinkers. But how, therefore, do we understand this sudden attention given once again to the atheistic impulse? The growing recognition of the significance of spirituality within Western societies and the continuing presence and indeed growing strength of religion within the South have largely undermined the secularization thesis first posited by Peter Berger. While organized and institutionalized religion is on the decline in the Post-Christian West, religious belief is as alive as ever.

Accordingly, New Atheism could be understood in one of two ways. On the one hand, it could viewed as a yet another heroic, but ultimately destined to fail, assault by Enlightenment thought upon religious faith and belief. In this case, one could contend that the reductionist ontological naturalism offered by its advocates is really only the domain of a select elite comprised of University lecturers and "left-wing" public intellectuals. Yet, as appealing as such an explanation maybe, a growing number of intelligent and reflective people (including, as my co-editor notes, theological students) are attracted to the explanatory power of such a narrative. Perhaps therefore, following Judith Brown's suggestion we would do better to understand belief and unbelief as existing dialectically. Maybe belief is always present in unbelief (atheism)—as in the case of Bloch—and so too, perhaps unbelief is always present in belief. Indeed, Thomas refuses to believe in the resurrection of Jesus on the testimony of his fellow disciples, requiring hard evidence to overcome his very clear doubts (John 20:24–29). So too, Mark's Gospel offers a striking account of this dialectic in its recounting of the story of a loving father, whose son has been afflicted since childhood. Breaking himself free of the undoubtedly theodicean debate taking place between scribes and the disciples, the Father asks for the pity and assistance of Jesus. His cry is one I suspect that resonates with all of authentic religious faith: "I believe; help my unbelief" (Mark 9:24).

And yet, despite this entanglement of belief and unbelief, the contributors to this work have reminded us that ultimately within the Christian tradition, "belief" is not purely an intellectual comprehension of concepts. True knowledge, Irene Alexander has argued, consists of academic, relational and inner knowing. Such a holistic knowledge leads us on a journey towards our "truest selves" and is evidenced in a life engaged with the world.

There are, I would suggest a few defining marks that will tend to be evident amongst those engaged on such a journey of faith. The naturalistic scientific materialism advocated for by New Atheists contends that humanity is simply an evolved species consisting of atomized selves, whose traits of altruism can be explained by the evolutionary drive for survival.

Likewise, science tells us that one day in the distant future all of life in our solar system will come to an end (either with a big bang or a slow whimper). In contrast, the theology that has begun to be sketched out in this volume suggests the need for a "recovery of the sacred within the created order" and advocates for an awareness and reclamation of wonder, depth, mystery and hope. While a journey of faith will be one that is punctuated by doubts and unbelief, it will also be characterized by an attitude of wonder and sustained by a deep hope.

Such a faith, aware of its own doubts, will, as well as seeking to grow in its understanding, also engage respectfully with those who do not share such faith. Respect and gracefulness, not rhetorical violence should characterise our debate with those of non-belief. But perhaps even more significantly such belief will be characterized by an obedience demonstrated in lives of suffering and sacrifice. True biblical faith involves not violence towards the Other but rather a casting of our lives into the arms of a mysterious God, confident that the one who raised Christ from the death will also bring resurrection life and reconciliation to all of the created order. It is such hope that inspired the aforementioned monks of Algeria to choose obedience and thus death. So too it is such hope that is required by those of faith as they seek to live peacefully and faithfully in a world, which beset with intra-human violence and ecological destruction, faces an uncertain future.